cha LEABHARLANN me
RARIE

the **great big**
veg *challenge*

**photography
by pete jones**

Vermilion

For Chris – without his love and good humour, the Great Big Vegetable Challenge would have stalled at the letter A.

1 3 5 7 9 10 8 6 4 2

Published in 2008 by Vermilion, an imprint of Ebury Publishing

Ebury Publishing is a Random House Group company

The Random House Group Limited Reg. No. 954009

Addresses for companies within the Random House Group can be found at **www.rbooks.co.uk**

A CIP catalogue record for this book is available from the British Library

The Random House Group Limited supports The Forest Stewardship Council (FSC), the leading international forest certification organisation. All our titles that are printed on Greenpeace approved FSC certified paper carry the FSC logo. Our paper procurement policy can be found at **www.rbooks.co.uk/environment**

Printed and bound by Tien Wah Press

Designed and typeset by Smith & Gilmour, London

ISBN 9780091923594

Copies are available at special rates for bulk orders. Contact the sales development team on 020 7840 8487 or visit **www.booksforpromotions.co.uk** for more information.

To buy books by your favourite authors and register for offers, visit **www.rbooks.co.uk**

The publishers have made every reasonable effort to contact the copyright owners of any extracts reproduced in this book. In the few cases where they have been unsuccessful they invite copyright holders to contact them direct and corrections can be made in reprints.

The Department of Health advises that eggs should not be consumed raw. This book contains dishes made with raw or lightly-cooked eggs. It is prudent for more vulnerable people such as pregnant and nursing mothers, invalids, the elderly, babies and young children to avoid uncooked or lightly cooked dishes made with eggs. Once prepared, these dishes should be kept refrigerated and used promptly.

Remember before and after handling raw meat it is important to thoroughly wash your hands.

Both metric and imperial measurements have been given in all recipes. Use one set of measurements only, and not a mixture of both.

Standard level spoon measurements are used in all recipes, unless otherwise stated.
1 tbsp = one 15 ml spoon
1 tsp = one 5 ml spoon

Medium eggs are used throughout, unless otherwise stated.

Ovens should be preheated to the specified temperature. If using a fan-assisted oven, follow the manufacturer's instructions for adjusting the cooking time and the temperature.

Contents

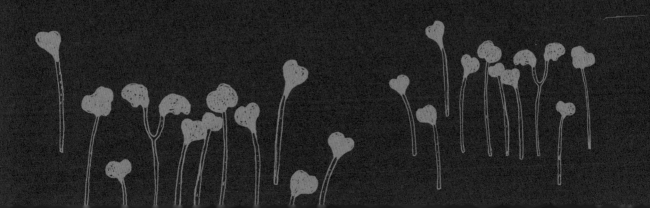

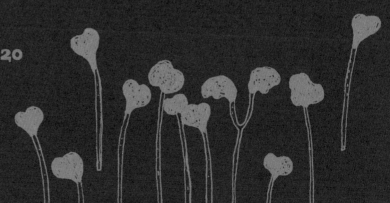

Introduction

It all started with a drama over peas. It was a scene that had been repeated night after night. What happens is that a very, *very* small portion of whatever vegetables the rest of us are eating is placed nonchalantly by me on Freddie's plate. I have taken on board the whole 'take the heat out of eating' line and never refer to the offending articles of greenness on his plate. He eats around them like a small bird pecking out bits of breadcrumbs. And at the end of the meal, of course, the peas are still there … waiting.

He looks up at me and the bargaining begins. 'If I eat two peas is that enough?' I am used to him starting the bids low.

'Now Fred, there are only seven peas on your plate, can't you just eat them?' He then starts to turn pale, slumps down into his chair and fiddles with his cutlery, accidentally on purpose knocking them onto the floor to create a diversion. I remain very calm and come in with my next bid. 'Try five peas. Just eat five small green peas and you can have pudding.'

I don't care if this breaks every child-rearing rule if it works. The trouble is it doesn't work. To cut a long drama very short, it is peas or bust. No peas, no pudding. By then all of us have finished our meal. My husband has tried reasoning with him. We do the Mr Nice, Mrs Nasty routine. My daughter has offered to eat them for him in return for two puddings and they are now elbowing each other. What became of the nice family meal? I don't know how the Waltons did it. I don't remember them arguing at the kitchen table over peas. And there were five times as many of them.

In the end, Freddie's love of puddings triumphs over his dislike of peas. He eats four of them. No more, no less – just four measly specks of green. And to cap it all as he places them in his mouth he retches. Then I feel sorry for him. Does it matter if he eats them? Well no, of course not. In the grand scheme of things, it matters zippo. But it was the same WHATEVER vegetable I gave him. We had dramas over peas, carrots, courgettes, broad beans, green beans, avocados,

tomatoes, mushrooms, onions – everything but potatoes. Sweetcorn he would eat reluctantly. He picked everything off pizza, sieved soup, searched in casseroles to extract any trace of vegetable. It was not a pretty sight. If it really were just peas that caused him to retch, he wouldn't have to try them. But surely he can't ban every wretched vegetable on the planet.

I was facing a powerful adversary. And that night I decided to admit that I needed help. I couldn't do this on my own. But as I sat in front of my computer feeding my eBay addiction, I realised the answer lay in front of me … why not look for help on the World Wide Web? People find romance, old friends and vintage frocks on the internet – why shouldn't I find help for my veg-phobic son?

Let me start with the basics. I am a mother of two children who represent polar opposites in their relationship with vegetables. My daughter, who is eleven, has always enjoyed food, relished new tastes and even been prepared to eat foods that she doesn't particularly enjoy. My son however, who has many talents, cannot count vegetable-eating among them. In his eight years he has been nothing if not consistent – consistently refusing all vegetables barring potatoes and sweetcorn.

Now I do realise that in the grand scheme of fussy-eaters he wouldn't warrant a second glance. I have read about a boy who lived off an exclusive diet of jam sandwiches, of a girl who would only eat food that is brown in colour. My son at eight wouldn't even get a nomination in the 'Fussy-Eating Oscars' compared to those two. But I don't want his determination to avoid vegetables to be underestimated. It shows real dedication and sticking power. All I wanted to achieve was to cajole, charm or even trick him into eating just a little more than potatoes. I read that there are two hundred types of vegetables to choose from and thousands of variations to try. There had to be something that he would like. And given all the pressure on parents to get children to eat healthily, it's beginning to feel like a legal obligation to at least try. No doubt in twenty-years time there will be newspaper reports of children suing their parents for failing to instil healthy eating habits. Maybe a passive-snacking law will be passed to protect the impressionable dears from being exposed to unhealthy eating.

In the pioneering spirit of the World Wide Web, I started a blog that evening. I named it the Great Big Vegetable Challenge and opened it up to 'all of you parents out there who have tried and succeeded to introduce your offspring to the joys of carrots, peas, lettuce, spinach, asparagus, beetroot, green beans – in fact any vegetable. Any ideas gratefully received. (See www.greatbigvegchallenge.blogspot.com)

The morning after the Great Big Vegetable Challenge was conceived, I checked my blog and experienced what must be very special to all fledgling bloggers – a buzz from the fact that people had visited the site and left their thoughts. There was commiseration from Canada, suggestions from Singapore and nuggets of wisdom from far-flung Norfolk.

With a spring in my step, I went down to breakfast which is prepared with military precision by my husband at 7 am. He runs our house as if it were a kind of bootcamp for weaklings. We are yelled at to get dressed quickly, asked whether we have the right equipment for the day – sports kit, Oyster Card, coat, correct shoes, etc. But then his bootcamp has a softer edge. Classical music is piped into the kitchen. All tastes in bread are catered for. And for me there are added privileges. I get coffee and newspapers. I am very, very lucky. I mentioned to everyone my small triumph in the world of blogging. Chris, my husband, was impressed but worried about the implications of time-wasting in the morning if I was checking my blog rather than getting ready for his 7 am-sharp breakfast. My daughter Alexandra asked why her brother (and not her) had inspired a blog. Sibling rivalry is big in our house. And Freddie? Well he looked up from his brown toast with honey (always the same, every single breakfast) and said. 'Twenty-eight visitors? You still have something like six billion to go then.'

Freddie likes statistics and he has an unerring knack of bringing me back down to earth with a bump. But I was undeterred. I decided I needed a strategy to make the Great Big Vegetable Challenge work. As Freddie systematically refused nearly every single vegetable, I was going to systematically introduce him to the entire alphabet of vegetables. The rules of engagement were established. We would try at least two recipes per vegetable and post the results on the blog. He would score the recipes out of ten. And the momentum of following the alphabet would keep us going.

First stop, the artichoke.

A is for... Artichoke

Trying to track down fresh globe artichokes became a search for the unholy grail. All I could find were pasty-coloured knots floating in olive oil. I suspect if I presented those at the dinner table, Fred would faint.

And I didn't want the Great Big Vegetable Challenge to fall at the first hurdle. But then as I emerged from the tube in Kentish Town I was confronted by a mob of globe artichokes glaring at me from a market stall. So far as you can humanise a vegetable, globe artichokes really do look quite angry. They are prickly-looking creatures who seem a little reluctant to let you enjoy them. I felt a bit uneasy about them and I wasn't sure what to do with them. I knew it was a case of boiling or steaming them for about 30 minutes. And then cutting off the stalk and somehow pulling off the prickly leaves and dipping the ends in butter.

Artichoke fans speak in hushed tones about the bit in the middle. How I get to that bit is unclear; globe artichokes should be sold with an instruction manual. I brought them home and put them in pride of place in the kitchen. Fred was interested. He thought they looked like something out of *Jurassic Park* and asked if they had meat inside. Maybe that's what the artichoke junkies get all breathless about.

Artichoke-Friday, as it became known, took on the air of a pagan ritual. The chosen ones were crouching on their sacrificial plate. I had four cookery books at the ready. I chose the simplest option. Chop off the stem, pick off the outer leaves, trim the top and plunge into boiling salted water. Twenty-five minutes later it was D-day. When I took them out I had to squeeze out the water which rather took the glamour out of the artichoke – reducing it to the status of any old boiled vegetable. Freddie was enthusiastic. There was a generous knob of butter on his plate and he joined in the dipping of the leaves. In fact butter was crucial to the whole thing. There was no retching. No tears were shed and no arguments started. He happily sucked the butter off the artichoke and scraped a little bit of the flesh with his teeth, only grimacing when he bit into the heart. As a challenge to eat butter it was a resounding success. In terms of vegetable consumption it was a rather more modest achievement.

I posted our first vegetable success. Already people from all over the world had left comments on the blog. Many of them extolled the virtues of culinary subterfuge. Hide the vegetables! Coat them, purée them, ketchup them, mash them, blend them – just don't let on to Freddie. I do like the glamour of secrecy, the curious feeling of power as I trick my unwitting infants into eating their worst nightmares. But the truth is it hadn't worked. Maybe I'm not made out to be a mother-turned Mata Hari. I had tried without success such tactics in the past. But the Great Big Veg Challenge is about a new approach. It's about trying to inspire change. I had to learn new ways of cooking. I was going on an adventure to find out what works in other homes. So with this new spirit of glasnost,

I returned the following night to artichokes. This time they were tinned artichoke hearts.

Freddie and Alexandra were given bowls of passata, mozzarella, basil leaves and two pizza bases. I opened the tin of artichoke hearts and rinsed them. They looked like clumps of cardboard. I sliced them thinly and the children arranged them on a pizza base. It actually worked. Freddie handled the artichokes, knew what they were and most importantly ate a few on his pizza. A modest success without the need for subterfuge.

tip

When selecting fresh globe artichokes, choose the ones that are undamaged. They should feel heavy for their size which means that they haven't dried out with age. And the leaves should be tightly-closed.

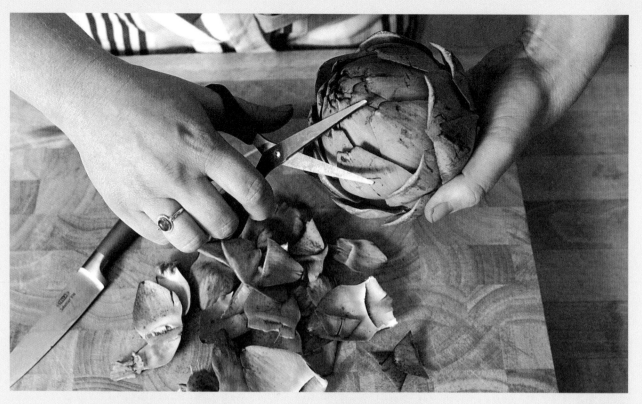

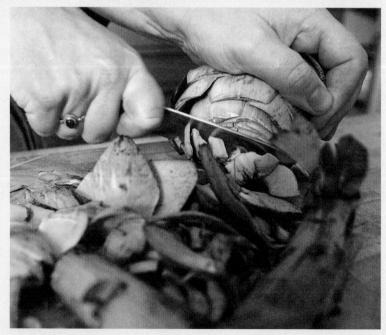

How to prepare a globe artichoke

Before you start, have ready a large bowl of water with lemon juice added. The lemon juice will prevent the artichoke from discolouring.

1 First, snap off the stalk at the base of the artichoke and remove any woody bits. Remove any browned or wilted outer leaves and some of the toughest outer leaves.

2 Cut off the top 2.5 cm (1 in.) of the artichoke so it has a flat top. Using kitchen scissors, trim off the spiky tip of each petal.

3 Place in a pan of boiling water with some lemon juice and simmer for 30–35 minutes. They should lie on their bases.

4 They are ready when you can easily pull out a leaf from the centre. Remove from the pan and drain upside down.

...and how to eat it!

1 Melt some butter to serve with the artichoke. Or, if you prefer, you can use mayonnaise or hollandaise sauce. Once they are well drained, place them on a plate, stalk-end down.

2 One by one, pluck off each petal and dip the petal base in butter. Using your teeth, scrape off the white flesh at the base of each petal. This is the only bit of the petals you eat.

3 When you have plucked off all the petals you will see that the centre of the artichoke has a thistlelike core, tinged with purple. This is the choke and is inedible. With a teaspoon scoop out all the spiny hairy bits until you reveal the much-desired artichoke heart. This is the most delicious bit which you can eat dipped in a little more melted butter!

Artichoke Pizza with Pesto and Pancetta

These pizza recipes use tinned artichoke hearts. You can buy more expensive artichoke hearts in oil, but these taste just as good on a pizza.

Serves 3–4
Large ready-made pizza base, 30 cm (12 in.) in diameter
400 g (13 oz) tin of artichoke hearts, drained and rinsed

115 g (3½ oz) rashers of pancetta
3–4 tbsp green pesto
1 tbsp olive oil
3 tbsp freshly grated Parmesan cheese

1 Preheat the oven to 220°C (425°F) Gas 7.
2 Slice each heart lengthways into 5 mm (¼ in.) slices. Sprinkle the pizza base with a tablespoon of the Parmesan cheese. Arrange the sliced artichoke hearts and rashers of pancetta over the top.
3 Drizzle pesto over the artichokes. Lightly brush the edge of the pizza base with the olive oil. Sprinkle the rest of the Parmesan over the top.
4 Bake for about 15 minutes until the pancetta is lightly crisped.

So far as you can humanise a vegetable, globe artichokes really do look quite angry.

Artichoke Pizza with Tomato and Mozzarella

Getting children involved in making the pizza – arranging the different ingredients on the top – is a great way of ensuring success.

Serves 3–4

Large ready-made pizza base, 30 cm (12 in.) in diameter
5–6 tbsp passata (sieved tomatoes)
200 g (7 oz) small mozzarella balls (bocconcini)

400 g (13 oz) tin of artichoke hearts, drained and rinsed
A generous handful of fresh basil leaves, roughly torn
Parmesan cheese shavings
Salt and freshly ground black pepper

1 Preheat the oven to 220°C (425°F) Gas 7.

2 Spread the passata evenly over the pizza base. Thinly slice the artichoke hearts lengthways and halve the mozzarella balls. Scatter the mozzarella and artichokes over the pizza.

3 Scatter the torn basil over the pizza. Season with salt and pepper and add a scattering of Parmesan shavings.

4 Bake the pizza for about 8–10 minutes or until the pizza base is well cooked and golden brown.

tip

Pizza provides the perfect setting to introduce unfamiliar vegetables to a fussy-eater. One thing they hate is the loss of control over what they are eating, so involve them in the process of making the pizza. Provide a ready-made pizza base with bowls of their favourite toppings alongside some new vegetable interlopers. Even if they are only making the pizza for others to eat, it's a start. Next time they may be persuaded to taste something new themselves.

A is for... Asparagus

Spears

'Asparagus inspires gentle thoughts,' wrote the poet Charles Lamb. And although he has been dead for well over a century, I worry for him. Firstly, what is a 'gentle thought'?

Frollicking lambs, sleeping infants, lapping waves – those are the sorts of things that spring to mind. But not asparagus. Speargrass, spargel, esparrago, asperge, asparago, espargos: whatever you call it, it is far from gentle in appearance or inclination. In its second year, asparagus spears can reportedly shoot up as much as 25 cm (10 in.) in 24 hours.

One evening asparagus achieved god-like status. Freddie liked the fact they looked like spears: a vegetable fit for a warrior. I served them with melted butter and lemon juice and he nibbled on the spears. I suspect that, much like artichokes, butter was the main attraction, but if it works, what is the harm? Our tiny triumph was greeted with delight by German visitors to the blog. This is a country that celebrates the asparagus in a big way, holding Spargelfests. Apparently, German towns vie for the title 'Asparagus Capital of the Year'. What an inspiration to vegetable eaters.

The Great Big Vegetable Challenge had started to change the kind of conversations I was having at work. The blog had a fierce appetite of its own and needed a supply of recipes. Instead of house prices and reality TV, the gossip turned to vegetables. My colleague Anna is Swedish and a wonderful cook. I told her that we were trying out asparagus. She started to reminisce. In Sweden, she liked to serve her asparagus wrapped in a spiral of puff pastry. By the water-fountain, Anna described in detail how to make what we have called Anna's Asparagus Twists. My daughter, Alexandra, took charge of recreating this dish. Having nibbled on asparagus dipped in butter, Freddie was even happier with puff pastry and awarded a 9 out of 10 for this delicacy.

The asparagus recipes came in thick and fast. We rose to the challenge of one blogger, Christa, who championed the cause of vegetables for breakfast. We held our own Breakfast Spargelfest with two dishes –

a bcthedgreatebigfveggchallengehijklmnopqrstuvwxyz

asparagus soldiers with a boiled egg and asparagus wrapped in ham, sprinkled in Parmesan and topped with a poached egg.

Freddie was seriously impressed. He seemed to appreciate the effort I was putting into cooking all these new vegetables. Even when he was busy refusing food, he operated a kind of doublethink and was touchingly loyal. He would boast to his friends about his fathers' qualities as a chef, based entirely on one dish, scrambled eggs. So when we rolled out our breakfast vegetable challenge he became quiet. And not the kind of quiet that is usually accompanied by a dramatic slump back into his chair, eyes lifted to the ceiling in disgust. Oh no – *this* time he was impressed. And he ate every bit. Who would have thought that two vegetables into our Great Big Veg Challenge we had already found a favourite?

tip
Choose asparagus stems that are firm and not woody. They shouldn't be bendy or have wrinkles but should snap easily. The spear tips should be tightly closed.

tip
How to cook asparagus
1 Bend the asparagus spears about 2–5 cm (1–2 in.) from the end of the stalk. They should snap easily. This will remove the woody end which takes longer to cook, but you can use these to make an asparagus soup.
2 Wash well. Tie the stalks in a bunch with a piece of string and stand the cut ends in 5 cm (2 in.) of water in a tall-sided pan.
3 Steam for 5–8 minutes. The stems should be tender but still have bite. Don't overcook asparagus as it becomes soggy and mushy. Drain well and serve with a little melted butter drizzled over.

Another method is to drop the stems into a large pan of boiling water with a pinch of salt and boil for just a few minutes. If the stems are thicker this might take longer. They should be just tender but still with a little bite.

Anna's Asparagus Twists

Asparagus quickly became one of Freddie's favourites, which could have something to do with the fact that it resembles a weapon.

Serves 4
500 g (1 lb) ready-made puff pastry
1 egg, beaten

50 g (2 oz) Parmesan cheese, finely grated
bunch of asparagus, approximately 12 slender spears

Baking tray lined with baking parchment

1 Preheat the oven to 180°C (350°F) Gas 4.

2 Roll out the puff pastry into a rectangle approximately 28 x 22 cm (11 x 8½ in.), to a depth of 5 mm (¼ in.) or the depth of a pound coin. Cut into ribbons, 1 cm (½ in.) wide and a little longer than the asparagus stems in length. Cut 2.5 cm (1 in) from the woody stalk of the asparagus.

3 Carefully wrap the ribbon of pastry around the asparagus stem at an angle so that it looks like a spiral. Press the end of the ribbon against the asparagus so that it is sealed.

4 When all the asparagus spears are twisted with pastry, place on the prepared baking tray. Brush the pastry with the beaten egg and then sprinkle the asparagus twists with the Parmesan cheese. Carefully roll the spears in any excess parmesan so that they are well coated.

5 Place in the preheated oven for 15–20 minutes until the pastry has puffed up and is golden brown. Make sure the asparagus tips don't burn. Serve hot or cold.

tip

This recipe works well dipped in the Romano Pepper Houmous (see page 203) and with Guacamole Dip (see page 208), which is included under P for Plantain.

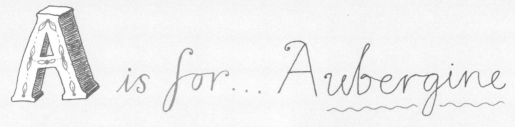

A is for... Aubergine

It was time to move on to aubergines. I had been working in Cardiff and living off conference food. Old-style school dinners have already been discredited by Jamie Oliver. But conference food makes school lunches look like haute cuisine.

This was a public health conference. Without irony, the caterers served six deep-fried snacks to delegates: a dish labelled 'Chicken Firecrackers' glistened menacingly under the fluorescent lights, accompanied by ranks of filo-covered deep- fried prawns. And all this while people tried to find inspirational solutions for improving public health. I returned home with a new sense of purpose.

Inspiring Freddie to try something new meant taking inspiration from wherever it was offered. I had to get under the skin of the vegetable-phobic. I showed him a plate full of these glossy purple creations. 'They look poisonous,' said Freddie as he picked them up and sniffed them. I didn't mention to him that the aubergine belongs to the family of nightshade plants, that its cousin is no less than the deadly nightshade. 'Well let's ask for help on the blog, see how other people eat them,' I suggested.

A day later and Freddie read out the contents of the comment box. One person recommended brushing aubergine slices with teriyaki sauce and grilling them. Others reminded us that in America they were known as eggplants. 'That's what Shaggy eats in *Scooby Doo*!', said Freddie. Thank God for Hanna Barbera. 'Shaggy and Scooby make eggplant burgers with chocolate sauce. Can we have those?'

Alexandra and I worked together to create an aubergine burger worthy of *Scooby Doo*. Freddie tried it and reluctantly admitted that he liked it. His score was a cautious 7 out of 10. It would have been higher if we had added chocolate sauce.

I turned to the arch-enemy of Turkey Twizzlers, Jamie Oliver, for my next aubergine recipe. His cookbook includes a recipe for penne or rigatoni pasta with sweet tomatoes, aubergine and mozzarella. I made sure Freddie was really hungry, keeping his appetite keen so that the chances of rejection were slightly minimised. Had the Scooby Burger endeared him to aubergines?

He liked their flavour, which was something, but complained that they were chewy. There seems to be no logic to the fussy-eater. At least he didn't resort to his old trick of retching. He just ignored the aubergines, picking round them. I needed a recipe where the aubergines couldn't be shuffled around or picked out so I made some grilled aubergine houmous which I served with long strips of crispy pitta bread. The reputation of the aubergine was salvaged and Freddie gave the dip 8 out of 10.

tip

When buying aubergines, choose the ones with bright, shiny skins without any wrinkles or shrivelling near the stem. The stem should not be dried out or brown.

Grilled Aubergine Houmous

Transformed from a vegetable that looks 'poisonous' into an innocent dip, the sinister-looking aubergine became a hit.

Serves 4
2 medium aubergines
1–2 tbsp olive oil
1–2 tbsp teriyaki sauce
400 g (13 oz) tin of chickpeas, rinsed and drained

3 tbsp light tahini
Freshly squeezed juice of 1 lemon
Freshly squeezed juice of 1 lime
1 clove of garlic, crushed

Ridged griddle pan

1 Slice the aubergines lengthways into thin strips and brush them all over with teriyaki sauce.

2 Heat one tablespoon of olive oil in a large ridged griddle pan and lay the aubergine slices flat on the pan. Turn frequently so that both sides brown and cook evenly. They will need about 3–4 minutes for each side, depending on the thickness of the slices. Add a little more olive oil if necessary.

3 Add the chickpeas to a food processor and blend with the tahini, lemon and lime juice, remaining olive oil, crushed garlic and grilled aubergine slices until perfectly smooth. Serve with wholemeal pitta bread strips.

I showed Freddie a plate full of these glossy purple creations. 'They look poisonous,' he said, as he picked them up and sniffed them.

abcthedgreatebigfveggchallengehijklmnopqrstuvwxyz

tip
How to make pitta bread strips for dipping

1 Preheat the oven to 180°C (350°F) Gas 4.

2 Slice the wholemeal pitta bread lengthways into 2.5-cm (1-in.) wide strips. Place on a baking tray and drizzle a little olive oil on top.

3 Bake in the oven until they start to crisp. They make great dippers for houmous.

tip

You can use grilled aubergines in many other ways. They taste good on a pizza: follow the recipe for the artichoke pizzas (see page 12), adding the grilled aubergine slices instead of artichokes. Freddie gave the aubergine pizza 9 out of 10.

Or you can make an aubergine bruschetta. Brush a slice of crusty country bread with some olive oil and lay the grilled aubergines on top. Scatter some shavings of Parmesan cheese on top and put under the grill for a few minutes until the bread is golden brown.

Scooby Doo Aubergine Burgers

Inspired by Shaggy and Scooby Doo's eggplant burgers, this recipe proved a success with Freddie, despite the omission of the chocolate sauce.

Serves 4
1 large aubergine
4 tbsp teriyaki sauce

2 tbsp olive oil
8 slices of mozzarella cheese
4 burger buns

Ridged griddle pan

1 Cut eight slices of aubergine from the middle of the vegetable, to get the widest circumference. The slices should be about 1 cm (½ in.) thick. Brush both sides with teriyaki sauce.

2 Heat the griddle pan and put in one tablespoon of olive oil. Carefully place the slices of aubergine in the pan and cook on a medium heat. Aubergines absorb oil like a sponge, so add the second tablespoon of oil when you turn over the slices to cook the other side. It should take about 10 minutes each side. When you turn them over, brush them once more with the teriyaki sauce.

3 The slices should be nicely browned and when they are ready the flesh will have become very soft. Turn down the heat to low. Place a slice of mozzarella on each aubergine and then add another aubergine slice and then top with another slice of mozzarella. You should have four towers of aubergine and cheese.

4 Turn off the heat. The mozzarella will melt from the heat of the aubergine. Put the tower in a bun and serve.

a bcthedgreatebigfveggchallengehijklmnopqrstuvwxyz

B is for... Beetroot

The A to Z of vegetables continued with beetroot. Not a vegetable often given to children but we are challenging the norm. Apart from concerns over allergies and choking, why is it that we only seem to offer children a really narrow choice of vegetables?

There seems to be a premier league of vegetables beyond which I never used to venture with Freddie: peas, carrots, sweetcorn, potatoes, broccoli and beans. I would rotate them without thinking. Freddie would in turn reject them without a thought.

Online, I summoned beetroot lovers to come out from their purple bowers and inspire us. It was a cake-loving neighbour who provided the perfect idea. It was only a matter of time before the Great Big Vegetable Challenge became the Great Big Cake Challenge. I am not proud of it. I was instantly led astray. I baked it in a heart-shaped silicon case – it was a shameless attempt to tug at the heart-strings.

The beetroot combined with the chocolate lured Freddie into a false sense of security. He embraced beetroot like a long-lost friend. His score was 10 out of 10. And he could boast that he likes beetroot.

At this point in the Great Big Vegetable Challenge, I had introduced Freddie to four new vegetables. More importantly, I had watched as he parked some of his suspicions and tried new tastes. Technology and vegetables make strange bedfellows but something about this challenge really worked. Freddie was just eight years old, believed (quite rightly) in Father Christmas, the tooth fairy Jeffrey and the heroism of premiership footballers. And now, the Great Big Vegetable Challenge had taken on a similar status in his mind. He monitored the visits by people around the globe, danced around the kitchen when someone from Baku browsed and felt a responsibility to his virtual public to face up to the challenge of putting fork to mouth.

So in this spirit we tried a beetroot risotto recipe left by one of our blog visitors. It was no longer just a meal delivered by his nagging mother but much, much more than that. It was an offering from one of his many followers and so had to be treated seriously. Freddie had developed a new politeness at the meal table which meant that beetroot risotto was tasted and at least half-eaten with quiet respect. So the blogged-offerings made by people across the planet were slowly beginning to work their magic.

Beetroot Risotto

This recipe was inspired by one of our visitors like a magic spell lying dormant on the blog. It produces a dish with a beautiful orangey-pink colour – an added attraction.

Serves 4
2 onions, chopped
2 cloves of garlic, crushed
225 g (7½ oz) cooked beetroot (2–3 medium beetroot), diced into small cubes

400 g (13 oz) arborio risotto rice
4 tbsp olive oil
1.2 litres (2 pints) vegetable or chicken stock
4 tbsp freshly grated Parmesan cheese
Salt and freshly ground black pepper

1 Put a large saucepan on a low heat and heat up the olive oil. Add the onion and garlic to the pan with the cooked beetroot. Sauté on a low heat for 6 minutes, stirring constantly until the onion is soft.

2 Add the risotto rice and stir for 3 minutes. Keep the stock gently simmering in a pan and add 100 ml (3½ fl oz) of stock to the rice. Stir the rice constantly and keep adding the stock in stages as the rice absorbs the liquid. Stir frequently.

3 The process will take about 25 minutes until the rice is a lovely creamy texture without being sticky. Season to taste and sprinkle the grated Parmesan on top and serve.

tip

Once you learn to make a risotto, you can introduce all sorts of vegetables this way. The basic risotto recipe is the same, simply feature a different vegetable. It is a bit like pizza, giving you another safe setting to challenge your vegetable-hater. Instead of beetroot, experiment with finely chopped mushrooms, courgettes, asparagus or butternut squash.

Beetroot and Chocolate Cake

This is the recipe that won the day – Freddie embraced beetroot like a long-lost friend. After cooking, the cake becomes a beautiful chocolate-mauve colour.

Serves 8
250 g (8 oz) butter, at room temperature
325 g (11 oz) dark muscovado sugar
4 eggs, beaten
250 g (8 oz) plain flour
2 tsp baking powder

2 heaped tbsp cocoa powder
450 g (14 oz) raw beetroot, finely grated
115 g (3½ oz) grated dark chocolate (minimum 70% cocoa content)
½ tbsp vanilla essence
icing sugar, to decorate

23 cm (9 in.) deep-sided cake tin, greased

1 Preheat the oven to 180°C (350°F) Gas 4.
2 In a bowl, mix together the softened butter and muscovado sugar until light and fluffy. Add the beaten eggs little by little, mixing well.
3 Sift the flour, baking powder and cocoa powder into the cake batter and stir together well.
4 Add the grated beetroot to the cake mix together with the grated chocolate. Stir well to combine and add the vanilla essence.
5 Pour the cake batter into the prepared cake tin and bake for 50–65 minutes, depending on your oven and the depth of the cake tin. Check whether it is ready by carefully piercing the centre of the cake with a skewer. It should come out relatively clean. If you can still see pink batter on the skewer, it needs longer. Cover the top of the cake loosely with foil to prevent it from burning whilst the middle cooks. Allow to cool in the tin for 10 minutes, then turn out on to a wire rack to cool completely. Serve dusted with icing sugar.

Dark chocolate and beetroot were clearly meant to be together

B is for... BROAD Beans

The ancient Greeks and Romans liked to use beans not just for eating but for voting. A white bean was a 'yes', a black bean a 'no' vote. For Freddie, being able to vote on each vegetable recipe was a major part of the appeal. It gave him a feeling of power.

It also got me off the hook. Under the old regime he would vote with his mouth, which wouldn't open. I would take the rejection personally and the whole mealtime would deteriorate. But this way, he has to taste the vegetable to get the right to vote.

There are so many types of beans, we chose a representative by placing the names of various beans in a hat. The winner was the broad bean. It's also known as a fava bean, a fact I remember from the film, *The Silence of the Lambs*. Hannibal Lechter, who I suspect was not a fussy-eater as a child, claims to have eaten the liver of one of his victims 'with some fava beans and a nice Chianti.'

Our first broad bean recipe leapt out from the website of Riverford Organic Vegetables, with the irresistible claim that it was 'a soup for children who hate broad beans!'. Freddie had a pathological hatred of broad beans. But this recipe really did live up to its claims. Broad beans were transformed into something quite exquisite. And I can say with all confidence that my son – he of the turning-up-nose, eyes-screwed up, pale face – tucked into a bowl of broad bean soup as if he had been born into a vegetarian commune. 'This,' he declared, 'is something I will be wanting again!'

When Alexandra had taken her 11 plus exam, we celebrated with a film and a meal out. We chose a new Lebanese restaurant. It was all going so well. The movie had been a touching, comforting sort of film. We were in a good mood. But then the restaurant refused to give the children a glass of water. The warm fuzzy Sunday mood evaporated. The manager explained, with what looked suspiciously like arrogance, that his restaurant had a water meter and he charged us a pound a glass for tap water. We should have walked out. But in reality we were too hungry and I was looking forward to eating my favourite Lebanese broad bean dish.

This is something I first tasted as a student when I shared a house with a Lebanese woman, who served me broad beans cooked in lemon juice, garlic and coriander. By the end of the summer I had learnt how to make this delicious dish. I made it for Freddie and Alexandra. 'I don't like broad beans much but if I did, these taste miles better than the ones in that mean restaurant,' said Freddie.

a *b* c t h e d g r e a t e b i g f v e g g c h a l l e n g e h i j k l m n o p q r s t u v w x y z

Broad bean Soup for Children who Hate Broad Beans!

The Riverford recipe warns you not to skimp on the cream and I suspect that it was this creaminess that ensured Freddie gave it a confident 8 out of 10. (See www.riverford.co.uk)

Serves 4
50 g (2 oz) butter
125 g (4 oz) onion, chopped
1–2 cloves of garlic, chopped
375 g (12 oz) shelled broad beans
900 ml (1½ pints) vegetable stock

Freshly chopped sage or parsley
3 clean, good bean pods
Sugar, to taste
6 tbsp double cream
Salt and freshly ground pepper

1 Melt the butter and cook the onion and garlic gently for about 3 minutes without colouring. Add the beans and stock, together with a tablespoon of chopped sage or parsley and the pods.

2 Simmer until the beans are cooked (about 10 minutes). Discard the pods and pour the liquid into a hand-blender or liquidiser. Blend well until smooth.

3 Season to taste, adding one or two teaspoons of sugar. Reheat and stir in the cream. Serve on its own or with croutons.

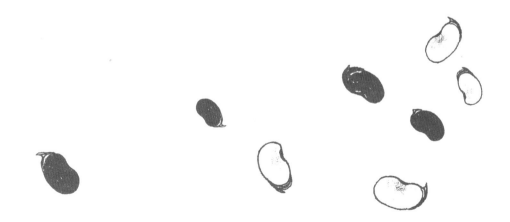

Lebanese-style Broad Beans

Freddie's pathological hatred of this particular vegetable was tamed a little by this old favourite from my student days.

Serves 4
4 tbsp olive oil
3 medium onions, chopped
500 g (1 lb) shelled broad beans (fresh or frozen)
Freshly squeezed juice of 2 lemons

A pinch of salt
60 ml (2 fl oz) water
3 cloves of garlic, crushed
50 g (2 oz) freshly chopped coriander

1 Heat the olive oil over medium heat and fry the onions for 4 minutes. Make sure they don't burn.
2 Add the broad beans and sauté for 10–15 minutes.
3 Add the lemon juice, salt, garlic, measurement water and 40 g (1½ oz) of the chopped coriander.
4 Cook the beans for another 20 minutes, allowing it to simmer on a medium-low heat. (If it looks as if the dish is becoming too dry, stir in a little more water.)
5 Just before serving, add the rest of the chopped coriander leaves. This is delicious served with grilled chicken or salmon.

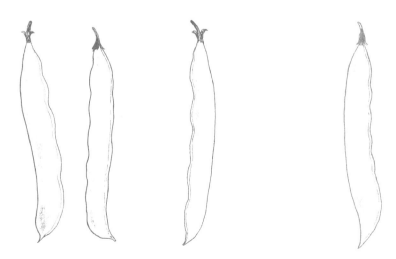

a *b* cthedgreatebigfveggchallengehijklmnopqrstuvwxyz

B is for... Broccoli

← trees?

In March 1990, President George W Bush Senior held a press conference in which he told the press corps, 'I do not like broccoli. And I haven't liked it since I was a little kid and my mother made me eat it. And I'm President of the United States and I'm not going to eat any more broccoli.' Yah boo sucks!

In February 2007, a small boy stood on a chair and delivered a similar diatribe in my kitchen. He wasn't president but he wielded a disproportionate amount of power. Clearly I had a duty to do a better job than the President's mom. An appeal on the blog prompted a flurry of ideas. Freddie liked to help pick out the most desirable recipes. But with broccoli, he looked through them and rejected them one after another.

'I'd like this one if you can leave out the broccoli,' said Freddie pointing out a chicken, cashew nut and broccoli stir-fry.

'We're not leaving out the broccoli – what is wrong with broccoli?'

'It's too green.' Well he has a point. It's the epitome of green, which if you don't like vegetables must make it untouchable.

Things hadn't always been this difficult. At 20 months old, Freddie had been willing to bite into broccoli, carrots and peas. When he turned two it all changed. I blame a birthday present. It was a white plastic spoon with wings, in the shape of an aeroplane.

'Here's a flying one,' my husband would say as he attempted to land a spoonful of broccoli into Freddie's mouth.

'Open the aircraft hangar!'

Freddie's mouth clamped shut.

The spoon with its cargo of vegetables was turned away and left to circle around in the air. Permission to land was never granted. Chris's aeroplane commentary became more elaborate. The toddler became more resolute. 'The airport is shut' was one of his first sentences. Eventually the aeroplane spoon found its way to join the bath toys.

We did try the broccoli stir-fry without much success. In effect, Freddie edited the broccoli out of the recipe by leaving it in the bowl, uneaten. We then tried steaming the florets lightly and offering them as dippers. He sucked off the dip, leaving the floret intact. But our third attempt was different. In the comment box, someone had suggested making a broccoli pesto sauce. Where the aeroplane spoon had failed, the hand-blender succeeded. Broccoli was blitzed into a smooth pesto sauce and served with spaghetti. Freddie was delighted. We should really forward this recipe to George W Bush Senior.

Broccoli Pesto

Blitzed into a bright green sauce for pasta, Freddie was won over.

Serves 4 as a pasta sauce
2 heads of broccoli
50 g (2 oz) pine nuts
1 clove of garlic, chopped
A handful of fresh basil leaves

A handful of fresh coriander leaves
50 g (2 oz) freshly grated Parmesan cheese
4 tbsp olive oil
A pinch of salt and freshly ground pepper

1 Follow the packet instructions to cook the pasta of your choice.

2 Remove the tough stalk from the broccoli and break the head into florets.
Place them in a pan of salted boiling water for about 3 minutes. Drain.

3 Put the broccoli in the bowl of a food processor or hand-blender, along with
the pine nuts, garlic, basil, coriander and grated Parmesan. Blend until smooth,
drizzling in the olive oil, little by little. Season with a little salt and pepper,
if preferred.

4 Add the broccoli pesto to the cooked and drained pasta, while it is still hot
from cooking. Stir until the pasta is well-coated and serve.

tip
Choose broccoli which has tightly-packed florets. They should be a deep-green
colour without any signs of yellowing.

B is for... Brussels Sprouts

look like v. small cabbages

On Christmas Eve we have a tradition. We make twelve fish dishes, light lots of candles and wade manfully through everything from Cromer crab to squid. The whole feast is served on special fish plates which come out once a year.

It is not so much a meal as an aquarium. But Freddie and Alex look forward to it and family Christmas traditions have a habit of persisting, however bizarre.

On Christmas Day, we are more conventional, serving turkey and all-the-trimmings which include of course, the Brussels sprout. Like many fussy-eaters, Freddie's fears about vegetables would often revolve around the texture. Once more I turned to my trusty hand-blender and made a simple sprout purée. This was a success. It is sweet and goes well with a slice of turkey. Freddie, full of Christmas spirit, gave it 8 out of 10.

If fussy-eating is genetic, I must take some of the blame for Freddie's loathing of vegetables. As a child my least favourite vegetable was the Brussels sprout and I would go to any lengths to avoid eating it. At eight years old, I managed to keep an intact sprout in my cheek and eat my pudding around it.

After the meal I climbed up to the top of the house and threw the sprout out of the attic window. Thirty years on and I am sitting in my own kitchen attempting to rustle up a bit of seasonal cheer with a plate of sprouts. On New Year's Eve we still had a large bag of them. We know how to have fun: a couple of leftover crackers and a Brussels sprout stir-fry. Actually, I learnt that sprouts *can* be made to be enjoyable. And it was all thanks to someone from Finland who suggested on the blog that I should stir-fry my sprouts. I looked at Freddie who was busy arranging his football cards. He ate this meal without any dramas. His eyes were focused on Wayne Rooney. Sprouts, having been puréed, shredded and nibbled raw had undergone their final manifestation as a stir-fry. Freddie rated it 7 out of 10.

Putting so much effort into the humble sprout was a bit like customising a Morris Minor. It is a simple, noble and modest vegetable without airs or graces. And to add the culinary equivalent of go-faster stripes is slightly insulting. Freddie must have sensed this because in the end the biggest surprise came when he popped one simply steamed sprout into his mouth and declared that sprouts tasted good.

Brussels Sprout Purée

This simple purée gives a new twist to this traditional Christmas vegetable.

Serves 4 as a side dish
10–12 Brussels sprouts, approximately
  500 g (1 lb), quartered
A generous knob of butter

A handful of fresh basil leaves
3–4 tbsp crème fraîche or double cream
Salt and freshly ground pepper

1 Bring a pan of water to the boil, add the sprouts and cook them for about
5 minutes.
2 Remove the sprouts and place in a bowl. Keep back a few leaves.
3 Add the butter, basil and two tablespoons of crème fraîche or double cream
to the sprouts. Using a food processor or hand-blender, whiz them to a purée.
4 Season and serve, decorating the edge of the bowl with the sprout leaves
that you kept back.

Stir-fried Sprouts

This recipe from Finland turns the humble sprout into a tempting dish that
may convert the hardiest sprout-hater.

Serves 4
2 tbsp sesame oil
500 g (1 lb) Brussels sprouts, stalks removed
  and chopped

50 g (2 oz) bacon lardons
½ tsp freshly grated ginger
2 cloves of garlic, finely chopped
A splash of light soy sauce

1 Heat the oil in a wok or large pan until hot. Throw in the sprouts and stir-fry
for 3 minutes.
2 Add the bacon, garlic and ginger and continue to stir-fry for another 2 minutes.
3 Add a splash of soy sauce and serve immediately with rice or noodles.

C is for... Cabbage

When we moved from B to C, I hadn't realised how unfairly vegetables are distributed within the English alphabet. For some reason the letter C has the lion's share.

We chatted over breakfast about the next victim and Freddie took a deep breath. He spoke quietly, 'I think it is time to get cabbage over with, quick.' He also asked if it was possible to be given an anaesthetic so that he could sleep through the experience and wake up when it was all over. So we took it gently.

Apparently the ancient Greeks recognised hidden depths in a cabbage. This was a vegetable that sprang from the fallen tears of a Thracian king waiting to be killed by the god of wine, all because he had uprooted a couple of his measly grapevines. In tribute to this tragic myth, Freddie was sombre when I served braised red cabbage with guinea fowl. The fowl went down a treat but the red cabbage sat uncomfortably on his plate, knowing that young Master Fred was avoiding it.

He did finally do the gentlemanly thing. He forked a paltry amount into his mouth, swallowed it and uttered the word 'Yuck!'. This felt suspiciously like the old days, the days before the Great Big Vegetable Challenge had started to widen his culinary horizons.

Over 50 years ago, Elizabeth David wrote about cabbage in *French Country Cooking*. She complained about the 'far too notorious' ways that boarding-schools, railway dining-cars and hospitals served cabbage. Sadly, boiled cabbage is still with us. So I was relieved when the blog's comment box filled up with more imaginative suggestions. Cabbage fans were springing up across the globe.

Jack from Nebraska opened our eyes to the wonders of the Runza; a cabbage and meat delicacy. In 1949, the first Runza drive-thru was opened in Lincoln Drive, Nebraska. Now the

state is covered in Runza-outlets. Some look like bread rolls, others a little more like pasties. We made our own version one wet Thursday evening in London. And considering they are stuffed with large quantities of cabbage, they were surprisingly good. Freddie rated it a Runzatic 9 out of 10.

Then came Hannah Miles's recipe for Savoy Cabbage and Sausage Meat. Hannah was a finalist in the BBC Masterchef show; someone who can strut her stuff in front of a tableful of Michelin-starred chefs creating gold-flecked millefeuilles and wafer-thin tempered chocolate. But that is nothing compared to what she can do with a cabbage. In fact she became *the* Queen of Cabbages in our house. Freddie took one forkful and announced, 'Tell Hannah that she has made the cabbage taste as good as the sausage!'

We walked a mile up the road to visit the local Saturday farmers' market to buy more cabbage. London is not flushed with farmers.

Bankers, lawyers and film stars maybe – but farmers haven't really featured big there for at least two centuries. So a cast of farmers is imported from across Britain for a Saturday morning. There is something infectious about the enthusiasm from the apple growers, cheesemakers and oystercatchers. Freddie and Alex like this trip because it invariably means sampling lots of food and juice. Freddie was swigging apple and beetroot juice, chomping on pear slices and nuggets of goats' cheese. I had to ration him.

We made a quick exit with our cabbage to try out a Colcannon recipe from Alanna Kellogg who blogs 'A Veggie Venture' from Missouri. Her recipe for Colcannon made a school boy happy. 'This is heaven,' said Freddie, who asked me, 'Are you sure there really *is* cabbage in this?' There was a tonne of cabbage in this dish and he loved it.

Savoy Cabbage and Sausage Meat

Hannah Miles's recipe converted Freddie to cabbage, without the need for anaesthetic. (See www.hannahscountrykitchen.blogspot.com)

Serves 4
1 Savoy cabbage, leaves separated
10–12 good quality sausages or 670 g (1½ lb)
sausage meat

50 g (2 oz) salted butter, diced
Salt and freshly ground pepper

1 Preheat the oven to 180°C (350°F) Gas 4.
2 Blanch the cabbage leaves for 3 minutes in boiling salted water until soft. Drain and set aside.
3 Remove the skin from the sausages and mix the sausage meat together.
4 In a cast iron casserole dish, line the bottom with some of the cabbage leaves, place a third of the sausage meat on top and then continue layering the cabbage leaves and sausage meat, seasoning between each layer and ending with cabbage leaves on top.
5 Sprinkle the diced butter over the top cabbage layer. Place a sheet of greaseproof paper on top. Press down and fold in at the sides so that it forms a tight lid. Place the casserole lid on top and cook in the preheated oven for approximately 40 minutes.
6 Serve in slices with warm crusty bread.

ab_cthedgreatebigfveggchallengehijklmnopqrstuvwxyz

Potato, Cabbage and Rapini Colcannon

Alanna uses rapini in this recipe, also known as broccoli rabe. We found some at the farmers' market but you could use young spinach leaves instead. (See www.kitchen-parade.com)

Serves 6
225 g (8 oz) potato, unpeeled and diced
450 g (14 oz) cabbage, roughly chopped
115 g (3½ oz) rapini (or young spinach leaves),
   thick stems removed and chopped

1 tbsp soured cream
60 ml (2 fl oz) light or reduced-fat cream
Salt and freshly ground pepper

1 Heat a pan of water on medium high and add the potato and cabbage before the water boils. Bring to the boil then reduce the heat to medium, cover and simmer for 15 minutes or until the potatoes and cabbage are soft.
2 Add the chopped rapini or spinach and cook for about 3 minutes, until soft but still bright green.
3 Drain the potatoes, cabbage and rapini and return to the hot pan. Mash with a hand-blender. Add the creams. Season to taste and serve.

'This is heaven,' said Freddie.
'Are you sure there really is cabbage in this?'

C is for... Carrots

The Great Big Vegetable Challenge turned orange the same night as the lunar eclipse. We all stayed up to watch the moon turn a muddy carrot colour and baked a carrot cake in its honour. I know people might think that cake is a cheat's way of eating vegetables.

Maybe they're right. But I like to think that making cakes with vegetables is a kind of aversion therapy for fussy-eaters. The more exposure to vegetables, the less hysteria. If Freddie enjoys carrot cake, he can't claim to hate carrots. Besides, these were desperate measures. We ate our first slice, warm from the oven, looking up at the orange moon. You can taste the carrot, apple and cinnamon and it has a wonderful moist texture.

Our next carrot recipe, Potage Crecy, was a recommendation from someone in France. There are apparently two 'Crecy' towns in France, both celebrated for the quality of their carrots. How nice to be well known for something so wholesome.

The least I could do was to recreate a little bit of rural France in my urban kitchen. There are many recipes for Potage Crecy so here is our version. This one has rice added and is delicious. Because of his earlier experience with carrot cake, Freddie was feeling generous towards carrots and in a better frame of mind to try this Potage Crecy. But as always he looked suspiciously at the soup as I served it.

'This doesn't look very nice.'

'Just try it. Close your eyes and taste it,' I suggested. He took a spoonful and opened his eyes with a smile.

'You know that line, face of an angel, spawn of the devil?' said Freddie, who watches far too much television.

'Yes?' I said, waiting for the killer verdict on my potage.

'Well this soup has the face of the devil but is the spawn of an angel,' said Freddie. 'It's really, really good as long as I don't actually look at it.' His score was 9 out of 10.

Our third carrot recipe was a bit of an experiment. I wanted the Great Big Vegetable Challenge to be exciting to the taste buds so I created the Carrot and Chorizo Tart. Freddie had started to adopt a statesmanlike air at the dinner table. Before this meal he uttered the words, 'I'm doing this for My People.'

tip

If you buy carrots with the green tops still on you can tell if they are fresh – avoid them if they are wilting or yellowing. If you are buying pre-packed carrots with tops removed, look for those that are firm, not bendy.

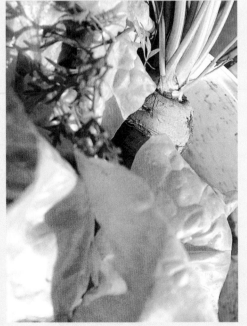

Carrot Cake with Polenta

For this recipe, I added some grated apple for sweetness and half a cup of polenta which gave it a slightly crunchy texture.

Serves 8
115 g (3½ oz) margarine or butter, melted
150 g (5 oz) soft dark brown sugar
225 g (8 oz) self-raising flour
2 tsp baking powder

1½ tsp ground cinammon
50 g (2 oz) polenta
1 eating apple, peeled, cored and grated
200 g (7 oz) carrots, peeled and finely grated
2 eggs, beaten

20 cm (8 in.) round cake tin, greased

1 Preheat the oven to 180°C (350°F) Gas 4.
2 Melt the margarine or butter and stir in the soft dark brown sugar. Take the pan off the heat.
3 Sieve the flour, baking powder and cinnamon into a large bowl and add the melted fat and sugar. Stir well. Add the beaten eggs and polenta and stir in.
4 Add the grated carrots and apple and mix together well. Pour into the cake tin and place in the middle of the oven.
5 Bake for 45 minutes until well risen and golden brown. Leave to cool in the tin for 10 minutes before turning out onto a wire rack to cool completely.

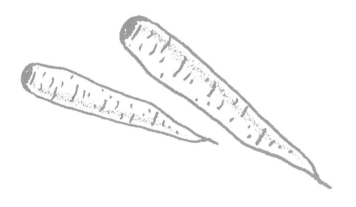

ab_c**the**d**great**e**big**f**veg**g**challenge**hijklmnopqrstuvwxyz

Potage Crecy

Freddie's verdict: '…this soup has the face of the devil but is the spawn of an angel.'

Serves 4–6
3 tbsp olive oil
1 onion, sliced
1 large leek, sliced (white part only)
1.5 litres (2½ pints) vegetable or chicken stock
750 g (1½ lb) small carrots, peeled and sliced

2 tsp tomato purée
2 bay leaves
75 g (3 oz) long grain rice
5 tbsp reduced-fat crème fraîche, plus extra
  to serve
Salt and freshly ground pepper

1 Heat the olive oil in a pan and sauté the onion and leeks for 5 minutes.
2 Pour in the chicken or vegetable stock and bring to the boil. Add the carrots, tomato purée and bay leaves. Turn down the heat to medium-low and allow the soup to simmer for 30 minutes.
3 Turn off the heat. Remove the two bay leaves and discard. Then pour the soup into a food processor, or use a hand-blender. Blend the mixture until smooth.
4 Pour the soup back into the saucepan and add the rice. On a medium-low heat simmer for about 15–20 minutes until the rice is cooked.
5 Season with salt and pepper and stir in the crème fraîche. Serve with a small dollop of crème fraîche on top.

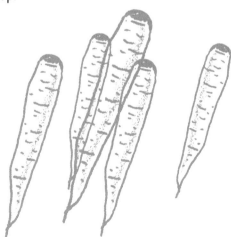

Carrot and Chorizo Tart

This tastes a little smoky and mildly spicy. Freddie didn't notice the carrot but loved the chorizo.

Serves 4–6
375 g (13 oz) ready-rolled shortcrust pastry
2 medium carrots, finely grated
½ tbsp olive oil
75 g (3 oz) chorizo sausage, chopped
115 g (3½ oz) bacon lardons

3 eggs, beaten
200 ml (7 fl oz) reduced-fat crème fraîche
60 ml (2 fl oz) milk
75 g (3 oz) finely grated Parmesan cheese
Salt and freshly ground pepper

23 cm (9 in.) flan tin
Baking beans

1 Preheat the oven to 190°C (375°F) Gas 5.
2 Line a quiche or flan tin with the pastry. Prick it and bake it blind for 10 minutes, using greaseproof paper with baking beans on top.
3 Squeeze out excess moisture from the grated carrot. Add the olive oil to a pan and gently fry the carrot with the chopped chorizo and bacon for 10 minutes. Season.
4 Add the crème fraîche and milk to the eggs and beat together. Stir in the Parmesan cheese.
5 Spread the carrot and chorizo mixture evenly across the pastry case. Pour the egg mixture on top.
6 Bake in the oven for 30 minutes or until golden brown on top.

C is for... Cauliflower

The cauliflower, in Freddie's eyes, benefits hugely from not being green. We started with Cauliflower Cheese, which I remember from my childhood. Like all the best recipes I know, I was taught how to make it by my mother.

The trick is to make sure you don't overcook the cauliflower, use a strong Cheddar cheese and make a crispy topping.

There was a new confidence about our family meals. The nervousness that used to linger at the kitchen table when Freddie refused anything new had dissipated. His wary eye hadn't left him but he was more adventurous. He tucked into the cauliflower cheese and looked proud.

'Well, I have my 5,000 visitors from across the world to think of.'

I was industrious with this cloudlike vegetable. Cauliflower is so easy to prepare; it's not a high-maintenance vegetable like an artichoke or a sensitive soul like an asparagus tip. And it makes perfect finger food, which suits Freddie's simian ways. With our Friday-night film we snacked on Cauliflower Crunch. Freddie and Alex munched away happily as if it were popcorn.

tip

When buying cauliflower, look out for black spots in the florets which means it is past its best.

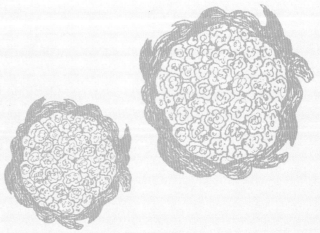

Enjoying the great
outdoors took on
a whole new meaning
when we embarked on
a foraging trip.

Cauliflower Cheese

With an old tried-and-tested family recipe and a good strong Cheddar, you're almost guaranteed success.

Serves 4
1 large or 2 medium cauliflower heads
25 g (1 oz) plain flour, sifted
25 g (1 oz) butter
575 ml (18 fl oz) milk
115 g (3½ oz) mature Cheddar cheese, grated

1 tsp mild French mustard (optional)
Salt and freshly ground pepper

For the topping
5 tbsp coarse breadcrumbs
25 g (1 oz) mature Cheddar cheese, grated

1 Preheat the oven to 180°C (350°F) Gas 4.

2 Wash the cauliflower and remove the outer leaves and discard the tough parts of the stalk. Break up the head into florets that fit in the palm of your hand and cook in boiling water for about 6 minutes. Drain well.

3 Gently melt the butter in a pan on a low heat. Stir in the flour and keep stirring until it forms a smooth paste. Add the milk and whisk constantly until the sauce thickens. Allow the sauce to boil for a minute or so.

4 Turn down the heat and add the cheese and mustard and stir well until it melts. Season.

5 Put the cauliflower into an ovenproof dish and pour the cheese sauce on top. Make sure the cauliflower is well coated in the sauce.

6 To make the topping, mix together the breadcrumbs and grated Cheddar and sprinkle it evenly over the cauliflower. Cover the dish loosely with foil.

7 Place in a preheated oven for 30 minutes. For the last 5 minutes take off the foil to allow the topping to crisp and become golden brown. Serve immediately.

tip

Try steaming the florets for 8–10 minutes to prevent your cauliflower retaining too much water and becoming soggy. Also try using some broccoli florets in this recipe along with the cauliflower.

Cauliflower Crunch

Freddie and Alex like to munch away on this as if it is popcorn.

Serves 4
1 large cauliflower head
3 tbsp olive oil
1 tsp smoked paprika

115 g (3½ oz) fine breadcrumbs
Salt
Olive oil cooking spray

1 Preheat the oven to 180°C (350°F) Gas 4.
2 Break the cauliflower head into small popcorn-sized florets. Put them in a bowl and add the olive oil. Make sure the florets are well coated with the olive oil. Then add the smoked paprika, breadcrumbs and a couple of pinches of salt. Stir so that the cauliflower is evenly coated.
3 On a baking sheet, spread out the florets evenly, well spaced and put in the oven for 20 minutes. After 10 minutes turn them over and spray lightly with more olive oil. The trick is to cook them until they crisp up and are golden brown but not burnt.

tip

Cauliflower Crunch is perfect snacking food. It is hard to persuade children who are used to snacking on biscuits and crisps to try something healthier. It may seem brutal but the first step is to clear out your kitchen cupboards so that the biscuits and crisps just aren't available. Then try leaving out bowls of cauliflower crunch, carrot sticks, apple slices, pumpkin seeds or rice cakes.

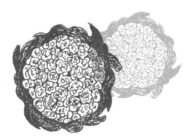

C is for... Celeriac

We moved on to celeriac. The children thought it looked like a huge brain. Its skin is covered with what seem to be traces of ganglia and veins. This was the first celeriac I had ever cooked.

My opening gambit was very easy, largely because I discovered an internet site called 'Videojug'. Videojug could, if you wanted, run your life for you. As well as recipes you can get golfing tips and guidance on how to give a man-to-man hug. I found a step-by-step video to make celeriac purée (see www.videojug.com). A hypnotic voice guided me through the stages of its creation complete with a video illustration. Think *Stepford Wives* crossed with *Listen with Mother* circa 1972. It is a somewhat surgical approach to cooking.

When introducing vegetables to a fussy-eater it helps if you can slip them onto the plate next to something irresistible. In Freddie's case this is red meat, preferably lamb. He came with me to the local butcher, standing in line looking at the raw meat with his tongue lolling out like a puppy. He chose lamb chops as the accompaniment to the celeriac purée, which tasted delicious. Freddie loved it. How something so ugly can be so delicious is beyond me. It has the consistency of potato with the delicate flavour of celery.

And it looks like a wart-covered boulder. Celeriac is the frog prince of vegetables.

An unexpected bonus of the Great Big Vegetable Challenge was that it boosted all of our mapping skills. A free bit of blogging software gave us a map of the world on which a red spot represented a visitor. Within time, it looked like it had caught measles. Freddie had his own map of the world stuck on the fridge and added a football sticker each time we had a visit from a new country. Clusters of dots appeared across Europe, North and South America, Asia and Australasia. Over supper we looked out through our kitchen window and thought about the view from the kitchens of our visitors in Greenland, Hawaii and the Falkland Islands. When someone from Bhutan visited we felt like we had established radio contact with Mars. Leaving only their red dot, most visitors visit and vanish. But when they left a comment, a word of encouragement or best of all a recipe tip, we felt as if we had made a new acquaintance. We were experiencing the unexpected: that vegetables can bring people together.

With a gratin from France and a Swiss-style rosti, Freddie was becoming a taste-explorer and gaining a good geographical grounding along the way.

Celeriac Purée

This recipe proves that its remarkably easy to turn something that resembles a body part into an instant hit.

Serves 4 as a side dish
1 large celeriac, peeled and cubed
Freshly squeezed juice of 1 lemon

50 g (2 oz) butter
100 ml (3½ fl oz) reduced-fat crème fraîche
Salt and freshly ground pepper

1 Put the cubes of celeriac in a pan of salted boiling water with the lemon juice. Cook for 15–20 minutes, until the celeriac is tender.

2 Drain the celeriac well and place in a food processor or the bowl of a hand-blender. Add the butter, which will melt with the heat of the celeriac, and the crème fraîche.

3 Purée until the celeriac is smooth. Season with a little salt and ground pepper.

Celeriac and Potato Bake

Someone from France suggested that we should try layering the celeriac purée with slices of potatoes, which we did.

Serves 4
Celeriac Purée (see page 53)
3–4 large potatoes, peeled and cut into 5 mm (¼ in.) slices
25 g (1 oz) freshly grated Parmesan cheese

1 Preheat the oven to 220°C (425°F) Gas 7.

2 Follow the recipe on page 53 to make Celeriac Purée.

3 Put the potatoes in a pan of boiling salted water for about 4–5 minutes until they are just beginning to soften. Don't allow them to overcook or become mushy. Carefully drain without breaking the slices.

4 In a round or oval ovenproof dish, arrange a layer of potato slices. Then add a third of your celeriac purée on top, spreading it evenly over the potato. Add another layer of potato slices, then a layer of purée and so on until you have used all your potato. Finish with a layer of purée.

5 Sprinkle the Parmesan cheese on top. Cook in the oven for 15 minutes until the top is a crispy golden brown.

How something so ugly can be so delicious is beyond me. It has the consistency of potato with the delicate flavour of celery.

Celeriac and Sweet Potato Rosti

Rosti are traditional in Switzerland and are simply a crispy fried 'cake' of grated potato. But you can make them from other grated root vegetables like celeriac, carrot, sweet potato or add ingredients like apple. Freddie gave these 8 out of 10.

Serves 3–4
1 medium celeriac, peeled and grated
300 g (10 oz) sweet potato, peeled and grated
1 large egg, beaten

1 tbsp plain flour
Mild chilli powder (optional)
Cooking spray oil or butter
Salt and freshly ground pepper

1 Squeeze any excess moisture from the celeriac and sweet potato. Put them in a bowl and stir in the beaten egg, then the flour and mix well. Season. If you like, you can add a pinch of mild chilli powder for extra flavour.

2 Heat up the oil or butter in a non-stick pan. Pat the celeriac into balls, the size of a golf ball and place in the hot pan. Carefully flatten them with a fish slice and cook for 2 minutes. Turn them over and cook the other side. They are ready when they are golden brown and are starting to crisp up on both sides.

3 Cook in batches and keep warm in a low oven. In between batches you will need to wipe the pan clean with kitchen paper and re-spray with oil.

tip

For a really simple supper, serve these with a poached egg on top or with lamb or pork chops.

C is for... CELERY

Is celery the only vegetable to be banned from a football match? Chelsea football fans have a noble tradition involving the waving of celery sticks whilst singing an unprintable chant.

Some fans have been banned for throwing their green sticks onto the pitch. There was even talk of a telephone hotline for people to report illegal salad tossing. Unfortunately for Freddie it couldn't be banned from the Great Big Vegetable Challenge, as the rules state that all vegetables must be tried, however stringy.

In *The Lion, the Witch and the Wardrobe* there is a point at which the creatures of Narnia start to notice the ground thawing and signs of spring emerging after a long dark winter. Well, something similar was happening in our home: small but significant changes in eating habits. Freddie, who used to operate a strict 'no bits' policy, ate raspberry jam on toast and then strawberry yoghurt 'with bits'.

Many parents will be familiar with this 'no bits' obsession that lots of children seem to have. Food products for children market themselves as 'smooth' with 'no bits'. Are the children of Britain alone in their hysteria over bits? Yoghurt has to be smooth with no unsettling scraps of fruit undermining it. Jam is out of bounds because of the likelihood of bitty seeds. 'Bits' is such an insignificant word and yet it has the power to bring a meal to a grinding halt. And despite signs of glasnost in our home, I wanted our first celery recipe to be smooth, in every sense. I made Celery and Apple Soup which is puréed to remove the stringiness of the celery. Freddie ate his and marked it 8 out of 10.

We went on holiday to Cornwall for Easter, taking with us a recipe for Baked Cheesy Celery. We enjoyed it, sitting outside in the warm spring sun. The recipe had been sent to us by David Hall, a chef from South Shields who is on a mission to persuade children like Freddie to learn to love cooking and enjoy vegetables and fruit. We met up with him later in the year at the Children's Food Festival in Abingdon, and watched him as he inspired and charmed a tent full of children and parents into eating more fruit and vegetables. Freddie gave Baked Cheesy Celery 8 out of 10.

I'm uncertain how his marking system works. Like all good judges, he is mysterious and highly impartial. He did say that the dish lost two marks because 'the celery is not very hidden'. If you are looking to pretend that you aren't eating celery, this isn't the recipe for you. But the celery has been tamed by being braised in chicken stock. It is tender to eat and the cheesy sauce makes it delicious.

Back home in London I made a Waldorf Salad. There aren't that many recipes starring celery and I did the hard-sell on this one, talking about the mâitre d', Oscar Tschirky, at the luxurious Waldorf Hotel in New York. We all visited New York last autumn and Freddie loved it, so I thought it might influence him. No such luck. (And I caramelised the walnuts so that they were delicious …) This is the closest thing to a salad that I had served Freddie so far during our Great Big Vegetable Challenge and it was a little too threatening, too green. Freddie's face said it all when he tried it. He gave it a mean 4 out of 10. But the rest of the family loved it and his sister Alexandra was impressed, so we included the recipe for others to judge for themselves.

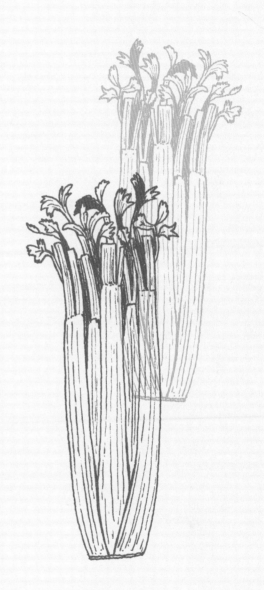

Celery and Apple Soup

This smooth, no 'bits' soup was a hit with Freddie and a good introduction to a vegetable that has been banned from at least one football club!

Serves 4
3 tbsp olive oil,
1 onion, finely chopped
2 cloves of garlic, chopped
2 large cooking apples, peeled, cored and diced
4 celery stalks, finely chopped

1 potato, peeled and diced
1.5 litres (2¹/₂ pints) vegetable stock
4 tbsp crème fraîche
Salt and freshly ground pepper
Chopped basil leaves, to garnish

1 Cook the onion and garlic in the olive oil on a medium heat until soft.

2 Add the apple, celery and potato to the onions. Cook for 5 minutes, stirring continuously.

3 Add the vegetable stock. Bring to the boil slowly, stirring so it doesn't stick on the bottom of the pan. Cover the pan and simmer on a low heat for 20 minutes until all the vegetables are tender. Remove from the heat and allow to cool.

4 Add the crème fraîche and using a hand-blender or food processor, purée the soup until it is smooth. Season.

5 Reheat gently and serve with some chopped basil leaves.

Baked Cheesy Celery

I made a small addition to this recipe by David Hall, sprinkling some breadcrumbs on top. (See www.bookthecook.blogspot.com)

Serves 4 as a side dish
2 heads of celery, washed, trimmed and each stalk cut into 3
Hot chicken stock, enough to just cover the celery
400 ml (14 fl oz) single cream
4 egg yolks
115 g (3½ oz) Cheddar cheese, grated
50 g (2 oz) finely grated Parmesan cheese
25 g (1 oz) coarse breadcrumbs
A little salt and freshly ground pepper

1 Preheat the oven to 200°C (400°F) Gas 6.

2 Put your celery into a shallow pan and pour on the stock until just covered. Bring to the boil then turn down to a very low heat and put on the lid. Simmer for approximately 15–20 minutes, or until the celery becomes slightly tender.

3 Mix the cream, egg yolks and Cheddar cheese together. Season but go light on the salt.

4 Drain the celery and tip into a gratin dish. Pour on the cheese mixture and finish off with the Parmesan. Bake for 15–20 minutes on a high shelf or until golden and bubbly.

Here the celery has been tamed by being braised in chicken stock. It is tender to eat and the cheesy sauce makes it delicious.

Waldorf Salad

This was a hit with Freddie's big sister, Alexandra – aided and abetted by caramelised walnuts.

Serves 4
3 red apples, cored and sliced
Freshly squeezed juice of ½ lemon
325 g (11 oz) celery, roughly chopped
1 round lettuce
75 g (3 oz) walnut pieces, caramelised
(see tip below) and chopped

For the dressing
4 tbsp reduced-fat crème fraîche
1 tbsp freshly squeezed lemon juice
1 tbsp reduced-fat mayonnaise
1 tbsp walnut oil
Salt and freshly ground pepper

1 First make the dressing. Whisk all the ingredients together in a bowl. Leave for a moment.

2 Place the apples in a bowl with the lemon juice and mix together. Add the celery and season.

3 Line a salad bowl with the lettuce leaves and spoon in the salad mixture, pour over the dressing and scatter the walnut pieces on top.

tip
How to caramelise walnuts

To caramelise nuts like walnuts or pecans, take 125 g (4 oz) of walnut halves, 50 g (2 oz) of caster sugar and a teaspoon of butter. Place a small, heavy-based frying pan or skillet on a medium heat. Add the butter and sugar and stir until the sugar starts to caramelise and turns golden brown. Add the walnuts and stir well until covered in the caramelised sugar. When well-coated, transfer the caramelised walnuts to a piece of non-stick parchment paper to cool. As they cool, they will harden with a crispy caramelised coating.

C is for... Chard

Rainbow Chard is a psychedelic little number that looks as if nature got a bit liberal with the food colouring bottle. If a toddler were to design a vegetable, this is what it might look like. There is a more staid version with plain green leaves known as Swiss Chard, Rainbow's sensible older sister.

We bought our multi-coloured chard in the holidays, from Lostwithiel farmers' market in Cornwall. It was perched on a stall, fanning its multicoloured stalks, like a parrot. Freddie and Alexandra were drawn in by the dazzling colours. The stall holder explained that they sold it in loose bunches so that the leaves don't get bruised. This is the joy of farmers' markets: the person who sells to you is often an enthusiast. The lady in Lostwithiel told Alex and Freddie how to make a rainbow pizza. Just use the brightly-coloured chard stalks to decorate the pizza, and serve the dark green leaves, quickly sautéed with a little lemon juice and butter, as an accompaniment.

There were just three days of the Easter holidays left. Freddie was pinging around our tiny back garden like a ball-bearing in a pinball machine. In his mind it is Wembley Stadium. Every now and again he stops and asks me what is for lunch. It is the strangest sports commentary.

'Smith passes to Giggs and Giggs curls the ball into the top corner! Mum what's for lunch? Alan Smith just taps the ball to Giggs and the Welsh wizard completely whacks it in the net.'

'It's chard and lentils,' I reply.

'Chard? And its a GOOAAAL! Manchester United take the lead with a smashing goal from Giggs. Mum, do I like chard?'

The imaginary match was won, the lunch was ready. Freddie peered at it and told me it looked unpleasant. But he offered rather generously to close his eyes and see if it tasted better than it looked. And it did. He loved it in fact. But only if he didn't actually look at it. Which is strange but I can work with that approach if it means he is enjoying vegetables.

'A good eater must be a good man; for a good eater must have a good digestion, and a good digestion depends upon a good conscience.' So said the Victorian Prime Minister Benjamin Disraeli. His old vegetable garden in Buckinghamshire is undergoing a renaissance under the care of the National Trust. Because chard is not a common vegetable, not something children see everyday, we thought we would try and see it growing in Disraeli's walled kitchen garden at Hughenden Manor.

'Do you think Queen Victoria came round and ate some of these vegetables?', asked Alex. In this old walled garden, Freddie and Alex could work on developing good digestion, conscience and eating habits by seeing chard in all its glory growing in the soil. A volunteer helped them to plant seeds. Freddie lay back in the grass and communed with nature as his sister did all the digging and planting. That evening we went back home with our chard and made a plate of chard and basil fritters.

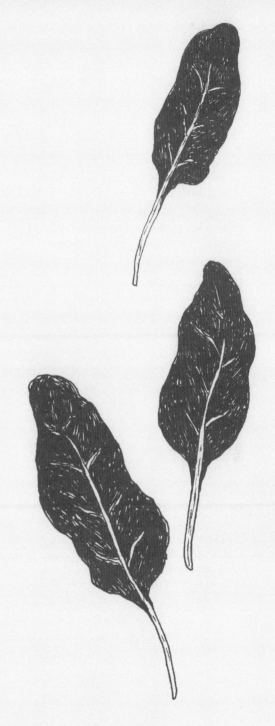

Rainbow Pizza

This psychedelic-looking vegetable gets to show off it's best assets on a pizza.

Serves 4

Large ready-made pizza base, 30 cm (12 in.)
   in diameter
1–2 tbsp olive oil
2 tbsp finely grated Parmesan cheese
1 bunch of rainbow chard stalks, green
   leaves removed
1 clove of garlic, crushed
Mini mozzarella balls (bocconcini), or whole
   mozzarella torn into pieces
Salt and freshly ground pepper

1 Preheat the oven to 220°C (425°F) Gas 7.

2 Put the pizza base on a lightly greased baking tray. Drizzle the olive oil across the pizza base and sprinkle the grated Parmesan cheese on top.

3 Finely chop the coloured chard stalks and sauté in a little olive oil for 3 minutes, stirring constantly. Scatter them on top of the pizza with little balls of mozzarella.

4 Bake in the oven for 10 minutes until crisp and golden.

Sautéed Chard

This farmers' market recipe makes a great accompaniment to the Rainbow Pizza.

Serves 4

Chard leaves, stems removed
1 tbsp of olive oil
½ clove of garlic, finely chopped
A squeeze of lemon juice
Salt and freshly ground pepper
A knob of butter

1 Cut the washed chard leaves into ribbons. Heat the olive oil in a pan and sauté the leaves for 5 minutes with the garlic. The leaves will wilt.

2 Squeeze a little lemon juice on top of the leaves, season and add a knob of butter before serving.

abcthedgreatebigfveggchallengehijklmnopqrstuvwxyz

Chard and Basil Fritters

Originally made with chard from Hughenden Manor, Disraeli would have been proud to see two good eaters wolf this down 125 years later.

Serves 4
Leaves of a chard, finely chopped
1 generous handful of fresh basil, finely chopped
1 clove of garlic, finely chopped
1 tbsp olive oil
125 g (4 oz) self-raising flour

A pinch of smoked paprika
2 tsp caster sugar
2 eggs, separated
200 ml (7 fl oz) milk
30 g (1½ oz) butter, melted, plus extra
  for frying

1 Cook the finely chopped chard leaves, basil and garlic in a pan with olive oil, stirring constantly to prevent burning. Do this for 3–4 minutes. Remove from the heat and put aside.

2 Sift the flour and paprika into a bowl and add the sugar, egg yolks, milk and melted butter. Beat until everything is combined.

3 In a separate bowl, whisk the egg whites to soft peaks and then gentle fold into the batter mixture. Stir in the chard and basil.

4 Melt a little butter in a large frying pan and place spoonfuls of the batter a small distance apart in the pan. Cook until golden, turning over halfway through cooking when the batter is almost cooked on the top side of the fritter.

5 Keep the fritters warm in a low oven until you have cooked the remainder of the batter.

C is for... Chicory

The C vegetables seemed to go on for months and chicory was one of the last ones. Buying it proved difficult. At the first supermarket, I spent 20 minutes playing 'hunt the chicory', scanning the shelves for their albino leaves.

'I'm looking for chicory. Do you have any?' I asked the shop assistant.

'Chicky? What's that then?' he replied.

'Chicory,' I repeated.

He smiled at me, gently took me by the arm and led me to the meat counter. Then followed an embarrassing episode in which I attempted to spell the word chicory out loud to the bemused shop assistant, watched by a small crowd of shoppers who clearly thought I was on day release. So I left and in the next supermarket asked the same question.

The store manager quizzed me, 'Is that produce then?' She didn't have a clue what I was talking about, offering me chicory coffee. In the third and final store, a rather doleful manager told me he had asked Head Office *three times* to stock it but the promised chicory had never arrived. Conspiracy theories have been started on subjects of lesser importance than this.

So I gave up for the day and bought vegetable crisps instead. Chicory is a vegetable in need of an identity card. In British English it is called chicory, in the US it is known as Belgian Endive but it also known in countries like Belgium as Witloof. Can you really trust a vegetable with so many identities?

The next day I tracked down the Scarlet Pimpernel of vegetables in Waitrose, where there were mounds of them. A label said they were grown in Britain and sported the smiley face of a farmer called Mark. So before they made a getaway, I took them home and turned them into soup.

Building on the success of the soup, we became braver. Two visitors to the blog recommended caramelising chicory. We did this by blanching the chicory in salted boiling water for 2 minutes, then draining it and putting it on a baking tray with knobs of butter on the bottom. Then we added two teaspoons of honey and put it in the oven at 180°C (350°F) Gas 4, for 15 minutes, basting it and then baking for another 15 minutes. Freddie was unusually optimistic about this recipe, as it contains two of his favourite foodstuffs (honey and butter).

Given it had an unattractive stringy and slimy consistency he did well to eat it. Then he said, 'I don't like my vegetables sweet.' You can't win sometimes. He gave it 5 out of 10, which is a pass. I have to say it tasted medicinal, like antibiotic syrup. I half expected matron to enter the kitchen and take our temperatures. My husband liked it but he did spend seven years in a boarding school, so he has a soft spot for matron's cooking.

Freddie regained confidence in this vegetable when I combined it with chicken.

'This is how you should always disguise the vegetables, Mum,' he said. Clearly, I could learn a trick or two about disguises from Mr Witloof.

I was about to move on from chicory and the endless convoy of C vegetables when an email arrived from a lady called Penny Wesson, with a recipe for chicory cooked in ham and cheese. Back in the 1960s, Penny was working as an au pair in St Germain-en-Laye in the suburbs of Paris. Over 40 years on, she remembered this recipe and passed it on to me and my children. Freddie and Alexandra were becoming fond of chicory and appreciated the addition of ham and cheese. Penny's recipe was awarded 8 out of 10.

Chicory and Flageolet Bean Soup

Freddie's rating for his first chicory recipe was 10 out of 10. Chicory, though elusive, is clearly worth the effort of tracking it down.

Serves 4
3–4 chicory stalks, ends removed
2 cloves of garlic, chopped
2 tbsp olive oil
400 g (13 oz) tin of flageolet beans in water,
   drained and rinsed

500 ml (17 fl oz) chicken or vegetable stock
4 tbsp reduced-fat crème fraîche
Salt and freshly ground pepper

1 Separate the chicory leaves and blanch in salted boiling water for 3 minutes.
2 Meanwhile, sauté the garlic in olive oil until soft.
3 Remove the chicory with a slotted spoon and roughly chop it, then add it to the garlic and oil. Sauté for 4 minutes on a gentle heat.
4 Transfer the mixture to a bigger pan. Add the stock and heat gently. Put aside a quarter of beans and purée the remainder with a hand-blender. Add to the soup. Stir and gently simmer for 15 minutes. Purée the whole soup if your child dislikes unfamiliar textures.
5 Season. Add crème fraîche and the remaining flageolet beans and warm through without boiling. Serve hot.

'This is how you should always disguise the vegetables, Mum,' said Freddie. Clearly, I could learn a trick or two about disguises from Mr Witloof.

Chicory with Herby Chicken

I adapted this from a recipe on the BBC food website for chicory baked with sage and chicken. (See www.bbcgoodfood.com/recipes)

Serves 4

3 heads of chicory, stalks removed, quartered
2 tbsp olive oil
4 tbsp chicken stock
4 skinless and boneless chicken fillets,
   cut into small cubes
1 tsp clear honey
1 tsp dried oregano
1 tsp dried basil
1 tsp dried thyme

2 cloves of garlic, finely chopped
1 medium onion, finely chopped
1 tbsp plain flour
25 g (1 oz) butter
300 ml (½ pint) milk
150 ml (¼ pint) reduced-fat crème fraîche
2 tsp French wholegrain mustard
Grated Cheddar cheese, to sprinkle on top
Salt and freshly ground pepper

1 Preheat the oven to 180°C (350°F) Gas 4.

2 Lay the chicory leaves in a lightly greased ovenproof dish. Pour over the stock and a little olive oil. Cover with a lid or foil and bake in the oven for 10 minutes.

3 Heat a tablespoon of olive oil in a pan and add the chicken with the honey and herbs and sauté for 5 minutes. Season to taste.

4 Add the garlic and onion. Cook, stirring all the time for 3 minutes.

5 Take the chicory out of the oven and add the chicken mixture to it. Put it aside and make the sauce to go on top.

6 Melt the butter in a pan, add the flour on a gentle heat and stir. Add milk a spoonful at a time. Keep stirring until the sauce thickens.

7 Remove from the heat and stir in the crème fraîche and mustard. Pour this over the chicken and chicory and sprinkle the Cheddar on top. Return to the oven for 25 minutes. The cheese should look nice and golden on top.

Chicory in Ham and Cheese

Originating in the suburbs of Paris, this recipe from the blog charmed Freddie and Alex into awarding it a high score.

Serves 4
8 chicory hearts
Vegetable bouillon powder
8 thin slices of ham

For the cheese sauce
15 g (½ oz) plain flour, sifted
15 g (½ oz) butter
225 ml (7½ fl oz) milk
50 g (2 oz) mature Cheddar cheese, grated, plus extra
1 tsp mild French mustard
Salt and freshly ground pepper

1 Preheat the oven to 180°C (350°F) Gas 4.

2 Place the chicory hearts in a saucepan and cover with boiling water with a little vegetable bouillon powder and cook on a medium heat for about 10 minutes.

3 Meanwhile make the cheese sauce. Gently melt the butter in a pan on a low heat. Add the sifted flour and stir until it forms a smooth paste. Add the milk and whisk constantly until the sauce thickens. Allow the sauce to boil for a minute or so. Reduce the heat and add the cheese and mustard and stir well until it melts. Season.

4 Drain the cooked chicory and wrap each one in a slice of ham. Line them up in a shallow baking dish and cover in the cheese sauce. Grate more cheese on top and bake for 30–40 minutes.

 tip

Penny suggests you can add some breadcrumbs on top for added crunch.

C is for... CORN

'Come see the butter fly!'

Now that's the kind of exhortation I like. A friend had sent me a link to the town called Millersport, off Ohio's Route 24. This is Freddie's kind of town.

It is a place where men and women are rewarded for gorging themselves on corncobs. According to their website, the Millersport Annual Sweetcorn Festival even has its own Festival Queen with her court and they tour as ambassadors of this revered vegetable.

And why not? I particularly like the fact that one of the previous reigning queens was a young lady called Natalie, from a place called Licking Heights. You couldn't make it up. I think I may have to send Freddie to Licking Heights, as he has a very special relationship with buttered corn on the cob. He could be the Prince to Queen Natalie.

Our first corn recipe was the simplest. It is the best way to cook sweetcorn on the cob. We bought the corn still in its husks, placed it under a hot grill, turning it regularly until the husks were blackening. Then, we split open the husks and served the corn with discs of chive butter. Millersport would have been proud of us.

The following day we gorged on Corn and Coriander Fritters, using a recipe from Hannah Miles. This is the lady who introduced Freddie to the delights of Savoy cabbage layered with sausage meat. She should be honoured for her services to vegetables.

I was side-tracked by a recipe on Oprah Winfrey's site for vanilla creamed corn. This had the potential to be revolting. It's not a pretty dish but it gave me an excuse to use a vanilla bean which had been lurking in the kitchen cupboard. Two of my children's friends, Rebecca and Patrick, came to stay for the weekend, so we had a four-strong tasting panel. I had cunningly ensured they had built up a healthy appetite at the playground. They all had seconds. It was delicious. I wouldn't have thought to put vanilla seeds and puréed sweetcorn together but it does work.

Freddie was relaxed this week. Sweetcorn was safe territory; one of the few vegetables that he would always eat. I overheard him chatting to a neighbour who asked him, 'So what's changed with you Fred? Why are you trying all these vegetables?'

'I haven't changed. I am just the same boy as I was before the Great Big Vegetable Challenge – it's just that I'm eating differently.'

He was probably right. I had done the most changing. I was cooking far more, trying out new things and not being quite so bad-tempered when he turned his nose up at something. In return, he was entering into the spirit of things. It was the opposite of a vicious circle.

tip

When you are used to preparing food for a fussy-eater it is very easy to start mirroring their behaviour. They narrow down what they are prepared to eat and you find yourself narrowing down what you cook. Try and break that cycle by trying out new vegetables and new tastes on a regular basis. It takes a long time to introduce change so don't be despondent if your attempts are rejected at first.

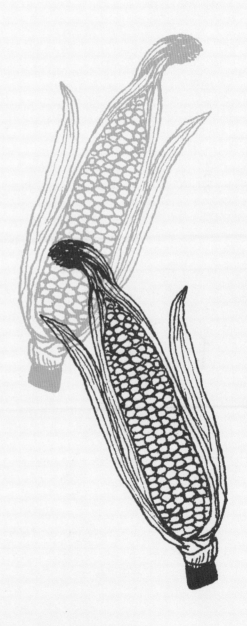

Corn and Coriander Fritters

Another wonderful recipe from Hannah Miles, that transformed this revered vegetable into another successful incarnation.

Serves 4
115 g (3¹/₂ oz) self-raising flour
2 tsp caster sugar
2 eggs, separated

200 ml (7 fl oz) milk
50 g (2 oz) butter melted, plus extra for frying
330 g (11¹/₂ oz) tinned sweetcorn, drained
A handful of fresh coriander, finely chopped

1 Sift the flour into a bowl and add the sugar, egg yolks, milk and melted butter. Whisk until everything is incorporated.
2 In a separate bowl, whisk the egg whites to soft peaks and then gently fold into the batter mixture. Stir in the sweetcorn and coriander.
3 Melt the butter in a large frying pan and place spoonfuls of the batter a small distance apart in the pan. Cook until golden, turning over halfway through cooking when the batter is almost cooked on the top side of the fritter.
4 Keep the fritters warm in a low oven until you have cooked the remaining batter mixture.

tip
Larger supermarkets sell both tinned sweetcorn and creamed sweetcorn. If you are using the ready-made creamed sweetcorn, it often contains corn starch and sugar. But you can make your own creamed sweetcorn very quickly, without the need to add any sugar.

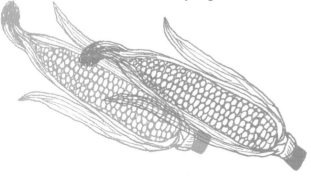

Vanilla Sweetcorn

I adapted these recipes from the Oprah Winfrey site, www2.oprah.com. It is good served as a side dish with some sausages, pork chops or chicken thighs.

Serves 3–4 as a side dish
Version 1: Using tinned creamed sweetcorn
400 g (13 oz) tin of creamed sweetcorn

200 g (7 oz) tin of sweetcorn kernels, drained and rinsed
½ vanilla pod

1 Add the creamed sweetcorn to a pan with the sweetcorn kernels.
2 Scrape the seeds from half a vanilla pod into the corn and stir over a medium heat for about 5 minutes. Serve hot.

Version 2: Using sweetcorn kernels
500 g (1 lb) tinned (drained weight) or frozen sweetcorn

A knob of butter
½ vanilla pod

1 Heat up the sweetcorn kernels in a pan over a medium heat in a little water. Drain well.
2 Remove 300 g (10 oz) of the sweetcorn and place in a food processor with a knob of butter and blend until smooth and creamy. Put back in the pan with the rest of the sweetcorn.
3 Scrape the seeds from the vanilla pod into the pan and stir in. Heat gently for 2 minutes, stirring well. Serve hot.

Grilled sweetcorn with flavoured butter

1 Preheat the grill to high.

2 Place the cobs of sweetcorn still in their husks under the grill. If you prefer you can do this on a barbecue. Turn the cobs every minute under the grill so that all sides cook evenly. The husks will blacken but make sure they don't get so close to the grill that they catch fire.

3 After about 10 minutes the corn should be cooked. Split open the husks with a knife and peel back. They taste delicious just like this, nothing added, or you can serve with discs of chive butter.

tip
How to make chive butter

1 Put 115 g (3½ oz) butter in a bowl. Warm a fork under some hot tap water and use it to soften the butter.

2 Finely chop a generous handful of fresh chives. Mix into the butter with the fork.

3 Using your hands, roll the butter into a small cylinder. Wrap in a piece of foil and put it in the fridge to harden.

4 When hard, cut into small discs and serve with the corn.

Some other flavoured butters for grilled corn

Lime and Paprika Butter
Soften 115 g (3½ oz) butter in a bowl, add the finely grated zest of one lime and 1 teaspoon of mild ground paprika.

Parsley or Basil Butter
Soften 115 g (3½ oz) butter in a bowl, add 25 g (1 oz) of finely chopped parsley or basil and mix together.

Roasted Garlic Butter
Soften 115 g (3½ oz) butter in a bowl, add 1 roasted garlic bulb (see page 115).

Spring Onion Butter
Soften 115 g (3½ oz) butter in a bowl, add 3 finely chopped spring onions.

C is for... Courgette

'Children aren't happy with nothing to ignore, And that's what parents were created for.' (Ogden Nash)

I know my place as a mother; issuing orders that evaporate within a few inches of my children's ears or ranting unheard about the merits of washing hands, tidying up and eating vegetables. But what Ogden Nash didn't say was that children curiously consider *other* adult's advice more compelling than their own parents'. On the blog, on a number of occasions, visitors from the United States had spoken about quesadillas and how it was possible to persuade children to eat vegetables when cooked this way.

The courgette, which is a baby marrow, is a perfect ingredient for quesadillas. Freddie liked the fact that this advice came to him from families in America. The Courgette Quesadillas became a favourite. Freddie scored them 10 out of 10.

I'm sure that having a healthy appetite helps to maximise the chances that something new will at least be tried. I realise that it doesn't look great to compare a child with a small puppy but there are parallels. I have a friend with a greedy dog who refused its dog food and preferred to snack from their table. They were advised by her vet that they should keep him hungry between meals so that he actually ate what was in his bowl. It worked. And I suspect it works with small boys as well. Freddie, if kept keen for his meal, is more willing to eat what is on his plate. The moment his appetite is sated, his attitude shifts and he starts picking out the green bits. So, I cunningly introduced our next courgette dish after a particularly exhausting game of football in the park.

I hadn't realised that courgettes come in other shapes and colours. In the supermarket I found round yellow courgettes that looked like tennis balls. After the success of quesadillas, we tried bruschetta topped with courgettes. In its simplest form in Italy, bruschetta (pronounced brusketta) would have been a slice of well-toasted country bread, with newly pressed olive oil drizzled on top, the bread having been rubbed with a clove of garlic. Then everyone else joined in around the world and added fancy toppings. Which is a perfect excuse for us to join in, too. Bruschetta, topped with thinly sliced courgettes, were eaten without any resistance and scored 9 out of 10.

Courgette Quesadillas

Buy the smaller-sized tortillas, rather than the larger ones so that you can serve a whole one for each child.

Serves 4
2 tbsp olive oil
1 onion, finely chopped
5 medium courgettes, coarsely grated
2 cloves of garlic, crushed

1 tsp freshly grated ginger
8 small tortillas
225 g (7½ oz) Cheddar cheese, grated
1 large carrot, grated
Salt and freshly ground pepper

1 Preheat the oven to 200°C (400°F) Gas 6.

2 In a frying pan, heat the olive oil on a medium heat. Add the onions and fry for 3 minutes until they start to soften and become translucent.

3 Add the grated courgette, garlic and grated ginger. Sauté for 3 minutes, stirring continuously. Make sure the courgette and onion mix does not burn. Turn off the heat and season.

4 Lightly brush one side of each tortilla with oil. Place four tortillas, oiled side down, on a sheet of baking parchment paper on a baking tray. Take half of the cheese and sprinkle it evenly amongst the four tortillas. Divide the courgette mixture equally between your four tortillas and sprinkle it on top of the cheese. Then add the remaining cheese on top. Place another tortilla on top. Gently press with a spatula to compress the quesadillas.

5 Place in a preheated oven for 8–10 minutes, until the edges of the quesadillas curl up slightly. Slice into quarters and serve hot.

The courgette, which is a baby marrow, is a perfect ingredient for quesadillas. Freddie liked the fact that this advice came to him from families in America.

Bruschetta with Courgettes

Try and buy some crusty Italian country bread to make the bruschetta or you can use ciabatta.

Serves 4
Olive oil
1–2 courgettes, thinly sliced
4 slices of Italian country bread or ciabatta

1 clove of garlic
Parmesan cheese shavings
Balsamic glaze (optional)
Sea salt and freshly ground pepper

Ridged griddle pan

1 Heat a ridged griddle pan with a little olive oil and carefully cook the courgette slices for a few minutes.
2 Place the slices of bread on a baking tray under a hot grill for a few minutes each side, until they are well toasted.
3 Remove and rub the bread with the side of a cut garlic clove. Then drizzle olive oil on each slice.
4 Top the bread with the grilled courgette slices and add some Parmesan shavings. Season with some freshly ground pepper and a little sea salt. Drizzle a little balsamic glaze on top, if liked, and serve immediately.

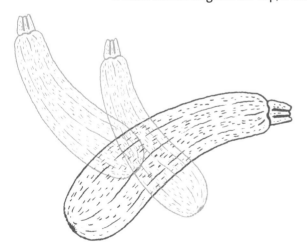

C is for... Cress

The vegetable cress has a great claim to fame. Captain Cook's crew apparently ate something known as 'scurvy grass' to keep them healthy and it belongs to the cress family. Clearly salad cress is a rather more domestic version.

It sits in a plastic box looking like a grass lawn in the suburbs. And this was the next vegetable in our challenge.

No one ever said the Great Big Vegetable Challenge had to be sophisticated. Egg and Cress sandwiches are simplicity itself, completely unthreatening to the veg-phobic Freddie. In fact, I put these down in front of him, turned round and when I looked back the sandwiches had gone. The boy must have an 'inhale' mode which bypasses normal eating methods in favour of speed. 'What's our blog recipe today Mum?' he asked. 'That was it.' He seemed relieved. The score was 10 out of 10.

I have learnt that if I make a soup smooth, Freddie will enjoy it. I still tell him exactly what the soup is made from. But nothing scary lurks in the bowl. Now if I get this right,

he eats more vegetables. Over our smooth, sweet Cress and Potato Soup we were discussing the daft names that some employers use in job adverts, asking for an 'education centre nourishment production assistant' when what they needed was a dinner lady, or recruiting a 'vision clearance executive' instead of a window cleaner. We reached the conclusion that I was no longer a mother but a Vegetable Enjoyment Facilitator.

We all spent the day running the second-hand toy stall for a May Fair in Notting Hill. We had eight trestle tables piled high with other people's cast-offs. You could make a study of the collective neuroses of parents in West London. There were Teach your Baby to Read flashcards, Bach and Beethoven music units for toddlers, IQ enhancing cot mobiles and three unopened 'Basic Electronic Sets' for 8 plus. We sold out. That evening we made our last cress recipe with a quiche.

'Most quiches I don't eat properly but this one I did,' said Freddie. His friend gave him some cress seeds which he is growing on the kitchen windowsill.

Freddie's Favourite 10/10

Egg and Cress Sandwiches

These were honoured with a 10 out of 10 and seemed to disappear so quickly that they could have barely touched the sides.

Serves 2
3 hard-boiled eggs
1 tsp low-fat mayonnaise
1 tsp crème fraîche

1 punnet of salad cress
A handful of basil leaves
Salt and freshly ground pepper
Your choice of sliced bread

1 Mash the hard-boiled eggs in a bowl with the mayonnaise, crème fraîche and a pinch of salt and pepper.

2 Cut off the salad cress, wash it, drain and dry, then finely chop.

3 Tear the basil leaves into smaller pieces and add to the mixture. Spread on your sandwich bread.

tip

For smaller children, or those who are young at heart, cut out different sandwich shapes using biscuit cutters.

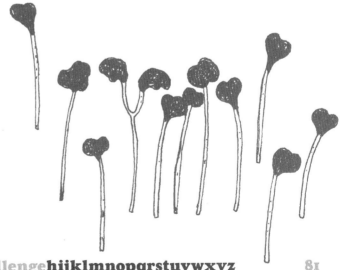

Cress Quiche

Not a great fan of the quiche, Freddie ate this one 'properly'.

Serves 4–6
500 g (1 lb) ready-made shortcrust pastry
2 punnets of salad cress, finely chopped
3 medium eggs, beaten
1 egg yolk

200 ml (7 fl oz) milk
175 ml (6 fl oz) cream
½ clove of garlic, crushed.
25 g (1 oz) Cheddar cheese, grated
Salt and freshly ground pepper

23 cm (9 in.) flan dish
Baking beans

1 Preheat the oven to 200°C (400°F) Gas 6.
2 Roll out the pastry to a depth of 5 mm (¼ in.) and line a 23 cm (9 in.) flan dish. Bake the pastry blind by placing a large circle of baking parchment on top of the pastry weighed down with baking beans. Bake for for 12 minutes. Remove and allow to cool. Reduce the oven temperature to 180°C (350°F) Gas 4.
3 Whisk the beaten eggs with the egg yolk. Stir in the milk and cream. Season and stir in the garlic. Add the chopped salad cress and mix together well.
4 Pour into the pastry case and sprinkle a little cheese on top. Bake in the oven for 30–35 minutes until just golden brown and set. Serve warm or cold with salad.

'Most quiches I don't eat properly but this one I did,' said Freddie.

ab_cthe_dgreat_ebig_fvegg_gchallenge**hijklmnopqrstuvwxyz**

Cress and Potato Soup

Like a lot of children, Freddie is suspicious of unfamiliar textures and so I have learnt that if I make a soup smooth, he will enjoy it.

Serves 4
2 tbsp olive oil
1 medium onion, finely chopped
1 clove of garlic, crushed
1 small courgette, finely chopped

2 large potatoes, peeled and sliced
1 litre (1³/₄ pints) vegetable or chicken stock
2 punnets of salad cress, finely chopped
3 tbsp crème fraîche
Salt and freshly ground pepper

1 Heat the olive oil in a large pan and gently fry the onion. Add the garlic. When softened, add the courgette and potato. Stir over medium heat for 4 minutes.
2 Add the vegetable stock. Bring just to the boil and then reduce the heat and leave to simmer very gently for 25 minutes until the vegetables are all soft.
3 Remove from the heat and allow to cool a little. Using a hand-blender, purée the soup mix. If you think it looks too thick, add a glass of water.
4 Add the salad cress. Stir and add the crème fraîche and warm over gentle heat for another 2 minutes, stirring. Serve with croutons and a sprinkle of cress.

C is for... Cucumber

'A cucumber should be well sliced, and dressed with pepper and vinegar, and then thrown out, as good for nothing.' (Samuel Johnson, *Journal of a Tour to the Hebrides*)

Samuel Johnson was right. There is something a bit prissy about the way we slice and dress cucumbers, pampering them like princesses. Cucumbers are clearly the 'it-girls' of the vegetable world. Freddie had tried cucumber juice, which was greeted with the violent response, 'Are you trying to torture me?' It was time for our next attempts. The sun came out and my daughter marched off and bought a beach dress, bikini and flip-flops and I prepared a cucumber summer tea, in April.

I chose Pain de Mie from the bakers. I spread it with lightly salted butter and thin slices of cucumber. Knowing Freddie's over-sensitive attitude to green vegetables, I also made some Tuna and Cucumber Paté. As it happened, he enjoyed both. The cucumber was sliced very thin and the butter very thick, which might be the key to our success.

To accompany the cucumber sandwiches, I made a gazpacho soup. I consulted with a Spanish neighbour and decided to use sweeter red peppers, lime juice and a little honey to make it irresistible. I was trying to find recipes for cucumber that would give it a less prominent role. It has to be more of an off-stage backing singer rather than the star of the show. I think the cucumber secretly wants to have a break from being 'sliced and dressed' and so gazpacho soup was perfect.

We sat outside in our fleeces basking in the barely warm spring sun, sipping chilled soup. Alex wore her new beach dress and flip-flops. The net curtains of neighbouring houses were twitching. That's the trouble with living in a city: it is hard to hide your eccentricities.

Freddie loved the taste of gazpacho and didn't believe that it contained the evil cucumber. He did ask me, apologetically, if I could put his bowl in the microwave. And of course I did. It was good and earned an 8 out of 10. It was a success and I don't care what the neighbours think.

Tuna and Cucumber Paté

Blended together, the tuna and cucumber were a successful combination.
It would work equally well with tinned salmon. I adapted this recipe from one
on the website of the Association of Cucumber Growers, which has a useful
recipe page. (See www.cucumbergrowers.co.uk)

Serves 4
½ cucumber
200 g (7 oz) tinned tuna or salmon, drained
115 g (3½ oz) cream cheese

50 g (2 oz) fresh breadcrumbs
2 tbsp lime juice
Salt and freshly ground pepper

1 Peel and deseed the cucumber then chop roughly.
2 Using a hand-blender or food processor, blend the cucumber with the drained
tuna or salmon, cream cheese, breadcrumbs and lime juice. Add a little ground
pepper and salt to taste and blend until it is smooth.
3 Place in the fridge to chill for 30 minutes. Spread on fresh bread.

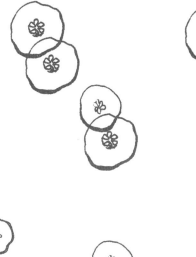

Easy Gazpacho Soup

My Spanish neighbour suggested that I use sweeter red peppers, lime juice and a little honey to make this classic cold soup irresistible. It worked, and even came out top after being warmed through, too.

Serves 4
1 large tomato
1 clove of garlic, chopped
1 red onion, chopped
1 red pepper, seeded and sliced
½ green pepper, seeded and sliced
1 medium cucumber, peeled and deseeded
400 ml (14 fl oz) tomato juice

1 tbsp lime juice
1 tsp honey
1 tbsp olive oil
1 tsp red wine vinegar
Sea salt and ground black pepper
Mild Tabasco sauce (optional)
Single cream (optional)

1 Simply put all the ingredients, apart from the Tabasco sauce, in the food processor and blend it all. We prefer it smooth because children often have a 'no bits' rule but you can blend it to a slightly chunkier texture if you prefer.
2 Pour it into a bowl and put it in the fridge to chill for an hour before serving. We like to add a dash of mild Tabasco sauce and a dash of single cream, but these are optional.

Freddie loved the taste of gazpacho and didn't believe that it contained the evil cucumber.

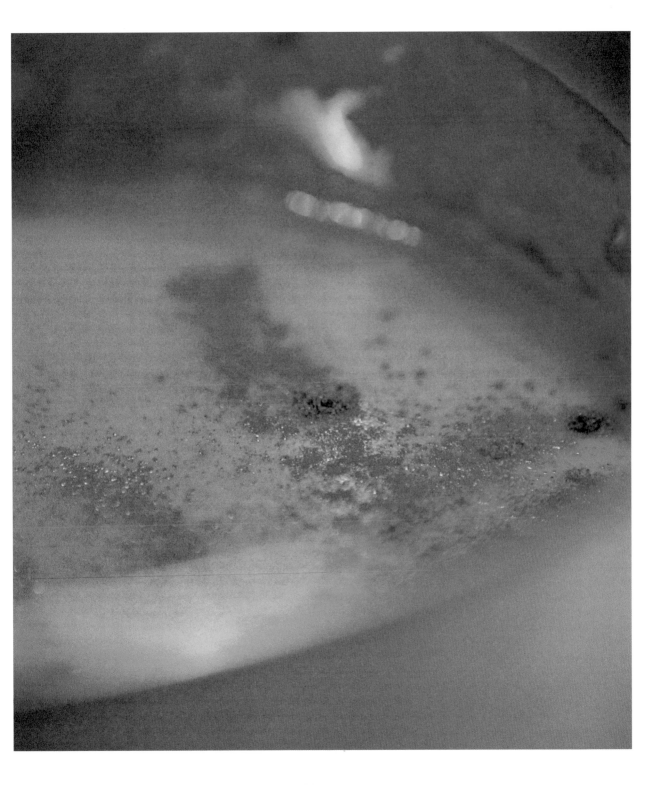

D is for... Daikon

D is a blighted letter; death, divorce, danger, distress. Whoever handed out the names for vegetables in the English language clearly felt uneasy about the letter D. Whilst its neighbour C has a cornucopia of vegetables, D stands out as a dunce.

All my hopes rested on daikon, a Japanese radish. It realises its value to the letter D and can consequently grow up to 90 cm (3 ft) in length and weigh up to 45 kg (100 lb), no doubt to make up for the lack of companions. Finding one presented Freddie and I with several challenges.

I woke up at six, Googled a picture of a daikon and made breakfast. The Great Big Vegetable Challenge would grind to a halt unless I could find a D vegetable. I walked the children to school and got on the tube, deciding to stop off in Chinatown. I had a twenty-minute window to spot a daikon and buy it before getting to a meeting in Westminster. No pressure or anything.

In my mind I had imagined that at nine in the morning, Chinatown would be bustling, a bit like a scaled down version of a Hong Kong market. It was in fact empty. So there I was with my picture, smudged in the rain, squinting through the windows of grocery stores, searching for the elusive daikon. I spoke to the men delivering boxes of produce. They were civil but clearly thought I was one sandwich short of a picnic. I forced my way into one store which hadn't properly opened. Inside were shelves full of produce that looked like it came from outer space. This was the space port bar in Mos Eisley in *Star Wars*: creatures with huge spiky points and lurid green skins. My daikon looked friendly in comparison. But he wasn't there, clearly too ordinary to feature in this shop. I was running out of time and ready to give up.

On my way out of Chinatown I passed a cornershop. And there they were. A crate of long white radishes tinged with green. I asked the shopkeeper what they were. He didn't speak English and I couldn't speak Chinese. I accosted other shoppers. A Malaysian man unplugged his iPod and gave the daikon a positive identification. I rushed to Westminster with the huge daikon lurking in my bag, only

abcthe *d* greatebigfveggchallengehijklmnopqrstuvwxyz

five minutes late. It is not an easy vegetable to conceal and I was working that day in one of the most security-conscious zones in London. Advice on wearing clean underwear 'just in case' should also be extended to taking greater care over the contents of your handbag. I hadn't thought through the challenge of having to empty my shopping bag for security officers in Whitehall. There was a queue of people, emptying their pockets of the paraphernalia of modern life; mobile phones, car keys and BlackBerrys.

'I don't have a BlackBerry,' I joked, trying to prepare the guard for the huge club-like white weapon of mass destruction that I pulled from my bag. 'But this is a daikon and it doesn't connect to the internet.' Security officers are not hired for their sense of humour. I tried to tell him about the Great Big Vegetable Challenge but he x-rayed the daikon all the same.

Back at home, the daikon had a brooding presence in our kitchen. Freddie picked it up and attempted to wallop his sister with it. It did look like a caveman's club. Nobody in the family had ever tried daikon before so this was a challenge for all of us. We tried it raw and

it tasted like a mild radish. I made a miso soup mix and added some rice noodles. I sliced some asparagus tips, a few spring onions and quickly fried prawns with some very thinly sliced daikon sticks, adding a splash of soy sauce. Freddie likes the taste of miso soup with noodles. He was suspicious of the daikon. 'This is a very new thing and I don't think I will like it,' said Freddie. But he did, which was good in itself. He rated the daikon a poor 4 out of 10 but enjoyed the miso soup.

The satisfaction I felt having tracked down the daikon was beginning to wear off. Chopping off a section for the miso soup didn't appear to have reduced its size. I worried that it may have the power to grow back overnight. A kind of gloom hung over its corner of my kitchen and even Freddie seemed a little too scared to pick it up and clonk his sister on the head. Having Googled 'Daikon', I think I know why. There are websites in Japan selling soft plush cuddly daikons. They come in various sizes and sport a variety of expressions. There is even the celebrated 'Dokonjo Daikon' that captivated the nation's attention when it grew through tarmac and featured on the nightly news. I didn't trust this vegetable in my home.

An email from Paula McIntyre rescued us from daikon-disaster. She is the resident chef on BBC Radio Ulster. Freddie had spoken about vegetables with her a few weeks before. We hacked off a huge chunk of daikon and made her recipe for Daikon Radish Salad.

Despite two outings, there was still a large torso of daikon left to eat. A fellow-blogger, Top Veg, left a useful comment on the blog. She had visited a Chinese neighbour for the inside knowledge on this veg-beast. 'The meat gives it good flavour. She kept repeating this … it is the opposite of our cooking where we add veg to the meat to flavour it during cooking. She told me to add the meat to the daikon in stews and casseroles. The meat will give the daikon a good flavour!'

So taking on board this advice, I bought some lamb neck fillet, cooked it for 5 minutes with some chopped red onions, a clove of garlic, a few mushrooms, herbs and seasoned it. I hacked the remaining daikon-boulder into cubes and boiled it for 20 minutes with a vegetable stock cube. I must warn you that Daikon can seem indestructible. It barely flinched in boiling water: the Freddie Krueger of veg. I drained it and added it to the lamb with a tin of chopped tomatoes and half a glass of red wine. It cooked in a casserole dish in the oven for an hour and a half.

The meat did make the daikon taste a little better. My husband, who will eat anything and rarely complains, muttered, 'Thank God that's finished.' Freddie ate all the lamb and two chunks of daikon and left the rest. I didn't have it in me to make a fuss. His score was 5 out of 10. As we finished the meal, the children started to sing a bowdlerized version of the song from *The Wizard of Oz*, 'Ding Dong! The Daikon's dead. Which old veg? The Wicked Veg! Ding Dong! The Wicked Veg is dead.' We all joined in. That's enough daikon for anybody.

abcthe *d* greatebigfveggchallengehijklmnopqrstuvwxyz

Daikon Radish Salad

With only a few salads successfully under his belt, Freddie bravely tackled this recipe from Paula McIntrye of BBC Radio Ulster and awarded it a respectable 7 out of 10.

Serves 4
500 g (1 lb) daikon, peeled and coarsely grated
4 spring onions, finely chopped
1 red onion, finely sliced

For the dressing
1 tbsp vegetable oil
2 chopped shallots
2 cloves of garlic

50 g (2 oz) freshly grated ginger
1 tbsp sesame oil
Freshly squeezed juice of 2 limes
1 tbsp clear honey
200 ml (7 fl oz) rapeseed oil
4 tbsp soy sauce
1 tbsp black sesame seeds
1 tbsp white sesame seeds
A handful of freshly chopped coriander leaves

1 Mix together the daikon and onions.

2 Make the dressing. Heat the vegetable oil and cook the shallots, garlic and ginger until golden.

3 Add the sesame oil, lime juice, honey, rapeseed oil and soy sauce and blend in a liquidiser to a smooth dressing.

4 Add the sesame seeds and toss through the daikon mixture. Leave for at least an hour before serving for the flavours to permeate. Just before serving, toss in the coriander.

D is for... Dandelions

One morning when the postman came, he delivered dandelions. They arrived carefully packed in a padded envelope sent by a lady known to me only as Purple Luv. I met her on a BBC internet food message board where I appealed for help with D vegetables.

In this virtual waiting room we chatted about dandelions with someone else known simply as 'Ian in France'. London dandelions punch their way through the gaps in the paving stones but I wasn't going to feed them to my family coated in diesel fumes and dog pee. So I needed a purer supply.

Purple Luv generously offered to pick them from a farm in Cheshire following Ian's detailed instructions. He advised blanching the leaves by placing a slate over the plants and waiting a few days before picking just the palest yellowy-green leaves. This makes them less bitter. Ian also had invaluable information for me, suggesting that I make a tepid salad as the French do, with a couple of bacon rashers cut into strips and some cubes of bread. I fried the bacon and when it was crisp kept it warm whilst I used the same fat to fry up the bread cubes to make croutons. With the bacon, the whole lot was tipped over the dandelions with a lemon, mustard and pepper dressing.

So this is what I did with my dandelions from Cheshire and my recipe from France, with some added asparagus tips. It was a perfect arrangement coaxed from the internet. And Freddie had been following the story of the dandelions as if it were a wonderful fairy tale. He imagines Purple Luv covered in purple dandelion flowers, a magical figure who is guided by Wizard Ian from his castle in France. And consequently Freddie, taken up by the magic of the whole story, ate dandelions. His score for the dandelion salad was 8 out of 10.

My next consignment of dandelion leaves arrived on the 7.52 from Pangbourne. Their courier was Helen, a work colleague who picked them from her back garden. She had taken extraordinary care with them. They had been washed, patted dry and lined up in neat rows, tucked in with kitchen paper. It seemed a bit cruel to remove them, let alone cook them. But the Great Big Vegetable Challenge has a momentum of its own.

We reserved these pampered greens for a very special Friday night meal. Alexandra had been away from home for a week on a school trip. So I made four dandelion tarts in heart-shaped tins. Freddie made a little welcome home card.

abcthe *d* greatebigfveggchallengehijklmnopqrstuvwxyz

For a second it felt like a Martha Stewart family moment. A split second. That was until I burnt my finger on the oven shelf, dropped one of the tarts and swore. Freddie looked up from his card-making with a withering glance.

I looked down at my heart-shaped tart splatted on the kitchen floor, muttered an apology and scraped it up with a fish-slice. That would have to be mine. Lots of well-meaning parenting guides say we have to lead by example. But you can bet that Freddie will not remember the fine example of my tart-cooking. The inappropriate swear word will however be lodged permanently in his mind. Oh well. Alexandra came home, talking ten to the dozen about her wonderful adventures, loved Freddie's little card and the Dandelion Tart. Freddie's score was 7½ out of 10.

By the time we finished D, The Great Big Vegetable Challenge was six months old. We had tried out 21 vegetables, over 60 new recipes. Sometimes it resembled a game of snakes and ladders with days when it seemed as if we had slithered back to square one. One day Freddie would try the exotic – the daikon and the dandelions – but another time something as simple as peas would trigger off a revolt.

Somewhere along the line, peas had assumed enemy status. Strenuous efforts were made to prevent them from entering his territory. If they broke through his considerable defences, the peas were cordoned off, banished to the outskirts of the dish. His knife and fork scuttled around his plate, scooping up all other food to the safety of his mouth. Then distraction techniques are employed. He gently nudged his plate towards his sister, knowing that she would happily hoover up his unwanted veg. If spotted, he claimed innocence. Then I would wade in with that stalwart of parenting lines. 'If you don't eat your peas, there'll be no ice cream.'

This isn't where I want to be. This is why I started the Great Big Vegetable Challenge. But as this goes through my mind, something more significant is happening across the table. Freddie looks at the pudding, looks back at me, takes a deep breath and stuffs the peas in his mouth. It's a truce. Now that wouldn't have happened six months before.

Dandelion Tart

I made this dandelion tart baked in a heart-shaped tin as a welcome home dish for Alex.

Serves 6
500 g (1 lb) ready-made shortcrust pastry

For the filling
A large knob of butter
1 medium onion, finely chopped
Smoked paprika

4 handfuls of small dandelion leaves, chopped
3 eggs, beaten
1 egg yolk
150 ml (¼ pint) crème fraîche
150 g (5 oz) Cheshire cheese, grated, or other
　white crumbly cheese
Salt and freshly ground pepper

23 cm (9 in.) flan dish (or heart-shaped tin), lightly greased
Baking beans

1 Preheat the oven to 200°C (400°F) Gas 6.
2 Roll out the pastry on a floured surface to a depth of 5 mm (¼ in.) and line the prepared flan dish and chill for 10 minutes.
3 Bake the pastry blind by placing a large circle of baking parchment on top of the pastry weighed down with baking beans. Bake for 10 minutes then remove the paper and beans. Return to the oven for 5 minutes until lightly browned.
4 Remove and let it cool. Reduce the oven temperature to 180°C (350°F) Gas 4.
5 Sauté the onion on a gentle heat until it is soft. Add a couple of pinches of smoked paprika.
6 In a small pan, melt a knob of butter and when it has just melted add your dandelion leaves, stirring until they wilt. Don't cook for longer than 30 seconds.
7 Layer the pastry case evenly with the onion and season. Scatter the dandelion leaves evenly over the case, reserving a few.
8 In a bowl, mix together the eggs, crème fraîche and cheese and season. Pour over the onion and dandelions and scatter the few remaining dandelion leaves on the top.
9 Bake in the oven for 30–35 minutes until slightly brown and set. Serve warm or cold with salad.

abcthe *d* greatebigfveggchallengehijklmnopqrstuvwxyz

E is for... Edamame Beans

'It is the magic bean that has virtually all the health benefits of eating meat, but none of the blood and gore.' (Daily Mail)

Our first E vegetable was the edamame bean. This is a vegetable that appears to have a PR machine behind the scenes working flat out. There are pronunciation tips (ed-ah-mah-may). It is described as a superfood, a magic bean, the 'only vegetable that contains all nine essential amino acids'. Having all nine essential amino acids sounds impressive. These beans are clearly part of a vegetable elite. I asked for them at three supermarkets with no success – so I went upmarket to an organic shop. This is the kind of place I find intimidating and a little confusing. It's a shop where you can't tell the food from the bath products. The basil and lemon shampoo looked good enough to dress a salad. The shop assistants smiled at me from behind their calico aprons. They looked like they were taking their edamame beans intraveneously. Their skin glowed, their hair shone and they had toned bodies like Lara Croft. They saw me and a look of pity crossed their faces. I tried to hide my shopping bag, worried that the Oreo cookies and steak might sully this temple to healthy eating. And I didn't want to be found out as a fake. A health-food charlatan.

The assistant ushered me to where the edamame beans were holding court in a freezer. £1.29 a bag seemed like a bargain. For the price of a cup of coffee I was buying an entrée into this vegetable powerhouse. At the till I added pumpkin seeds and carob bars. It was a pathetic attempt to inflate my healthy-eating credentials. I don't think the calico goddesses were convinced. It reminded me of my one and only visit to a weight watchers meeting. I talked the talk with the WW motivators, bought the low-cal snack bars, had myself weighed, my passport stamped and then walked off, never to return.

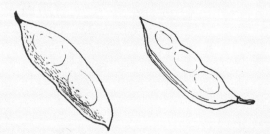

abcthedgreat bigfveggchallengehijklmnopqrstuvwxyz

I took my edamame beans home. The children have always inspected the shopping. Biscuits are leapt upon, vegetables groaned at. Ever since the Great Big Vegetable Challenge started, they want to know what is the latest vegetable in residence. I showed them the magic power beans and alluded to Jack and the Beanstalk. 'Looks like a broad bean,' said Alexandra. 'Are you going to put meat with it?' asked Freddie. I repeated the claim that the edamame bean is like eating meat with none of the blood and gore. 'But I like the blood and gore,' said Freddie.

Our first edamame bean recipe was a tortilla. Irrespective of its magic qualities, this dish scored an impressive 8 out of 10 from Freddie. And that was without any meat.

Our flirtation with the celebrity health bean continued. My husband, Chris, braved the calico goddesses at the temple of health. A comment left by a Japanese lady on the blog explained that edamame are simply baby soybeans, plucked from their mother-pod at an untimely age. They are like baby sweetcorn. Freddie and Alexandra looked a little sad when I told them. But that didn't stop them from slurping down edamame soup. The children named it Baby Bean Soup. Freddie gave it a confident 8 out of 10. I could now look the health-food shop assistants in the eye.

Our farewell to the edamame bean came from a blog comment left by someone called 'Wellunderstood'. We mixed the cooked edamame beans with penne pasta, grated Parmesan and ricotta cheese, a handful of bacon lardons and I added a generous sprinkling of chopped basil leaves. Freddie said 'These beans are as good as meat. And they're green!' This has to be the perfect food for a veg-phobic. Both children scored the meal a 9 out of 10.

Edamame and Potato Tortilla

The children have always loved tortilla and they provide the perfect cover for vegetables to sneak in.

Serves 4
2 tbsp olive oil
2 red onions, thinly sliced
250 g (8 oz) potatoes, diced into small cubes
250 g (8 oz) frozen edamame beans

6 large eggs
A small knob of butter
Freshly grated Parmesan (optional)
Salt and freshly ground pepper

1 Use a deep non-stick frying pan about 23 cm (9 in.) in diameter. Heat up the olive oil on a medium heat and add the onions and potatoes and stir well. Cover with a lid or circle of foil and cook gently for about 20 minutes, stirring frequently to prevent sticking.

2 Beat the eggs in a bowl with a pinch of salt and twist of ground pepper.

3 Cook the edamame beans in boiling water for 8–10 minutes. Drain them and in a bowl crush them a little with a potato masher. Add a small knob of butter.

4 Add the beans to the potato and onion in the pan. Stir over the heat for about 2 minutes. Transfer the onion, potato and bean mixture to the beaten eggs and stir. Return the frying pan to a medium heat, and add another tablespoon of oil.

5 Pour the whole onion, bean, potato mixture into the pan. Cook slowly without a lid on a low heat for about 20–25 minutes, depending on the depth of your tortilla.

6 Cook gently until the egg on the base sets and browns. Carefully draw around the edge of the pan with a palette knife, tipping any liquid left on the surface down the sides.

7 Now at this point decide how skilled you are. If you feel up to inverting the tortilla on to a plate and putting it back into the pan then go ahead. I know my limitations. I sprinkle a little Parmesan on top, turn off the hob and put the pan under a preheated grill to cook the top.

8 To serve, slice into quarters or cut into 5-cm (2-in.) cubes as finger food.

abcthedgreat bigfveggchallengehijklmnopqrstuvwxyz
e

Edamame Soup

Christened 'Baby Bean Soup' by the children, this tastes quite subtle and is easy to make.

Serves 4
1 tsp olive oil
1 medium onion, finely chopped
1 potato, peeled and cut into small cubes

750 g (1½ lb) frozen edamame beans, defrosted
1.2 litres (2 pints) vegetable stock
2 tbsp crème fraîche
Salt and freshly ground pepper

1 In a pan, sauté the onion and potato in the oil on a medium heat, stirring frequently. Cover and allow it to soften for about 4 minutes, until they have both softened. Stir to prevent the mixture from sticking and burning.

2 Add the beans and the vegetable stock. Put the lid on and simmer on a medium heat for 15–20 minutes until the beans are tender.

3 Liquidise in a food processor or with a hand-held blender. Stir in the crème fraîche, reheat gently without boiling and serve.

Edamame are simply baby soybeans, plucked from their mother-pod at an untimely age. Freddie and Alexandra looked a little sad when I told them. But that didn't stop them from slurping down edamame soup.

Edamame Bean and Bacon Pasta

Speed of consumption is a key indicator of approval in our house and this meal was eaten with indecent haste.

Serves 4
400 g (13 oz) penne pasta
200 g (7 oz) bacon lardons
325 g (11 oz) frozen edamame beans

250 g (8 oz) tub of ricotta cheese
50 g (2 oz) freshly grated Parmesan cheese
30 g (1½ oz) fresh basil leaves
Salt and freshly ground pepper

1 Cook the pasta in boiling water, following the instructions on the packet.

2 Sauté the bacon lardons for 3 minutes.

3 Cook the frozen edamame beans in boiling water for 3 minutes and drain.

4 When the pasta is ready, drain well and whilst the pasta is still hot, stir in the ricotta cheese, edamame beans, bacon lardons and Parmesan. Season. Tear the basil leaves and scatter over the pasta and serve.

You can find edamame beans, also known as soya beans, in the frozen section of the supermarket. If you can't find them you can substitute them with frozen peas, broad beans or even green beans.

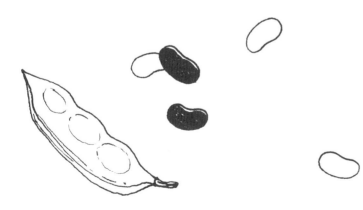

abcthedgreat bigfveggchallengehijklmnopqrstuvwxyz
e

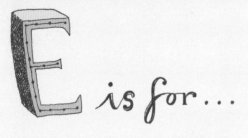

E is for... EDDOE

Sometimes when you are looking for one thing you find another. I was ready to move from E to F in the Great Big Vegetable Challenge. But as my daughter and I scoured the shelves at the supermarket, I caught sight of what looked like small mounds of elephant dung.

Individually they were small enough to fit in the palm of your hand. Their fibrous brown skins prickled with hair, like coconuts. If you look closely, they appear to be tattooed. These creatures looked friendly. The sort of vegetable we should take home. And, joy of joy, the label said 'Eddoe'. Even the name sounded cosy.

But there was a whispering campaign against the Eddoes. A fellow shopper sidled up to me as I placed them in the trolley. He grimaced at them and uttered one word in my direction. 'Slimy,' he said. 'They're really, really slimy when you cook them.' The defamation didn't stop. A woman brushed past with a grinning toddler. She smiled. 'I wouldn't recommend them. They're not worth the effort.' But having invited the eddoes home I couldn't change my mind. I went to the checkout. As they took their turn to be scanned, the shop assistant switched out of automatic pilot mode, stopping herself just in time from picking up the eddoes. She put on a pair of surgical gloves and then weighed them. Her nose wrinkled as if there was an unpleasant smell. The poor eddoe had become a supermarket pariah.

When we got home the first thing Freddie did was to sniff them, which seemed reasonable. 'Yuck! I'm not eating these.' A quick bit of research informed me that eddoes are a tuber crop related to Taro and Coco Yam and are used in Indian, Chinese and Caribbean cooking. This is what our challenge is all about, I told Freddie: new horizons, new tastes, new experiences. 'Yuck,' said Fred. Eddoes came with an instruction leaflet which invited me to treat them more or less like potatoes.

I have learnt that the best thing to do with a completely unfamiliar vegetable is to keep it simple. So we decided to bake them. About 50 minutes later the eddoes emerged. I cut a little cross in their hairy skin and peeled it back. The flesh of the Eddoe is greyish-white, not an attractive pallor. But there was no sign of slime. The flesh is like a sweet potato in texture. So it was eddoes for lunch with a dollop of butter or soured cream. With considerable bravery, Freddie and Alexandra tucked in. 'This is good,' said Freddie. 'It's tastier than a potato,' said Alex.

Freddie scraped off every last trace of the flesh and ate it, leaving the skin. And he gave it full marks. I plan to lurk in the 'unusual produce' section of the supermarket and start my own campaign to promote the poor eddoe.

Our adventures with our new friends continued. It's interesting how quickly children will get used to a new food. But then, so much is new to children, the hardest hurdle is probably the first recipe, the first taste. I am sure that one reason why the Great Big Vegetable Challenge was gradually taking away Freddie's fears, is the gentle pace we were moving at. He is given the opportunity to get to know a new vegetable, get used to its taste as a single entity and make up his own mind if he likes it or not. And he knows that whatever happens, we move on.

The baked eddoes had been delicious so I struck whilst the iron was hot and gave them another simple dish of mashed eddoe. Alexandra, who loves cooking, helped me. We first washed the eddoes and then placed them in boiling water in their skins. We boiled them, as you would a potato, for about 15–20 minutes, checking with a fork to see when they were soft. When they were ready, we took them out with a ladle and let them cool

a little on a plate. Then I carefully peeled off their hairy jackets to reveal the grey-white flesh. In a bowl, Alexandra mashed them with a generous knob of butter and 200 ml (7 fl oz) of milk and seasoned them with salt and pepper. We served it with sausages. Freddie and Alex were delighted with this meal.

'This mash is more filling than potato,' thought Freddie. But that didn't stop them from scraping the bowl so clean, it could have bypassed the dishwasher. It wasn't a pretty sight.

Now that we know the eddoe, he is going to be a regular visitor to our kitchen: a new friend. And just for the record, I have seen no evidence of a tendency to sliminess, at least not in our home where the eddoe will always be welcome.

tip
How to bake eddoes
Treat them like a baked potato. Wash the skin and rub in a little olive oil and salt. Place in the oven at 180°C (350°F) Gas 4, for about 50 minutes or until they are soft when you prick them with a fork. Peel back the skin and serve with a knob of butter or fromage frais. You can try them with some flavoured butter (see page 76). Don't eat the skins.

F is for... Farm visits

Every day that we are on holiday in Cornwall we drive past a large wooden box nailed to the wall of a farm. This is an honesty box, a way of shopping that we can't enjoy in London. It is special for two reasons.

Firstly, we are trusted as customers to put the right money in the jar and secondly we trust the farmers to offer what is fresh that day. We rarely catch sight of anyone but every morning the contents of the box magically change. We stop the car and Freddie and Alex peer inside to see what is on offer. There are freshly-laid duck eggs, potatoes, carrots, broad beans, beetroot, bags of fresh mint or peas in their pods. Sometimes there are surprises: huge field mushrooms the size of dinner plates. We choose something and put the money in the jam jar. The seasonal ingredients dictate what we eat for our evening meal. There is something strangely liberating about not having too much choice.

Four generations of this farming family live in and around Frogmore Farm. Over the years they have become our friends. The children love visiting and farmers Gill and Lorna show them around. They are introduced to the pigs, play fetch with the sheepdog Henry, feed the lambs, play in the barley, spot dragonflies and go pond-dipping. Gill and Lorna run farm visits under the Country Stewardship Scheme.

I told Gill about the Great Big Vegetable Challenge and she took Freddie and Alex to their vegetable garden in a field overlooking Lantivet Bay. Freddie's eyes glaze over in a supermarket. But the cling-film wrapped world of identikit vegetables is a long way away from the excitement of being on a farm. He dug up potatoes, pulled up carrots and onions and sat with Gill as she brought this field of vegetables to life. Alex and Freddie bit into carrots, fresh from the ground and wiped clean, and listened to Gill as she told them about the place where she has lived and worked all her life.

tip

Especially if you don't have a garden or allotment, seeing vegetables grow in a farm is all part of learning to enjoy eating them. There are several organisations that give details of farm visits or you can call the local tourist office for more ideas.
www.localfoodworks.org
www.face-online.org.uk
www.leafuk.org
www.rhet.org.uk
www.whatsonyourplate.co.uk
www.farmgarden.org.uk

F is for... Fennel

We celebrated our arrival at F with a Feast of Flattery. Fennel was our next vegetable companion and the timing was perfect. In Shakespeare's time, fennel was a symbol of flattery. The bright green, delicate leaves that top the fennel wilt very quickly, like the attentions of a flatterer. The reason for our feast was a visit by a very special guest, Leo, my stepson. Now, unlike his Dad and stepmum, Leo has a proper twenty-something social life with all sorts of exciting things going on. So when he comes across London to see us, it is a treat and a cause for celebration. Naturally, we want to impress him with a beautiful meal. So we went into overdrive with the fennel.

First off was Pear, Fennel and Parmesan Salad which is a combination of flavours that I have tasted several times before. Note the order of pear, then fennel in the recipe title. This is a cloak-and-dagger recipe. I wasn't kidding myself that Freddie would immediately like the very adult taste of fennel, which is a cross between mild aniseed and celery. I was hoping that the taste of pear, which Freddie loves, would wrap itself around the fennel, softening and sweetening some of that strong anise flavour. There is an added benefit of combining the pear with fennel. When sliced thinly and covered with olive oil and Parmesan, they look very similar. This hampers Freddie's ability to pick out the offending vegetable and avoid eating it. This wasn't so much a recipe, more an exercise in camouflage.

The Feast of Flattery continued and I think it was working its magic on Leo. He has always been a joy to cook for. He was slightly thrown by the bizarre practice of me photographing the food for my blog before it is eaten. The children sit in their places, in a near-hysterical state of hunger and I stand on the table in a pair of slippers with my camera, attempting to capture the best angle of each dish. I call for props, bowls of fruit, attractive place mats and demand that piles of homework are removed. In the end there is normally a revolt, led by Chris who brings me to my senses, takes my hand to help me safely off my kitchen pedestal and we start eating. In years gone by children waited for grace to be said before picking up their forks. In our house, they are waiting for their mother to get off the table.

There were two more fennel dishes. I baked chicken thighs alongside quarters of fennel, with a little chicken stock and covered the dish with foil, cooking it in the oven for an hour. Alongside I roasted fennel with Emmental cheese. This is simple and a blatant attempt to use the flavour of Emmental, much loved by Freddie, to attract him to fennel. And I am ashamed to admit that it worked. He gave this recipe a confident 8 out of 10.

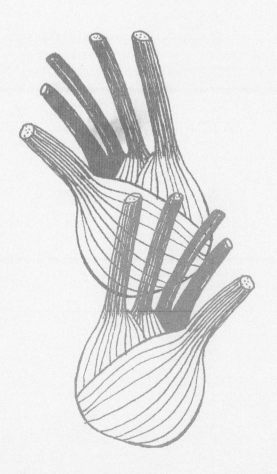

Pear, Fennel and Parmesan Salad

With this recipe you can alter the amount of fennel to pear. With Freddie, I wanted the pear to help lure him into tasting and enjoying the fennel: yet more flattery. He gave this dish a respectable 7 out of 10.

Serves 4–6
2 pears
½ fennel bulb
50 g (2 oz) freshly grated Parmesan cheese

2 tbsp olive oil
Freshly ground pepper

1 Core the pear and thinly slice it lengthways.
2 Cut off the stalk and base of the fennel and cut it in half. Slice thinly lengthways. Mix the pear and fennel together on a plate.
3 Add a splash of olive oil, a twist of ground pepper and the grated Parmesan. Carefully mix together to serve.

The taste of pear, which Freddie loves, wraps itself around the fennel, softening and sweetening some of that strong anise flavour.

abcthedgreatebig**f**veggchallenge**hijklmnopqrstuvwxyz**

Roasted Fennel with Emmental Cheese

Here I used the flavour of Freddie's favourite cheese to camouflage the grown-up taste of the fennel. It worked and was deemed a success.

Serves 4–5
2 fennel bulbs
2 tbsp olive oil

4 tbsp finely grated Emmental cheese
1–2 cloves of garlic, finely chopped
Salt and freshly ground pepper

1 Preheat the oven to 180°C (350°F) Gas 4.

2 Lightly oil a baking dish. Cut off the stalk and stump of the fennel and then slice it in half vertically. With each half, slice it into quarters. Put in the baking dish, add the rest of the olive oil, garlic and season. Cover the dish with a loose foil lid and bake for about 30 minutes.

3 Stir the mixture with a spatula halfway through. After 30 minutes, remove the foil lid, sprinkle and mix over the Emmental cheese and return to the oven for 10–15 minutes. Check to make sure the cheese doesn't burn. It should be golden brown.

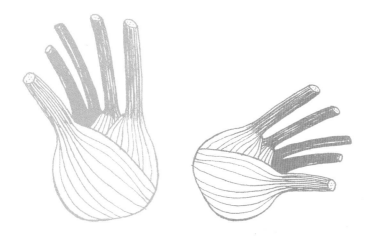

G is for... Garlic

After edamame, eddoe and even fennel, our next vegetable in the challenge should have been a breeze. I use it without thinking in so many recipes but the challenge was to make it the star of the show.

And this is where I came up against a huge impediment; my husband's deep-seated loathing of garlic. I warned him that a difficult week was approaching and tried to reassure him that I would segregate the food to prevent contamination. But his antipathy towards the stinking rose extends to the cooking smells and more specifically the smell of garlicky breath.

Freddie has not inherited the garlic-hating gene. In fact, he holds the Pizza Express children's record for the fastest consumption of a plate of garlic dough balls. He started training for this event as a toddler when we would carry him out, at arms' length, his hair smeared in garlic butter. We called him dough-boy. I would soap and shower him clean before presenting him to his Dad for a bedtime story, deodorised.

When I suggested to Freddie on his return from school that he could make our garlic bread for supper, he was delighted. And as he was scoring his own dish, it was 11 out of 10. Chris, of course, abstained.

Nobody ever told me that vegetables could lead you to lie. But that is what I did all week, so that Chris wouldn't realise his kitchen was being turned into a garlic factory. I took to hiding clumps of garlic in my bag, carrying it to and from work on the tube. I secretly researched garlic recipes and gossiped about the attraction of the stinking rose with colleagues. Even the children joined in with the deception.

I bought extra-minty toothpaste, introduced a rigorous routine of teeth-brushing and tongue scrubbing. I tried rubbing my hands on stainless steel spoons to take away the smell. (I can report that that old wives' tale didn't work.)

When I cooked Garlic Potato Bake, the kitchen door and windows were kept open: all to keep 'He Who Hates Garlic' in the dark. Of course it didn't work. He came in the house like the giant in Jack and the Beanstalk. 'Fee, Fi, Fo, Fum', sniffing out his vegetable enemy. Apparently, it is the sulphur compounds in garlic that make it so pungent. And there is no point trying to disguise them.

It was my neighbour, Erica, who suggested Chicken with Forty Cloves of Garlic. In France this is known as 'Poulet Quarante aux Gousses d'Ail'. The Great Big Vegetable Challenge tries to bring out the best in every vegetable, making it feel special so that it stands the strongest chance of impressing Freddie. And in this recipe the garlic is supercharged. If you have heard of the TV show, *Pimp my Ride*, this is *Pimp my Chicken*. And to make something involving industrial quantities of garlic, you need helpers. Alex and Freddie were given the task of breaking open the garlic bulbs and counting out the cloves as I set to work preparing the poor chicken. By now my husband had given up and resigned himself to having to defumigate the house, the children and his wife.

I always feel a little intimidated trying out traditional French recipes. I know how seriously these things are taken. We once had a holiday in Provence and rented a house belonging to a Mrs Tiggywinkle look alike, known as Madame P. She was many important things in the village but was best known for being the local aïoli-making champion. At the annual competition Madame P came first, several points ahead of her local rivals and a brave American visitor who scored just 3 out of 10. Madame P was overheard judging the American's aïoli as 'pas mal', adding that she

had committed the cardinal sin of using 'deux oeufs' or two eggs. The time-hallowed rule (unwritten of course) only allowed for the use of one egg.

There seem to be hundreds of versions of Chicken with Forty Cloves of Garlic. Some involve heart-stopping quantities of oil, others add interlopers like carrots and onions. I decided to keep it simple and a little less oily. I don't know whether the number 40 has some deep significance in the garlic world but Freddie and Alexandra thought 41 a more pleasing number. The garlic cloves stay in their skins and are roasted. The end result is smooth and mouth-watering.

The children loved the sweetness of the garlic which they squished and ate with their bread. And the garlic-fest didn't end there. There were around 20 leftover roasted cloves of garlic which we puréed and added to mashed potato. The following morning, the house reeked. Chris ate his breakfast in the garden as we gargled to sweeten our breath. 'Poulet Quarante aux Gousses d'Ail' is not for the faint-hearted. The recipe also introduced us to the delights of roasting garlic.

Garlic Bread

Oozing with buttery stickiness, garlic bread is often a big hit with children and getting them involved in its preparation only adds to their enjoyment.

Serves 4
1 French baguette
50 g (2 oz) butter, at room temperature

3 tbsp finely chopped parsley
1 medium clove of garlic, crushed

1 Preheat the oven to 180°C (350°F) Gas 4.

2 Slice the baguette down the middle lengthways but just stop short of severing the two halves completely. With the top half, score deeply into individual slices but again don't cut all the way through the bread.

3 In a bowl, mix the softened butter, parsley and crushed garlic together. The parsley should be chopped very finely.

4 When it is all mixed together, spread evenly in between the two halves of the baguette. Close the two halves and wrap in foil. Cook in a preheated oven for 15 minutes. Uncover the foil to cook for another 5 minutes. It should be golden brown. Don't allow to burn.

Garlic Potato Bake

Both of the children loved Garlic Potato Bake, but then again it would be hard not to. It is creamy and, well, garlicky…Not surprisingly, Freddie gave this a top score.

Serves 4
500 g (1 lb) potatoes, peeled and thinly sliced
½ vegetable stock cube
1 tbsp olive oil
150 ml (¼ pint) single cream

100 ml (3½ fl oz) milk
1 medium clove of garlic, crushed
50 g (2 oz) freshly grated Parmesan cheese
Salt and freshly ground pepper

1 Preheat the oven to 180°C (350°F) Gas 4.

2 Put the potatoes in a pan of boiling water. Crumble half a vegetable stock cube into the water. Cook for about 5 minutes. They should not be too soft, just lightly cooked. Ladle out 50 ml (2 fl oz) of the liquid and put aside. Carefully drain the potatoes so they don't break up. Allow to cool.

3 Lightly oil a shallow ovenproof dish. Arrange the potato slices overlapping each other around the dish until there are several layers.

4 In a small pan on a low heat, simmer the cream and milk with the garlic for a few minutes. Add a pinch of salt and pepper and stir in the reserved cooking liquid from the potatoes.

5 Pour the sauce evenly over the potatoes, making sure it is distributed well. Then sprinkle the freshly grated Parmesan on top. Bake for 30 minutes.

Poulet Quarante aux Gousses d'Ail

For this supercharged, 'pimped' chicken dish the children decided that 41 cloves of garlic were the key to it's success.

2 tbsp butter
1 chicken, jointed
41 cloves of garlic in their skins
3 tbsp of chopped parsley
3 tbsp of chopped thyme

3 glasses of white wine (approximately
  300 ml/^{1}/$_2$ pint)
2 tbsp olive oil
Salt and freshly ground pepper

1 Preheat the oven to 180°C (350°F) Gas 4.
2 Gently melt the butter in a large flameproof casserole dish. Add the chicken pieces and brown on both sides. Season with salt and pepper. Turn off the heat.
3 Add the garlic cloves, still in their skins, herbs, wine and the olive oil. Mix well.
4 Put the lid on the dish and bake in the oven for about 45–50 minutes. Halfway through cooking, baste the chicken and garlic with all the juices.
5 Serve with a warm baguette.

tip
How to roast garlic
1 Preheat the oven to 180°C (350°F) Gas 4.
2 Take a whole garlic bulb and place it on a small square of foil.
3 Drizzle a little olive oil on top and wrap it up in the foil parcel. You can put it in the oven at the same time that you are cooking something else. After about 45 minutes the garlic cloves will be roasted to a delicious mush. Squeeze the flesh from the skins.

Roasted garlic is a great ingredient for flavouring other vegetables. You can add it to mashed potato, sweet potato, parsnip or celeriac. It is delicious added to vegetable soup. Or, if you are a garlic-addict, like Freddie, rub it into some toasted ciabatta for instant garlic bread.

G is for... Garlic Scapes

Just when I thought it was time to move on from garlic, something new arrived on the scene: garlic scapes. Scapes are flowering stems that grow out of the crown or root of a plant.

If you ever see these curly stems on sale in markets or stores, buy them. They are the ultimate delicacy for garlic-lovers. Scapes are normally cut off by the farmer to allow the garlic to concentrate on producing a bulb. They are sweet-tasting, garlicky but without the pungency.

Anything that comes from garlic is going to be popular with Freddie, who loved the garlic scapes, quickly sautéed in butter and served with linguine pasta. A month later I went back to the same shop and there were no more scapes. I emailed the garlic farmers, Glen and Gilli Allingham who grow garlic at the foot of the Cawdor Hills in Scotland. Sadly, they explained, their scape season is one month long in June. The best scape-producing garlic are the Hardneck varieties that are closely related to wild garlic, producing more flower than bulb. The fact that the garlic scape season is fleeting made our discovery all the more enjoyable.

abcthedgreatebigfveg **g** challengehijklmnopqrstuvwxyz

Linguine with Garlic Scapes

This quick, simple dish uses pasta as the perfect foil for the delicate, garlicky flavour of the flowering stem.

Serves 4
300 g (10 oz) linguine
1 tbsp olive oil
1 bunch of garlic scapes, roughly chopped

A knob of butter
Freshly grated Parmesan cheese
Salt and freshly ground pepper

1 Follow the packet instructions for cooking the linguine pasta. Drain and add the olive oil.

2 Sauté the scapes for a minute or two in a knob of butter.

3 Add the scapes to the cooked linguine pasta and stir through. Season with salt and pepper and serve with Parmesan cheese sprinkled on top.

This simple pasta recipe can be adapted to other vegetables. If you can't find garlic scapes, you can use green beans. Top and tail them, slice them into smaller thinner strips and steam for 2–3 minutes. Stir them into the linguine pasta with the butter and Parmesan cheese.

Just when I thought we were moving on from garlic, something new arrived on the scene to feed our garlic habit.

G is for... Green Beans

We stumbled on eddoes and tracked down the daikon, so it seemed a little tame to be dealing with something as straightforward as a green bean. The letter G doesn't appear to have many vegetable candidates so I have promoted the green bean in the Great Big Vegetable Challenge.

For years I used to place the obligatory five green beans on Freddie's plate in the hope that he would eat them. He never did. He might grimace and self-consciously nibble on the end of a bean. More often, he would quietly edge them to the outskirts of his plate and then when, I wasn't looking, nudge them off the plate, onto the table and thence to the floor. At the end of the meal I would find green beans scattered at his feet. Like a scene from *Toy Story*, they were motionless but I knew that only moments before, with the help of this pint-sized veg-phobic, they had all been part of a brilliantly-planned escape.

They may seem to be harmless but there is a quality to green beans that provokes a violent reaction in my son. And he's not alone.

If you look on You Tube, there is a home video entitled 'The Green Bean Stand-off'. It's almost too painful to watch. No doubt some desperate mother posted it to share her frustration with the world. She is gently encouraging her young son to eat a few beans. His response is a professional outburst. If there were Oscars for tantrums, this boy would have wiped the floor. And all over a green bean.

Freddie told me that the reason he doesn't like green beans isn't their taste but their squeaky texture. So to give them a fighting chance I relied on my trusty hand-held blender. We call it the Bits-Blitzer. And it played a vital role in our Green Bean and Garlic Soup recipe, which scored a respectable 8 out of 10.

Our next move was to see if he could be persuaded to eat a green bean without pulverizing it. Green bean twists are based on something I made for asparagus spears (see page 18). I cooked the beans in boiling water for just 3 minutes, drained them and let them cool down. I thought if I could present the bean attractively, creating a bit of a diversion, the bean-hater might be bamboozled. The beans were divided into groups of four. I cut thin strips of puff pastry and wrapped them round the bean in a spiral. I brushed them with egg and sprinkled grated Parmesan on top and placed them in the oven for about 20 minutes at 180°C (350°F) Gas 4, until the pastry was golden brown.

Alexandra named them Green Bean Twisters. She already understands the importance of a catchy name for Freddie's vegetables. And it worked. Despite his distrust of beans, he liked the look of this dish. He even ate one without making a fuss. And another. That means he consumed eight green beans.

Parenthood is made up of small triumphs that no-one else can quite appreciate: using a potty, sleeping in a big bed, learning to tie shoelaces and in our house, eating eight green beans. However, Freddie was less generous with his scoring, giving 7 out of 10. 'And that is only for the pastry, not the green bean.'

A chance comment left on the blog led me to a recipe by Ed Bruske, the Slowcook from Washington DC. He describes himself as an urban insurgent and rails against fast food and the cult of the celebrity chef. 'It's time to take back control of the food we eat and the pace of our own lives'. He is passionate about eating good local food when it is in season and runs food appreciation and cookery classes for children.

Writing about green beans, he advises that you have to choose between flavour and colour and that slow-cooking the beans maximises the flavour. Inspired by Ed's recipe, I made some changes to suit Freddie's taste buds. He devoured the dish with a passion.

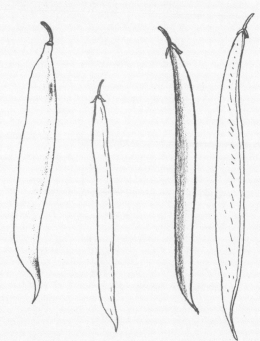

Green Bean and Garlic Soup

With hand-blender at the ready, this recipe quickly converts into a tasty dish that can be enjoyed by the 'no bits' crowd.

Serves 4
2 medium potatoes, peeled and diced into 2.5-cm (1-in.) cubes
1 small onion, chopped
1 tbsp olive oil
400 g (13 oz) green beans, topped, tailed and chopped

750 ml (1¼ pints) vegetable stock
3–4 cloves of roasted garlic (see page 115)
4 tbsp crème fraîche
Salt and freshly ground pepper

1 Gently sauté the potatoes in olive oil with the onion. When the potato has softened and the onion is translucent, add the green beans.
2 Add the vegetable stock and on a medium heat allow to simmer for 15 minutes with the lid on. Stir occasionally.
3 Squeeze the soft contents of your roasted garlic cloves into the soup. Gently simmer for another 5 minutes. Season to taste.
4 Remove from the heat and allow to cool for a few minutes. Using a hand-blender, or a liquidiser, purée the soup until smooth. Stir in the crème fraîche and serve.

Freddie told me that the reason he doesn't like green beans isn't their taste but their squeaky texture.
So to give them a fighting chance I relied on my trusty hand-held blender. We call it the Bits-Blitzer.

Slow-cooked Green Beans

Thanks to Ed's inspiration for this recipe, Freddie found a way of loving green beans. Not just putting up with them, or merely tolerating them occasionally but actually consuming them with passion. Freddie scored this 8 out of 10. (See www.theslowcook.blogspot.com)

Serves 4
2 tbsp olive oil
1 medium onion, finely chopped
½ tsp smoked paprika
400 g (13 oz) tin of chopped tomatoes

450 g (14½ oz) green beans, topped
2–3 slices of thick-cut bacon, cut into small chunks
   or use gammon steak
Freshly ground pepper

1 Use a flameproof casserole dish or pan with a tight fitting lid. On the hob, cook the onion in the oil on a medium heat until it is translucent and soft.
2 Add the paprika, tomatoes and green beans. Add the bacon pieces. Mix together and simmer on a low heat for at least 3 hours. You may have to add a very small amount of water every now and again if it looks dry. The beans will break down and become softer.

tip

I've read that it takes a child between 10 and 90 tastes of a new food to learn to accept it. I like to look at it differently. I don't think that simply offering the same food repeatedly is most effective. Presenting the same food cooked in very different ways, seemed to give us more success. In the past, Freddie and I made no progress when I just placed the five green beans on his plate. We would have the same stand-off; the meal time equivalent of *Groundhog Day*. But if you make the green beans look different, taste different, at least you are helping to create change and the reluctant eater can't react in exactly the same way.

H is for... Herbs

I know that herbs are not classed as vegetables but given that we use them to enhance their taste, they clearly deserve a mention. Freddie has always enjoyed growing herbs in pots in our tiny backgarden. As Head Gardener, he has also carefully avoided eating them.

So we organised a blind-tasting competition. We laid out plates of thyme, basil, mint, rosemary and sage. The blindfolded taste-explorers were encouraged to touch, smell and taste the herbs and guess what they were. As we travelled through the alphabet, Freddie's fear of new flavours has faded. 'As long as it doesn't taste of sick or earwax, I'll try it,' said Freddie. Both he and Alex correctly identified four out of five herbs which saved us from a sibling row. Freddie asked for a sudden death-by-herb play off but I resisted and we settled for a draw. And their prize was a huge plate of herb fritters for tea. The fritters scored 10 out of 10.

The blind-tasting contest had its benefits. We have a tiny patio garden in which Freddie re-enacts Premiership football matches. And in this miniature stadium he kicks a tennis ball around, muttering a commentary under his breath. At half-time he is the team manager, reviewing the performance of his imaginary players. Through the kitchen window, I caught sight of him picking from his herb plants and nibbling on the leaves like a rabbit. In fact, he was grazing on the herbs in the garden. His terror of all things green appeared momentarily to have vanished. After this half-time snack, the match resumed.

I made Herby Beefburgers for supper. For Freddie, under normal circumstances, the flavour of the fresh herbs would have ruined a perfectly good beefburger. But things had changed. With Alexandra, he savoured the taste of the herbs. Both of them showed off their new-found skills in herb-identification. And Herby Beefburgers scored 10 out of 10.

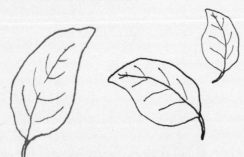

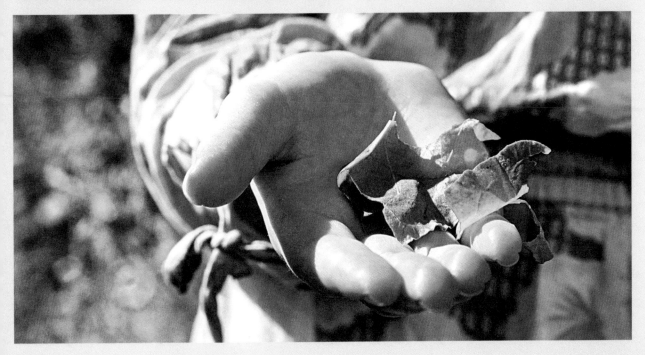

Herb Fritters

From windowsill to plate in a few simple moves – and they taste even better if the children have grown them themselves!

Serves 4
115 g (3½ oz) self-raising flour
2 tsp caster sugar
2 eggs, separated
200 ml (7 fl oz) milk

1 tbsp finely chopped thyme
1 tbsp finely chopped basil
1 tbsp finely chopped sage
1 tbsp finely chopped rosemary
50 g (2 oz) butter, melted

1 Sift the flour into a bowl. Add the sugar, egg yolks and milk. Mix everything together until it is smooth.

2 In a separate bowl, whisk the egg whites to form peaks. Gently fold into the batter mix. Stir in the finely chopped herbs.

3 Melt the butter in a large frying pan. Place small spoonfuls of the batter in the pan, carefully spaced apart. Cook on a medium to low heat until golden and turn them over halfway through cooking. Keep the fritters warm in a low oven until you have cooked the rest of the batter. Butter has a tendency to brown so you might want to stop between batches and wipe down the pan.

As we travelled through the alphabet, Freddie's fear of new flavours has faded. 'As long as it doesn't taste of sick or earwax, I'll try it,' said Freddie.

Herby Beefburgers

A little bit of sibling rivalry is no bad thing and trying to identify the different herbs in these burgers only added to Freddie and Alex's enjoyment of them.

Serves 4
500 g (1 lb) lean minced beef
1 tbsp finely chopped basil (or 1 tsp dried)
1 tbsp finely chopped sage (or 1 tsp dried)
1 tbsp finely chopped thyme (or 1 tsp dried)

1 tbsp finely chopped marjoram (or 1 tsp dried)
1 egg, beaten
Salt and freshly ground pepper
Bread rolls, to serve

1 Rinse your hands in cold water as it prevents the mince sticking.
2 Put the minced beef into a mixing bowl and mix the meat together with the finely chopped herbs by hand. You can experiment with different combinations of herbs. They taste far better if they are fresh, but dried herbs are fine, just use smaller quantities.
3 Add the egg to the meat and herb mixture. Mix thoroughly using a fork. Season with salt and pepper.
4 Shape into small patties of meat and lay out on a baking sheet. Cover with cling film and chill for at least 30 minutes in the fridge. This allows the herbs to flavour the meat.
5 Using a lightly oiled pan, carefully cook the burgers on a medium heat on the hob for 10 minutes. Turn over and cook the other side. Serve in a roll.

H is for... Horseradish

When did our High Street become an assault course? I was focused on buying one thing, which was horseradish. I had even been tipped off by a neighbour that I could find the fiery roots in the local supermarket. But before I got there, I was stopped in my tracks.

Three men dressed in commando jackets stood in my way. 'Do you have paintballing needs?' What sort of a question is that? I told them firmly and politely that, as yet, I had not discovered a need for paintballing. I walked on.

A minute later and a bright yellow t-shirt blocked my way, emblazoned with the words 'Fighting Poverty'. I side-stepped yellow t-shirt man and tried to refocus on the horseradish. But the obstacles came thick and fast. As I approached the last bend with the supermarket in my sights, a small woman dressed in what looked like a patchwork quilt drifted out in front of me.

'Can I show you the way of true love?' she asked with staring eyes.

'No,' I said. She looked crestfallen.

I marched into the supermarket, straight to the vegetables. I wouldn't have recognised the horseradish without the help of a label. They were thick, stumpy brown roots, tightly wrapped in cellophane. (Freddie thought they looked like wands from Hogwarts.) I bought them and headed home. In reverse order, the patchwork quilt woman and yellow t-shirt man tried once more to interrupt me. By the time I reached the paintball commandoes, I took the horseradish root in my hand. 'Do you have any horseradish needs?' I asked them. The commandoes were stumped. As I walked past them I overheard them muttering, 'There are some real nutters round here.'

Horseradish is the first vegetable that comes with a caution. Instructions on the internet included, 'Grate horseradish in a well-ventilated room' and 'Warning! The fumes are potent'. I should have paid more attention. I peeled the root. There were no fumes. I became complacent and began to grate the root vigorously. Thirty-seconds later a wave of tear-jerking fumes hit me. This was a thousand times worse than an onion. I flung open the kitchen door and scrabbled around in the drawer for a pair of goggles, leftover from a make-your-own volcano kit. I now know that grating the horseradish and even worse, grating it finely, crushes oils in the root, releasing this all-powerful stink. It's no surprise it also goes by the name of 'Stingnose'. To tame the stingnose, I made a sweet creamy sauce. This is after all for children to try.

I suppose I never really expected Freddie or Alex to like horseradish. It is a very adult taste but I was trying to give every vegetable a fighting chance: even the wretched stingnose. Chris and I loved these wraps and the horseradish was creamy and delicious with the salmon. The children however were less impressed. Freddie scored this 2 out of 10. Alexandra told me, 'This is the first vegetable recipe I haven't loved.'

To rescue the situation from complete disaster, I took inspiration from Collinsville, Illinois. Collinsville hosts the annual International Horseradish Festival and claims to produce 60 per cent of the world's horseradish each year. This is an event which endows celebrity status on the horseradish root. There are root-tossing and root-sacking competitions and a little Miss Horseradish beauty pageant. (All of the children looked delightful – I could see no resemblance to the stingnose). They promise 'a root-in tootin good time'. Now when a town is prepared to put this much effort into a vegetable, you have to sit up and listen. I wanted a root-in tootin good time in my kitchen. Alongside a host of horseradish recipes was the advice that when cooked, the horseradish loses a little of its bite. This was worth trying. The children had been unimpressed so far but I devised a quiche recipe that I hoped would rescue the root's reputation.

I didn't tell Freddie and Alexandra that this was another horseradish recipe because they would have written it off before tasting it. They scored it 8 out of 10. Collinsville would be proud of us. We still had half a root left in the fridge and we did what any self-respecting horseradish fan would do. We went to the local park and held our own root-toss. It wasn't as impressive as tossing the caber but it was, as they say in Collinsville, root-in tootin good fun.

Creamy Horseradish Sauce

This sweet, creamy sauce was an attempt to tame this all-powerful vegetable.

Serves 4
75 g (3 oz) horseradish
2 tsp freshly squeezed lemon juice

25 g (1 oz) caster sugar, or to taste
200 ml (7 fl oz) crème fraîche
A pinch of salt

1 Taking precautions against the fumes, finely grate the horseradish and add the lemon juice.
2 Mix in the remaining ingredients and stir well. Keep in the fridge.

Salmon and Stingnose Wrap

Having made the horseradish sauce, I created these wraps to present it in a familiar form to the children.

Serves 4
Wheat flour tortilla wraps
2 cooked salmon fillets (½ salmon fillet per wrap)

1 tbsp Creamy Horseradish Sauce (see above)
Shredded lettuce leaves

1 Combine the cooked salmon fillet with the horseradish sauce.
2 Spread the salmon mixture evenly over the wrap, sprinkle a few lettuce leaves on top, fold and serve.

abcthedgreatebigfveggchallenge_h ijklmnopqrstuvwxyz

Beef and Horseradish Quiche

This quiche rescued the horseradish's reputation and proved that the stingnose is gentler and more child-friendly when cooked in the oven.

Serves 4
375 g (12 oz) ready-made shortcrust pastry
1 onion, finely chopped
1 tbsp olive oil
3 eggs, beaten

150 ml (¼ pint) milk
2 tbsp crème fraîche
5 wafer thin slices of roast beef, cut into thin strips
2–3 tbsp Creamy Horseradish Sauce (see opposite)
Salt and freshly ground pepper

23 cm (9 in.) quiche or flan tin
Baking beans

1 Preheat the oven to 200°C (400°F) Gas 6.
2 Roll out the pastry on a floured surface to a depth of 5 mm (¼ in.). Line the flan or quiche tin with the pastry and chill in the fridge for 10 minutes.
3 Remove from the fridge and put a circle of baking parchment on top of the pastry. Weigh it down with baking beans and cook in the oven for 10 minutes.
4 Take out of the oven, remove the parchment and beans and bake for a further 5 minutes to cook the base.
5 Take out of the oven and lower the temperature to 180°C (350°F) Gas 4.
6 Fry the onion in a little olive oil until soft.
7 In a bowl, mix together the beaten eggs, milk and crème fraîche. Season. Scatter the onions around the base of the blind-baked pastry case. Scatter the strips of roast beef evenly over the case.
8 Pour over the egg, milk and crème fraîche mixture. Depending on your sensitivity to horseradish, carefully stir in the Creamy Horseradish Sauce.
9 Bake in the oven for 25 minutes until a golden-brown colour.

I is for Ice Lollies

The letter I might not be rich in vegetables but we were undaunted. We scoured the markets and searched the internet, and came up with Iceberg Lettuce. Now, although this is a noble lettuce, it will have to wait until it features under L.

But there was something in the word Iceberg that caught my imagination.

We had a hot, humid weekend in London and Freddie heard the cheery chimes of Mr Softee in the distance. We think that, at some time in the past, Mr Softee has attached a tracking device to Freddie so that wherever he is, the ice-cream van finds him. Mr Softee was getting closer and closer, the chimes were getting louder and louder until the van stopped two doors down. Target located. An hour later the ice cream had been bought and consumed. Freddie was thinking aloud.

'Wouldn't it be good if the ice-cream van sold healthy food so that parents didn't mind buying things?' And that is when the idea for Vegetable Ice Lollies was born. Our Food-Namer-in-Chief, Alexandra, christened them 'Veggie Lipsmackers'.

When I was a child in the seventies, Mr Frosty loomed large. My friend Becky owned one. We would sit in her porch tipping ice cubes into Mr F's head, turning the handle to produce the magic ingredient of crushed ice. Then we would pour undiluted orange squash on top and we would eat it super-fast until we yelled out 'Head Freeze' and collapsed on to the floor holding our foreheads.

In honour of the Prince of Cool, Mr Frosty, we turned our kitchen into a Veggie Lipsmacker production line. We sampled batches made from tomato, carrot, orange, beetroot, grape and apple juice. The most popular formulas were carrot and orange juice in equal measure and beetroot and apple. The children decided that they liked the colour of beetroot but the taste needed to be sweetened with apple juice. They poured the juice-mixtures into the moulds and froze them for a couple of hours. Mr Frosty would be proud of us.

Veggie Lipsmackers

These veggie-juice lollies were developed as a healthy alternative to the lure of the cheery chimes of Mr Softee tempting children from their homes.

Serves 4
Apple juice
Beetroot juice
Carrot juice

Orange juice
Purple grape juice
Tomato juice

Ice lolly moulds

1 Use any combination of vegetable and fruit juice that you like. We found that half and half carrot and orange was delicious. A quarter beetroot to three-quarters apple juice was popular. Or combine half grape juice with half beetroot for a purple-tastic lolly.

PS Don't tell Mr Softee …

tip

Try making some ice cubes from carrot or beetroot juice and add them to a glass of apple or orange juice. Its just a little taste of a vegetable, adds colour and helps to introduce new flavours to a child. Let them explore which combination of tastes they most like.

J is for... Jerusalem Artichokes

Rumour and confusion surround the Jerusalem artichoke. Freddie was adamant he had already 'done' artichokes. The thistle-like globe artichoke was the first vegetable he sampled for the Great Big Vegetable Challenge.

But the Jerusalem artichoke, as I explained to Freddie, is something entirely new. The name is misleading. It doesn't come from Jerusalem and it isn't an artichoke. It is actually the tuber from a type of sunflower. 'It looks like a potato with warts,' said Freddie. Apparently the Jerusalem artichoke is used to insults. In the distant past, people turned away from this poor vegetable because they thought it resembled a leper's fingers.

We were more charitable. I peeled the artichokes and sliced them very thinly and doused them in a few tablespoons of olive oil and lemon juice. The lemon juice keeps them from turning brown. We tried them raw. They are crisp and taste a bit like a nutty potato.

Freddie and Alex were unimpressed. But it is amazing what the mention of pizza can do to raise morale. I gave them a bowl of thin slices of Jerusalem artichoke covered in a little olive oil, some grated Parmesan and oregano, and let them get on with creating a pizza. Freddie's score was 10 out of 10.

I returned to the market to buy more Jerusalem artichokes, or 'sunchokes' as they are sometimes called. My friend, Emma, came along. 'You do know these things are evil?' she said. 'They can give you the most appalling wind.' On the blog, two more sinister warnings had been left. 'Seriously, use with caution' and 'You have been warned.' As with the warnings about horseradish, I thought I knew better. I made Roasted Rosemary Artichokes. They were sweet and subtle tasting. Freddie devoured them. He gave them 9 out of 10.

That evening we went to see Alexandra acting in a school production of *Romeo and Juliet*. It was during the second half that the trouble began. The action on stage became more intense, the theatre quietened. My husband turned to me and whispered in my ear, 'I think I'm going to give birth.' Freddie sniggered. I could feel these griping pains build up. This is what it must be like to be a colicky baby. The agony of the star-crossed lovers was nothing compared to our pain.

The walk home was bracing. I had been warned. There is a reason why these vegetables are known as 'fartichokes'. The cause is something indigestible called inulin. In 1621, the writer John Goodyer wrote, ' … in my judgement, which way soever they be drest and eaten they stir up and cause a filthie loathsome stinking winde with the bodie, thereby causing the belly to bee much pained and tormented … more fit for swine, than men.'* The last bit is a bit harsh. Wind is a small price to pay for the enjoyment of Jerusalem artichokes.

*Gerard's Herbal, cited in Davidson A. *The Oxford Companion to Food* (Oxford University Press, 1999).

Jerusalem Artichoke Pizza

Give a new vegetable a fighting chance by letting the children create a pizza with it – this one got top marks from Freddie.

Serves 3–4
1 large ready-made pizza base, 30 cm (12 in.) in diameter
4–5 Jerusalem artichokes, peeled

Freshly squeezed lemon juice
2–3 tbsp olive oil
4 tbsp freshly grated Parmesan cheese
2 tbsp dried oregano

1 Preheat the oven to 220°C (425°F) Gas 7.
2 Thinly slice the artichokes and put them in a bowl with a little lemon juice squeezed over to prevent discolouration. Add a little olive oil.
3 Arrange the slices overlapping on the pizza base, evenly scatter over the oregano, finely grated Parmesan cheese and drizzle a little olive oil on top.
4 Bake in the oven on a baking tray for about 10 minutes or until the pizza base is golden and crisp. Keep a close eye on it so that it doesn't burn.

The name is misleading. It doesn't come from Jerusalem and it isn't an artichoke. It is actually the tuber from a type of sunflower. 'It looks like a potato with warts,' said Freddie.

abcthedgreatebigfveggchallengehi *j* klmnopqrstuvwxyz

Roasted Rosemary Artichokes

Throwing caution to the wind (quite literally), I made this sweet and subtle-tasting dish which Freddie devoured with gusto.

Serves 4
500 g (1 lb) Jerusalem artichokes, peeled
2–3 tbsp olive oil

½ tbsp sea salt
6 sprigs of fresh rosemary

1 Preheat the oven to 200°C (400°F) Gas 6.

2 Cut the Jerusalem artichokes into wedges. Place them in a bowl and add the olive oil and sea salt.

3 Break up the rosemary sprigs and add to the artichokes, mixing it around so that they are evenly coated in oil, salt and rosemary.

4 Scatter the artichokes evenly across a baking tray. Roast in a preheated oven for about 15–20 minutes. Halfway through cooking turn the artichoke wedges so they cook evenly. Jerusalem artichokes flesh softens much quicker than potatoes so make sure they don't overcook. The outsides should be a little crisp, the inside soft.

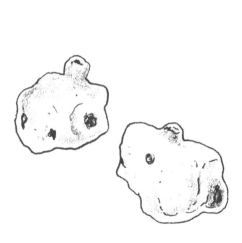

J is for... Jicama

It was my good friend Laura who suggested our next J vegetable, the jicama. Her family live in New Mexico and the jicama (pronounced hi-ka-ma) is a staple across Central America. It looks like a pale-skinned, tear-drop shaped turnip.

Tracking down the jicama was rather harder. I visited five different supermarkets, three street markets and then resorted to phoning grocers and specialist food shops in the yellow pages. 'Hello, do you sell jicamas? H-E-E-K-A-M-A – but it's spelt with a J. It is like a turnip. No, I don't want to buy a turnip…'

I offer jicama's other names; Mexican yam bean, ahipa, saa got, Chinese turnip, lo bok, and the Chinese potato. Eleven calls later and I find a man with several crates of jicama. But he is only prepared to sell me industrial quantities. I was sure Freddie would not appreciate having to eat through a tonne of unknown turnipy-style vegetables. The man with the jicama makes one helpful suggestion, a new American food store, Wholefoods, that

had opened in trendy Kensington. There in the glitzy vegetable department was a basket of jicama. They are possibly the most expensive vegetable I have ever purchased, at over £8 a kilogram. At that price it should have been diamond-encrusted.

At the checkout, an American shop assistant handled the jicama with care. 'I love this vegetable,' he said nostalgically. I did my usual thing of quizzing him on how to prepare it. 'We eat it raw. I like to grate it in slaw with swede and cabbage. And I add sweet red bell peppers because that's where I am in life at the moment.' I was intrigued, imagining what it must be like to know where you are in life by the vegetable you are eating. But then that is precisely what had happened for my family – a life marked by ever-changing vegetables.

Back at home I rang Laura, who suggested that we should first try to prepare it very simply: raw with lime juice. I sliced it into dipper shapes, doused it with lime juice and served it with houmous and taramasalata. Unless you are talking about rare red meat, Freddie is not a great raw-food enthusiast.

But jicama is mild and sweet-tasting and has a crisp texture like a water chestnut. He was happy to try it. 'It's ok,' he shrugged. 'But think how many football cards I could have bought with the money.'

The next day in the school queue I got chatting to a mum who comes from Mexico. I told her that I had found some jicama. Her eyes lit up. Everyone can name food that reminds them of home, of their childhood. For her, it was jicama. She said they could be cooked in casseroles but that it was a waste of jicama. Better to buy them small and juicy and cut them up in salads. 'We used to have them cut into batons with lime juice and a pinch of chilli powder and they are great with oranges or fresh pineapple.'

I'm a great fan of the school queue. Here, you can commiserate over lost sleep, compare notes on nits and have obscure conversations about Mexican vegetables. At home I returned to my jicama. The best ones are small and smooth. You can peel the skin away by hand. On their own, they taste slightly sweet but like a chameleon, they change when you add

other flavours to them. This isn't a vegetable that fights to keep its own identity. It's passive and seems to exist simply to take on the taste of its companion: more a handmaiden than a vegetable.

I created two dishes based on my friend's childhood memories and kept it very simple. One unfamiliar ingredient is enough for Freddie at any one time. The Simple Orange and Jicama Salad was sweet and juicy. Alexandra loved it. Freddie scored it 6 out of 10 but he gave 7 out of 10 to the jicama batons squeezed with lime and smoked paprika.

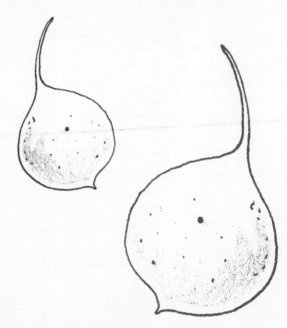

Simple Orange and Jicama Salad

This mild and retiring Mexican vegetable takes on a citrus twist in this salad.

Serves 4
4 small jicama
2 fresh oranges
1 lime

1 Peel the jicama, cut in half and into thin slices.
2 Peel the oranges, deseed them and cut into slices. Squeeze the juice of a lime over the salad and serve.

Jicama with Smoked Paprika

The smokiness of the paprika works well with the sweet lime juice. The adults liked the same, with chilli powder.

Serves 4
1 medium jicama
Freshly squeezed juice of ½ lime
½ tsp smoked paprika or mild chilli powder

1 Peel and cut the jicama into batons.
2 Squeeze over the juice of half a lime. Sprinkle the smoked paprika or chilli powder on top.

abcthedgreatebigfveggchallengehi *j* klmnopqrstuvwxyz

K is for... Kale

I don't know if it is just another urban vegetable myth, but the biggest consumer of kale in the United States is reportedly Pizza Hut, who use it to decorate the salad bar. I mentioned this to a fellow-shopper who was buying kale in the supermarket and she was unimpressed.

She came from Bremen in Germany and told me about the annual kale festival. Apparently the *really* keen ones compete to be crowned the King of Kale.

My children love trivia and I like to welcome a new vegetable with a few impressive facts. I went home and told them about the 'Kohl and Pinkel Fahrt' (Kale and Sausage Procession). This involves strolling around, decorated with sprigs of curly kale and stopping off at inns to enjoy kale with schnapps and a special sausage known as pinkel. Freddie giggled at the word 'fahrt' and Alexandra muttered 'losers'. But at least it introduced them to the curly kale that was sitting looking decorative in the corner of the kitchen.

Kale and cabbage are close relatives but it has long green leaves that grow up from the centre. We decided to serve our first kale recipe, Kale and Avocado, as a side dish to sausages and mashed potato. Sadly, there was no pinkel to be found. Savoy cabbage with its dark green leaves had been a surprise hit with Freddie early on in the challenge. He gave curly kale 8 out of 10, which surely made him a contender for King of Kale.

Our kale festival went from strength to strength with a recipe by Beth, who blogs at the Expatriates Kitchen. Her recipe for Kale Chips reminded us of the crispy seaweed served at Chinese restaurants. It had a light crispy texture and was tasty. The salt is needed to help the crisping up but go easy so that it isn't too salty for children to enjoy.

'I'm giving this 9 out of 10 because it doesn't taste anything like a vegetable,' said Freddie. Praise indeed. We didn't stop there with kale. We created a recipe without the salt, using Parmesan and breadcrumbs. This earned another 9 out of 10.

Kale and Avocado

We served this as an accompaniment to sausage and mash, in an attempt to recreate the 'pinkel' of the Bremen kale and sausage procession.

Serves 4
250 g (8 oz) curly kale
2 tbsp olive oil
1 clove of garlic, finely chopped

1 ripe avocado, peeled, stoned
  and chopped
½ lemon
Salt and freshly ground pepper

1 Wash and roughly chop the curly kale leaves, getting rid of any really tough stalks.

2 Heat the oil in a large frying pan on a medium heat. Add the finely chopped garlic and keep stirring. Add the curly kale to the pan and stir. The leaves should wilt in the heat. Sauté for about 7–8 minutes and stir continuously. The leaves will soften slightly.

3 Remove the pan from the heat. Transfer to a serving dish and add the chopped avocado. Squeeze the lemon on top. Season with salt and pepper and stir around so that it is evenly coated. Serve warm.

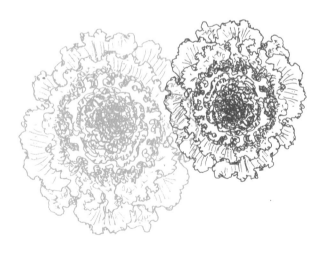

abcthedgreatebigfveggchallengehij**k**lmnopqrstuvwxyz

Kale Chips

This recipe came from Beth Bader at the Expatriates Kitchen blog and was a big hit with Freddie as 'it doesn't taste anything like a vegetable.' (See www.expatriateskitchen.blogspot.com)

Serves 4
200 g (7 oz) kale

Olive oil spray or 2 tbsp olive oil
Kosher salt or sea salt, to taste

1 Preheat the oven to 180°C (350°F) Gas 4.
2 Wash the kale, dry thoroughly in a salad spinner and tear into bite-sized pieces. Toss with the olive oil or spray to coat all the leaves. Rub the oil into the leaves to make sure they crisp up well. Oil a baking tray.
3 Put a single layer on the baking sheet. Sprinkle with salt. Cook in the oven for about 12–15 minutes. Remove crisp pieces as they form to allow the remaining kale chips to cook evenly and turn the pieces halfway through.

Cheesy Crispy Kale

We were on a roll following the success of the Kale Chips, and invented this recipe for anyone wishing to avoid salt.

200 g (7 oz) kale
Olive oil spray or 2 tbsp olive oil

50 g (2 oz) coarse breadcrumbs
25 g (1 oz) freshly grated Parmesan cheese

1 Preheat the oven to 180°C (350°F) Gas 4.
2 Prepare the kale following Step 2, above.
3 Add the breadcrumbs and Parmesan cheese and make sure the kale is well coated.
4 Spread the kale out on the baking tray and cook in the oven for about 10 minutes. Remove crisp pieces as they form to allow the remaining kale chips to cook evenly and turn the pieces halfway through.

K is for... Karela

I couldn't resist the karela. They were in the exotic vegetable pen, the part of the supermarket that looks more like a pet shop than a food counter. Their skins are reptilian, bright green like lizards with long thin bodies that taper off to a thin stalk.

Buying them was the easy part. Finding out what to do with them took a fortnight of research. Well I *call* it research but it consisted of lurking. I waited at the vegetable/pet counter waiting for someone else to buy them. Fifteen minutes passed and the security guard started to glare at me. I took them home and the karela became a vegetable freak show. Freddie and Alex surrounded it, patting and stroking the green skin, waiting for it to turn and snap at them. 'Can I have a tortoise, Mum?' asked Freddie. He likes reptiles.

On the internet I learnt that the karela is also known as the bitter gourd or bitter melon and is grown across Asia – including India, China and in Africa and the Caribbean. My daily commute became an intelligence gathering operation, weaving the karela into the conversation. It enlivened a meeting, caused a stir at the bus stop and sparked off a lively debate at a health-food store. But it was Shuba, a colleague at work, who finally helped me out. She rang her Mum who cooks karela for her Dad. Over the phone she relayed complicated instructions about salting, soaking and cooking the karela. I was warned that it was, as the name suggests, extremely bitter.

The karela requires nothing short of a full spa treatment to prepare. Skin has to be scraped, salt rubbed in, flesh soaked and then rinsed and squeezed to remove the bitterness. At the end of this process, I split open its middle and scraped out the pith and seeds and stuffed them with a mild lamb curry. I fried and then baked them in the oven.

A 'bitter gourd face' is a common Chinese phrase for an angry or serious face. When we

abcthedgreatebigfveggchallengehij**k**lmnopqrstuvwxyz

took a bite of this dish, all of us displayed the bitter gourd face. 'That is 0 out of 10.' This was Freddie's lowest-ever rating. Despite all the kind help and advice I had been given, I had failed to bring out the best in the karela. And no-one was prepared to let me try again. Well at least Freddie learnt exactly what we mean when we say 'it leaves a bitter taste in the mouth.'

And that is where our adventure with karela might have ended. Waiting to pick up Alex and Freddie at school, I chatted to Yamini. Her family comes from the Gujarat region in India but she spent most of her childhood in Uganda. Her mum, Pramila, taught her how to cook traditional Gujarati dishes when she was 11 years old. This was done without recipe books. Through the generations mothers passed on their detailed knowledge to their daughters. Yamini was disappointed that I had been defeated by the karela and offered to teach me at her home. Whilst Alex played with her daughters Ritu and Krishini, I was treated to a masterclass in Gujarati cooking. I watched Yamini, helped by their housekeeper Usha, carefully scrape, salt and rinse the karela. Yamini told me that it was important to prepare the karela well.

As she cooked, Yamini told me more about her mum Pramila. She described how for a while it had been too upsetting to cook her recipes after she had died. But gradually she had returned to these family dishes. Our evening was far more than just a lesson in taming the bitter gourd. The karela had been transformed by the onions, spices and then caramelised using jaggery – a traditional unrefined whole sugar. You slice it like cheese and it has a subtle sweet taste. You can buy it from specialist Asian food stores. If you can't buy it, you can subsitite dark brown sugar. When the meal was ready, Alex came down to join in the tasting. Freddie had ruled himself out of any more karela-tasting but Alex gave this 8 out of 10.

Yamini's Karela

This traditional Gujarati dish redeemed the karela and transformed it from a bitter gourd into a caramelised delicacy.

Serves 2 as a side dish
2 karela
2 tbsp vegetable oil
1/2 red onion, thinly sliced
1 tsp coriander seeds

1/2 tsp mild chilli powder
1/2 tsp ground turmeric
4 tbsp jaggery (or 3 tbsp dark
  brown sugar)
Salt to prepare the karela

1 Wash and dry the karela. With a small knife, scrape off the skin. Slice them in half lengthways. Scoop out all the seeds and pith in the middle. Chop the karela into thin strips. Apply salt and keep in a colander to drain away the bitter water.

2 Thoroughly wash all the salt from the karela, rinsing with fresh water. Squeeze out all the water.

3 In a small lidded pan, heat up the vegetable oil. Add the coriander seeds, then the karela and red onion with the spices. Stir well.

4 Reduce the heat a little, put the lid on and steam for 20 minutes, stirring occasionally.

5 Turn up the heat a little and stir in the jaggery. Continue to cook for another 5 minutes. The karela and onion will start to caramelise.

Freddie and Alex patted and stroked the karela's green skin, waiting for it to turn and snap at them.

K is for... Kohlrabi

This is a vegetable that knows how to make an entrance. I saw them piled up in a basket which looked like a graveyard of old Sputniks. Their long green antennae spring out of a smooth dome, the size of an orange.

I took them home. I half expected them to climb out of my bag with their long green limbs and launch an invasion of Planet Earth. When I got them into my kitchen, the children were impressed. Anything that looks as if it is an alien extra from *Doctor Who* gets brownie points in our house.

The kohlrabi is incredibly versatile. It may look a little scary but you can sauté, steam, roast, bake, stir-fry or simply grate it and eat it raw. Unlike some cabbages, it has a sweet mild taste. The green leaves and gangly stems can be eaten as well, like any green. But some kohlrabi fans claim that the real flavour of this vegetable only emerges when it is cooked.

Our first recipe for kohlrabi came from a farmer, Helen Thomas at Linscombe Farm in Devon, who grows organic vegetables with her husband Phil. They have three young sons who are her 'quality control experts'. Helen's recipe for Kohlrabi in Carrot Cream Sauce has passed the taste test with her children, so I tried it with Freddie – he gave it 7 out of 10.

I was drawn towards an advert on eBay: 'Enormous kohlrabi bulbs up to a foot in diameter! Sure fire state winner!' This belongs to the strange competitive world of giant vegetable growers. Apparently there is a farmer in Alaska who has grown a 'Kohlrabi Gigante' weighing in at over 43 kg (96 lb). Other smaller varieties of kohlrabi have glamorous names like the Kossack, the Grand Duke and the alluring Early Purple Vienna.

I took my modestly-sized kohlrabi, chopped off its green tendrils and peeled it. It has a mild turnipy taste and we discovered it makes good coleslaw. Freddie and Alexandra enjoyed the Kohlrabi-slaw, giving it 8 out of 10.

Kohlrabi in Carrot Cream Sauce

This recipe transforms a space-invader lookalike into a perfectly respectable terrestrial dish that is soft and sweet. (See www.linscombe.co.uk)

Serves 4
340 g (11½ oz) kohlrabi, washed and peeled
25 g (1 oz) butter
225 g (7½ oz) carrots, diced
300 ml (½ pint) chicken or vegetable stock

1 level tbsp cornflour
½ level tsp dried dill
150 ml (¼ pint) single cream
Freshly chopped parsley
Salt and freshly ground pepper

1 Cut the kohlrabi into 5-mm (¼-in.) slices.

2 Melt the butter in a large pan and sauté the kohlrabi and carrots for 5 minutes. Add the stock and seasoning, bring to the boil and cook for 10 minutes until tender. Put the vegetables in a serving dish and keep warm.

3 Blend the cornflour with a little cold water, add to the stock. Bring to the boil, stirring, and cook for 1–2 minutes.

4 Stir in the dill and cream, and reheat without boiling. Pour the sauce over the vegetables and sprinkle with chopped parsley.

tip

Helen told me, 'My children love nothing better than to select their own vegetable from the field for that evening's meal'. Her tip is to try and involve children in growing vegetables and to encourage them to choose vegetables to eat from the market or shop. She also advises people not to inflict their own tastes on their children, so that they get to experience a very varied range of vegetables.

Kohlrabi-slaw

Proving its versatility, eaten raw in a version of coleslaw, the kohlrabi came out on top again.

Serves 4 as a side dish
1 kohlrabi, stalks removed, peeled and finely grated
2 carrots, peeled and finely grated
1 red apple, cored and diced

4 tbsp raisins
3 tbsp plain yoghurt
3 tbsp low-fat mayonnaise

1 Mix the kohlrabi, carrot, apple and raisins together.
2 Add the yoghurt and mayonnaise and mix well. Serve immediately.

tip

If you like, try replacing half the grated carrot with some grated raw beetroot.

If you can't get hold of kohlrabi, cabbage would do just as well. Use conventional white cabbage, rather than something like Savoy.

The kohlrabi is incredibly versatile. It may look a little scary but you can sauté, steam, roast, bake, stir-fry or simply grate it and eat it raw.

L is for... Leeks

leaky leek

We reached L for Leeks the weekend we all went to Wales. This was Freddie's first visit, his first experience of a formal dinner party to celebrate my aunt and uncle's ruby wedding anniversary.

A year before and I would have had to sit next to him, whispering and negotiating with the waiters to fend off vegetables. This time was different. Freddie wore his first suit and sat amongst the adults. There was nobody there to protect him from the menacing plates of green.

It began well. They served him Welsh lamb and new potatoes. He flinched slightly at the mint sauce. The next vanguard of waiters sashayed towards him with the real test, the vegetables. The other guests knew about Freddie's phobia. His end of the table went quiet. The waitress smiled and presented him a platter of vegetables. He went slightly pink. 'I'll have a bit of everything please.' Everyone cheered. And not only did he invite the vegetables on to his plate: he ate them.

So we came home with a bunch of Welsh leeks and a new confidence. As a child I had always preferred leeks pinned to the blazer rather than served on a plate. They always seemed to be dished up in a slimy cheese sauce. Our first leek recipes were very

different. I paired the leeks with Caerphilly cheese, which is also known as 'the crumblies', and put them in a puff pastry tart. There was no hint of sliminess. Freddie and Alex both scored this 10 out of 10.

Apparently, Emperor Nero took his singing voice very seriously and followed a special diet, avoiding apples and eating large quantities of leeks. Because of this, his subjects nicknamed him the 'Leek Eater' or 'Porrophagus'. Maybe that is why the Welsh have such a fine choral tradition. Freddie also takes his singing voice very seriously, especially when it comes to football chants. So we made some Leek and Potato Singing Soup, boosted with roasted garlic. The soup was given 9 out of 10.

tip

Leeks are in season in Britain from November to April. Choose the medium or smaller-sized leeks rather than the huge monsters that are sometimes on sale. The larger leeks can sometimes be a bit tough and slimy to eat, which will discourage most children. Pick leeks with dark green leaves, without brown spots.

Remember to buy more than you need, as once you have trimmed off the ends and discarded the tougher leaves, you won't have as much leek as you thought!

Freddie's Favourite 10/10

Leek and Caerphilly Cheese Tart

Caerphilly cheese, also known as 'the crumblies', is the perfect partner for leeks.

Serves 4
375 g (12 oz) ready-made puff pastry
250 g (8 oz) leeks, finely sliced (weight after top
   and tails removed)
2 tbsp olive oil

1 clove of garlic, chopped
115 g (3½ oz) Caerphilly cheese, or similar white
   Cheddar cheese
Balsamic glaze (optional)

Baking tray lined with baking parchment

1 Preheat the oven to 200°C (400°F) Gas 6.
2 Roll out the pastry to a 33 x 23 cm (13 x 9 in.) rectangle, to a depth of 5 mm (¼ in.). Place on the prepared baking sheet. With a knife, lightly score 2 cm (¾ in.) in from the edge, all around the rectangle. This will rise to make a ridge when the pastry cooks.
3 Add the leeks to a frying pan with the olive oil and sauté with the garlic. Stir continuously on a medium heat for about 3 minutes. Don't let them burn.
4 Scatter the leeks evenly over the pastry within the inner rectangle.
5 Make shavings of Caerphilly cheese using a vegetable peeler or grater. Scatter the cheese over the leeks. If you like you can drizzle a little balsamic glaze on top.
6 Put in the oven and bake for 25 minutes or until the pastry is completely risen, cooked and golden brown. Serve hot or cold.

abcthedgreatebigfveggchallengehijk mnopqrstuvwxyz

Leek and Potato Singing Soup

Revered by Roman emperors and young boys with a penchant for football chants, leeks may hold the key to the perfect singing voice.

Serves 4
450 g (14 oz) leeks, finely chopped
350 g (11½ oz) potatoes, peeled and diced into
   small cubes
900 ml (1½ pints) chicken or vegetable stock

1 roasted garlic bulb (see page 115)
2 tbsp olive oil
4 tbsp reduced-fat crème fraîche
A handful of chopped chives, to decorate
Salt and freshly ground pepper

1 Heat the olive oil in a pan and sauté the leeks for 3 minutes on a medium heat.
2 Add the potatoes and cook with the leeks for further 5 minutes, stirring them to stop them burning.
3 Squeeze out all the soft garlic from the roasted bulb and stir in. Add the vegetable stock and bring to the boil. As soon as it reaches boiling point, reduce the heat and simmer for 20 minutes.
4 Stir in the crème fraîche and purée in a hand-blender or liquidiser. Serve with a little chopped chives and season to taste.

tip

For this soup recipe, you can substitute the potatoes for sweet potatoes or celeriac. This gives the soup a very different flavour but Freddie and Alex enjoyed these variations on the traditional Leek and Potato Soup.

L is for... Lettuce

When we reached L for Lettuce, Freddie came up with the idea for a League of Lettuce. We were confronted with too much choice at the supermarket. 'Let's put them into divisions like in football', he suggested. So the Lettuce League Tables were established.

There are apparently four main lettuce types which sound like they have come straight out of the Civil War: the Crisphead, the Butterhead, the Looseleaf and the Cos or Romaine. And within each group there are hundreds of varieties.

Alex and Freddie picked the lettuce teams: Little Gem, Round, Batavia, Green Oak Leaf, Iceberg, Frisee, Romaine and Butterhead Red. We came home on the bus with bags stuffed full of lettuces. Over the eight months since starting the Vegetable Challenge, Freddie had been growing into the role of Taste Explorer, the Marco Polo of the vegetable world. But he had a blind spot with salad. He couldn't see the point of it.

Back at home Alex and Freddie made team labels, arranged tasting plates and score sheets. Marks out of 5 were awarded for each lettuce based on taste and texture. Crunch was analysed, softness of leaf debated and flavour argued over.

After much deliberation the Raw Lettuce Table was announced. Little Gem was the winner, closely followed by the premier league of Round and Batavia whilst Freddie asked for the Butterhead Red to be relegated. Unwittingly, Freddie had eaten a salad, without any need for bribes or subterfuge.

The League of Lettuce meant that our kitchen looked like an allotment. At this stage, presenting a raw salad might have prompted a revolt, so our first recipe involved cooking a lettuce. I opened a 1936 edition of *Au Petit Cordon Bleu,* with recipes by Rosemary Hume and Dione Lucas: two of the best female chefs and cookery writers. We used four round lettuces which seemed like far too much lettuce but after boiling them and drying them, the poor things shrank. The end result was good enough to be a complete meal. Freddie gave it 8 out of 10.

Our tribute to Peter Rabbit came next. Lettuce Soup was sweet and mild-tasting and

Freddie gave it a confident score of 9 out of 10.

'It is said that the effect of eating too much lettuce is "soporiphic",' wrote Beatrix Potter. Well whether it was its sedative qualities or the repetitive boredom of preparing so many lettuce recipes that did it for us, we all slept like Peter Rabbit that night.

For a devout carnivore, Freddie was doing well. The pile of lettuces in the kitchen was shrinking. He had enjoyed the cooked lettuce recipes. Alex and I plotted the next move. As a Crisphead lettuce, the Iceberg had come out top for crunchiness. I read that it was given the name 'iceberg' because they used to be transported huge distances across America by rail, packed in ice to keep them fresh. We decided to be cunning. We made some of Freddie's favourite herby burgers and served them wrapped in a single iceberg lettuce leaf, secured with a cocktail stick. For him, red meat is irresistible, even if it involves crunching through a lettuce leaf. Actually, they both thought it was a good alternative to a bun. Edging a little closer to salad, I made an easy Chicken Caesar Pasta dish with our Romaine lettuce. Something about the way the lettuce

was introduced, first taste-tested and then incorporated into recipes, had taken Freddie on a journey that he would normally have resisted. His score: 7 out of 10.

tip

The iceberg lettuce leaf can also be used to serve a poached egg for children or as a little basket for servings of rice and chicken.

tip

The taste-testing session is a good way of exploring the tastes of different varieties of one vegetable. Sometimes children give up on the taste of a vegetable purely because they didn't like one variety. It is worth experimenting. We did this with mushrooms, potatoes and tomatoes. Give them the *X-Factor* treatment with the tasters scoring each one out of 10.

Braised Lettuce – adapted from *Au Petit Cordon Bleu*

In this thirties classic, the lettuces are cooked slowly and take on the flavour of the bacon.

Serves 4
4 round lettuces
8 rashers of unsmoked back bacon
1 carrot, finely chopped

1 medium onion, finely chopped
100 ml (3½ fl oz) vegetable stock
2 tbsp double cream or crème fraîche
Salt and freshly ground pepper

1 Preheat the oven to 180°C (350°F) Gas 4.

2 Discard the outer leaves of the lettuce. Put the four lettuces in a pan of cold water and bring to the boil. When the water is boiling, turn off the heat, take out the lettuces and drain. Carefully dry with a cloth, taking care not to ruin their shape.

3 Lightly grease a casserole dish and lay the bacon rashers across the bottom. Top with the carrot and onion, then lay the lettuce top-down on the bacon.

4 Pour the vegetable stock on top. Put the lid on and cook in the preheated oven for 40 minutes.

5 Place the lettuce and bacon on a serving dish. Pour the remaining stock and vegetables into a pan and place on the hob on a medium heat. Reduce the stock and stir in the cream. Pour over the lettuce and serve.

Peter Rabbit Soup

This mild soup was awarded the highest score from Freddie out of the lettuce recipes, perhaps because it least resembles a salad.

Serves 4
2 tbsp olive oil
2 medium courgettes, chopped
1 litre (1³/₄ pints) vegetable or chicken stock
2 green oak leaf or round lettuces, shredded

A bunch of mint leaves, finely chopped
¹/₂ tsp sugar
3 tbsp soured cream
Salt and freshly ground pepper

1 Heat the olive oil in a large saucepan and sauté the chopped courgettes for 5 minutes on a medium heat. Season.

2 Pour the stock over the courgettes. Add the lettuce and mint together with the sugar. Stir continuously and bring to the boil.

3 Reduce the heat to low and simmer with the lid on for 10–15 minutes.

4 Remove from the heat and allow to cool a little. With a hand-blender or liquidiser, blend the soup to a smooth texture. Serve with a dollop of soured cream on top.

tip

You can substitute the lettuce in this soup for the same quantity of spinach leaves. Leave out the mint and substitute with fresh basil.

Easy Chicken Caesar Pasta

Based on the traditional Caesar Salad, this pasta dish makes for an easy introduction for the salad-phobes.

Serves 4
300 g (10 oz) wholewheat penne pasta
4 skinless and boneless chicken breast fillets
1 clove of garlic, crushed
2 tbsp olive oil

5 anchovy fillets, chopped (optional)
1 Romaine lettuce, shredded
6 tbsp Caesar dressing
75 g (3 oz) freshly grated Parmesan cheese
A handful of croutons

Ridged griddle pan

1 Cook the pasta according to the instructions on the packet.
2 Cut the chicken fillets into strips and cook in a griddle pan with one crushed garlic clove for about 8 minutes till thoroughly cooked.
3 Add the chicken pieces and anchovy fillets, if using, to the drained pasta and stir to combine.
4 Wash the lettuce and dry in a salad spinner. Add the lettuce to the pasta.
5 Pour over the Caesar salad dressing and mix to ensure that everything is evenly coated. Stir in the grated Parmesan and scatter croutons on top. Serve immediately.

Whether it was its sedative qualities or the repetitive boredom of preparing so many lettuce recipes that did it for us, we all slept like Peter Rabbit that night.

M is for... Mangetout

eat *everything*

Mangetout ('eat all' in French) are simply peas cut off in their prime: immature pea pods. For Freddie, a pea-hater, they are a wolf in sheep's clothing. This is where we came in, with our drama over peas. It was one of the main reasons why we started the blog.

Only four letters away from his worst nightmare, mangetout became a kind of dress rehearsal. Instead of sneaking them in under P for Peas, we awarded them their own day of glory. We kept it simple. They make useful crudités for dipping in houmous (see Grilled Aubergine Houmous, on page 22 or Romano Pepper Houmous, on page 203).

Freddie was happy to use the mangetout as a kind of spoon, but it was more a case of *mange rien*. The next day I tried out a mangetout stir-fry. Stir-fries make great family meals and they take so little time to make, which is perfect after a day at work. This also gives Freddie, our resident fussy-eater, much less opportunity to study the ingredients and reject them. He hadn't really clocked that mangetout were peas until his sister almost told him. A sharp stare across the table from me stopped that. He scored this dish highly, giving it 8 out of 10, but I did notice a small pile of uneaten mangetout in the bowl.

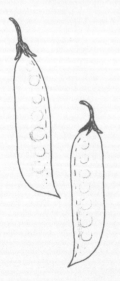

Mangetout Noodle Stir-fry

Stir-fry dishes smell delicious as they cook which helps to increase the appetite and hopefully make everyone feel more hungry – and receptive to the contents.

Serves 4
200 g (7 oz) mangetout
125 g (4 oz) baby corn
250 g (8 oz) dried spinach noodles, or plain noodles
3 tbsp sunflower oil

250 g (8 oz) frozen prawns, defrosted
2 cloves of garlic, chopped
2 tbsp sweet chilli sauce
2 tbsp light soy sauce
2 tsp sesame seeds

1 Cut the mangetout into strips and the baby corn into bite-sized pieces.
2 Cook the dried noodles according to the packet instructions, being careful not to overcook them. Drain and keep in their pan whilst you quickly stir-fry the rest of the ingredients.
3 Heat the oil in a wok or large frying pan. Add the prawns and garlic and stir-fry for 2 minutes, making sure that the garlic does not burn.
4 Add the mangetout and baby corn and stir-fry for 3 minutes. Add the sweet chilli sauce and soy sauce to the mangetout, prawns and baby corn.
5 Add the noodles and toss everything together until it is hot. Serve with a sprinkling of sesame seeds.

M is for... Marrow

If there is one thing more boring than the taste of a marrow, it has to be visiting seven superstores, three markets, two church fêtes and two farm shops to find one. And that was during the marrow season.

Normally, it's the sort of vegetable that people try very hard to give away, making hundreds of jars of marrow chutney or wine for the village fair. As a child, I was lucky that my parents had a vegetable garden. We weren't self-sufficient but I was so used to eating food grown in the garden that a Pot Noodle seemed exotic. Eating through a glut of vegetables was a feature of growing up. For what seemed like days on end, every meal would be a variation on a theme. A marrow glut was like water torture.

But this time round, chasing the marrow was like trying to apprehend a fugitive. Wherever I went, the marrow had just slipped away, moments before. I took to phoning stores in advance.

'Hello? Can you tell me if you have marrows in the store?'

'Let me check. Please hold.'

For five minutes I listened to a pan pipe rendition of *Greensleeves*.

'We have five left. And there's another order coming in tonight.'

I would rush round to the store, straight to the marrow pen but they had always flown. Someone had clearly tipped them off. In the end I asked the Co-op store to arrest them for me so that they couldn't get away. When I arrived they were grimacing at me from behind customer services with a label, 'Reserved for Charlotte.'

'We haven't had anyone reserve a marrow before,' said the manager.

Freddie looked suspiciously at the menacing marrow. 'It just looks like a huge courgette.' I was unusually honest with him. Normally I do the 'hard sell', inflating the image of each new vegetable but I didn't want to lie. 'This is a really boring vegetable which has grown far too big for its own good but I will try to make it taste better.'

I planned the marrow recipes with care. It has a tendency to be watery, a little stringy in texture and very, very bland. If there was an 'Extreme Makeover' programme for vegetables, the marrow would be a perfect candidate. My first attempt focused on overwhelming the marrow with the flavour of roasted garlic. Freddie gave it 6 out of 10, loved the taste but thought the texture of marrow was unpleasant. The rest of the family loved it.

Stuffing a marrow seemed like a last resort but in the end that is what I did. If you don't make an effort with a marrow the taste will send you to sleep. So I chose fragrant basmati rice, cinnamon and the sweetness of raisins to try and inject a bit of excitement. It seemed a bit like icing a stale bun. But the filling makes it worthwhile. Freddie edged his score up reluctantly with a 7 out of 10.

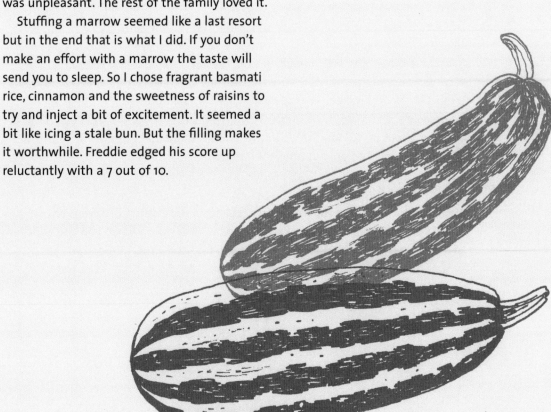

Roasted Garlic and Herb Marrow

In an attempt to give the mundane marrow a makeover, I devised this recipe using tried-and-tested roasted garlic to help it along.

Serves 4 as a side dish
1 marrow, chopped into 5-cm (2-in.) cubes
3 tbsp olive oil
1 tsp balsamic vinegar

1 tsp of dried oregano
1 tsp dried basil
1 roasted garlic bulb (see page 115)
Sea salt and freshly ground pepper

1 Preheat the oven to 180°C (350°F) Gas 4.

2 Place the marrow in a bowl with the oil, balsamic vinegar, herbs and a pinch of sea salt. Mix well.

3 Squeeze out all the soft garlic from the roasted bulb and add to the marrow, mixing it thoroughly to make sure the marrow chunks are well covered. Add a twist of ground pepper. Leave to marinate for one hour.

4 Spread out the marrow chunks evenly across a lightly greased baking tray and bake for about 25–30 minutes. Turn the chunks halfway through. The marrow will be very soft and golden brown when ready.

tip

The Roasted Garlic and Herb Marrow recipe can work well if you want to use chunks of courgettes instead of marrow. As well as marrow, you can add cubes of aubergine, which have been pre-steamed for 5 minutes, to the marinade with the roasted garlic and marrow and then bake altogether in the oven.

If there was an 'Extreme Makeover' programme for vegetables, the marrow would be a perfect candidate.

Stuffed Marrow with Basmati Rice and Raisins

This recipe was awarded a half-decent 7 out of 10, which owes as much to the fragrant combination of flavours as it does to the marrow itself.

Serves 4
1 marrow
3 tbsp olive oil
150 g (5 oz) basmati rice (uncooked weight)
½ tsp ground cinnamon
2 tbsp raisins
1 large onion, finely chopped

2 cloves of garlic, crushed
2 tbsp pine nuts
½ tsp mixed dried herbs
400 g (13 oz) tin of chopped tomatoes
1 tbsp clear honey
50 g (2 oz) finely grated Parmesan cheese
Salt and freshly ground pepper

1 Preheat the oven to 180°C (350°F) Gas 4.

2 Slice the marrow in half lengthways and scoop out the seeds. Lightly criss-cross the white marrow flesh with a knife and drizzle a little olive oil on top. Season and cook in the preheated oven for 15 minutes.

3 Meanwhile, cook the basmati rice according to the packet instructions. When cooked, drain and put the rice in a bowl with the cinnamon and raisins.

4 In a large pan on a medium heat, sauté the finely chopped onion, crushed garlic and herbs in the olive oil for about 5 minutes. Add the pine nuts and sauté until they are lightly browned.

5 Add the rice to the onion mixture and stir on a low heat. Add the chopped tomatoes and honey and stir for a further 3 minutes.

6 Take out the marrow halves from the oven and place each one on a piece of foil, large enough to create a parcel. Spoon half the rice mixture into each half and seal up the foil parcels. Bake in the oven for 25 minutes.

7 Unwrap the foil parcels, sprinkle with the Parmesan cheese and return to the oven for a further 5 minutes with the foil opened up. Serve hot.

M is for... Mushrooms

For a month in the summer we encouraged fungus to grow in our airing cupboard and cellar. I purchased a mushroom-growing kit on the internet. Now strictly speaking, mushrooms don't belong in a vegetable challenge as they are fungi, but it seemed a little mean to exclude them.

Back in the seventies, my father was very skilled at self-sufficiency. He grew all our own vegetables, made bread and yoghurt and would brew his own beer in huge plastic buckets. I can remember the smell of the malt extract which he poured like thick treacle out of large tins. There was one stage of the process when it was crucial that I didn't create any dust. I was allowed to sit on the kitchen table and watch but not fidget. 'If you make any dust, you'll turn the beer sour.'

He also grew his own mushrooms in trays under the shelf by the kitchen window. Everyday he would carefully spray them with water. I would lift the lid off to peek at the grey film which spread out over the soil. Slowly over the week it morphed into little pods of white mushrooms. One evening he announced they were ready. We went to sleep dreaming of fried mushrooms for breakfast. In the morning, there was a foul smell in the kitchen and soil was scattered across the floor. The cat was looking shifty. My father was furious. After that, he never bought another mushroom-growing kit.

A quarter of a century on and Freddie and Alex are checking the mushrooms lurking in our cupboard. We have no cat, so one hazard is removed but there is something slightly creepy about allowing fungi to grow in your home. There is a fungus in the Blue Mountains of Oregon which has stealthily grown to cover an area bigger than 1,600 football pitches. Clearly mushrooms are not to be trusted.

For Freddie, who had never knowingly eaten a mushroom, growing them was a perfect distraction. As we waited, I bought some huge flat field mushrooms that looked as if they had set their sights on challenging the monster fungi in Oregon. We made a selection of toppings which encouraged Freddie to at least taste his first mushroom. He gave it 7 out of 10, largely because of the toppings.

One of Freddie's best friends from school is Bertie, who is brilliant at loads of things, apart from eating mushrooms. That is, until his mum, Natasha, created a mushroom pasta sauce. The school queue is the original information superhighway and it was there that she told me about her recipe.

That evening I brought this irresistible mushroom sauce to life. An essential part of the recipe is not to let the mushroom-hater know it contains mushrooms until after it has been tasted. That was good advice. Freddie was hungry, after playing four hours of football, providing the optimum conditions for a new recipe. He ate the first bowl without looking up. Once the first fierce pangs of hunger had gone, he asked for seconds.

'What's this made of Mum?'

'Mushrooms,' I said as I filled his bowl with a second helping.

And before he could object I told him it was Bertie's recipe. He was straight on the phone to his friend. 'They tricked me into eating mushrooms. But your sauce was really good. I'm giving it 10 out of 10.'

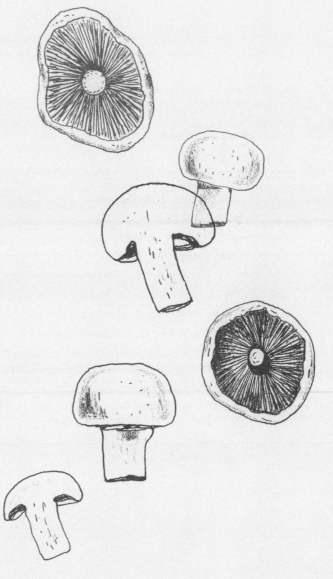

Field Mushrooms with Bacon and Parmesan

Topping these huge specimens of fungi with familiar ingredients is a great way to introduce them to a mushroom sceptic.

Serves 4 as a starter or 2 as a main course
4 large field mushrooms
Olive oil
Toasted muffin, to serve

For the topping
1 small onion, finely chopped
3 rashers of bacon, chopped
4 tbsp breadcrumbs
4 tbsp freshly grated Parmesan cheese
Olive oil spray
Salt and freshly ground pepper

1 Preheat the oven to 180°C (350°F) Gas 4.

2 Wash and dry the mushrooms. Cut off the stalks and chop them finely. Put to one side.

3 Place the mushrooms on a baking tray and lightly spray or drizzle with olive oil.

4 Heat a small amount of olive oil in a pan and add the onion, bacon and reserved chopped mushroom stalks and sauté for 4 minutes.

5 In a bowl, mix the breadcrumbs and Parmesan cheese together. Fill the mushrooms equally with the bacon and onion mixture and then sprinkle the breadcrumbs and Parmesan on top. Season.

6 Bake in the preheated oven for about 20 minutes until the mushrooms are cooked. Watch that the toppings don't burn. Serve on a toasted, buttered muffin.

tip
Mushroom toppings

You can make up your own irresistible toppings. Just remember to slice off the stalk so you have a nice flat mushroom platform. Here are some simple suggestions:

◉ Grill the flat mushroom by itself and then top it with a poached egg. Season with salt and pepper and serve on a slice of toasted ciabatta.

◉ Chop up some spinach leaves and quickly sauté in a little olive oil. Crumble some blue cheese in a bowl and mix with the spinach leaves. Top the mushrooms and place in the oven for 15–20 minutes.

◉ Drizzle pesto sauce onto the mushroom. Add a circle of goats' cheese to each mushroom. Place under a medium hot grill and cook for 8–10 minutes until the mushroom is cooked and the goats' cheese is slightly browned.

◉ Simply put a dollop of goats' cheese on each mushroom and sprinkle over chopped chives and place under a medium hot grill until the goats' cheese has melted and the mushroom is browned.

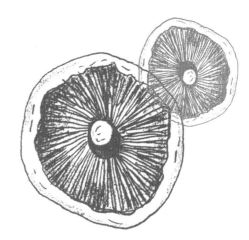

There's nothing
nicer than a
meal outdoors.

Bertie's Mushroom (but don't let on) Pasta Sauce

This recipe lived up to its reputation of converting mushroom-hating school boys into it's number one fans.

Serves 4 as a pasta sauce
450 g (14 oz) chestnut mushrooms,
    or white mushrooms
2 generous handfuls of chopped parsley
3 shallots or one medium onion, chopped
1–2 cloves of garlic, crushed

300 g (10 oz) dried spaghetti or linguine pasta
2 tbsp olive oil
100 ml (3½ fl oz) double cream or crème fraîche
50 g (2 oz) freshly grated Parmesan cheese
Salt and freshly ground pepper

1 Chop the mushrooms roughly and put them into a large bowl with the chopped parsley, shallots and garlic.

2 Use a blender or hand-blender to turn the mushroom mixture into a mush. At this point cook your pasta according to the packet instructions.

3 Heat the olive oil in a large frying pan and cook the mushroom mixture on a medium heat. Stir constantly with a wooden spoon. The mushrooms and shallots will soften and cook. Cook for at least 5 minutes.

4 Remove from the heat and stir in the double cream or crème fraîche.

5 When the pasta is al dente, drain and return to the pan with the mushroom sauce and stir round, coating the pasta thoroughly. Stir in the Parmesan cheese.

N is for... Nettles

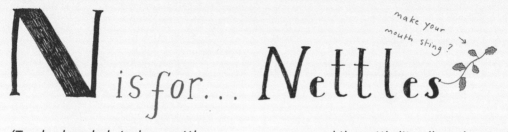

make your mouth sting?

'Tender-handed stroke a nettle,
And it stings you for your pains;
Grasp it like a man of mettle,
And it soft as silk remains.'
(Aaron Hill, Verses Written
on a Window in Scotland)

We went to pick nettles armed with a verse, a pair of gardening gloves and a Grandpa. London nettles come with an urban dressing of diesel dust and dog pee. Their country counterparts seemed more attractive so we visited my parents in Oxfordshire to find a better class of stinger. Grandpa carried out a reconnaissance trip, locating a clump of nettles where no weedkiller had been used. His foraging skills were honed as a child growing up in the countryside of Shropshire during the Second World War. He explained that the best time to pick nettles was in early spring and you have to pick the smallest, most tender top shoots. After some initial nerves, Alex and Freddie put on their gloves and

grasped the nettle literally and metaphorically. They presented me with a basket of nettles.

Nettles, like the pungent horseradish root, require some form of body protection to prepare. Cooking in gloves was challenging. I picked through the nettles, threw away other weeds, caterpillars and bugs. I made nettle soup. Cooking the nettles removes the sting, which was understandably Freddie's greatest fear. We all sat in Grandpa's garden sipping on our soup. Alex thought it was delicious. Freddie gave it 8 out of 10 but was convinced his lips were stinging.

Rather worryingly, Freddie's new found confidence with vegetables had developed into bravado. On a visit to a bog garden at Upton House in Warwickshire, Alex shrieked, 'Mum, Freddie's bitten into a bulrush!'

Over the years I have learnt to disregard *most* of the outrageous things that my children say about each other. But he had indeed done exactly that. Maybe because a bulrush looks like a sausage on a stick, Freddie had decided to take a bite. This was a clear sign that he now saw vegetation as a source of food rather than suffering. But I am not a wild food expert. Not knowing whether bulrushes were poisonous or edible, I flushed the brown bits out of his mouth with a bottle of water and lectured him on the dangers of putting strange plants in his mouth.

Someone should publish a manual of ready-to-deliver lectures for parents. Lecture 56 'Do not run whilst holding scissors.' Lecture 103 'Do not put your fingers into the electric socket.' I delivered Lecture 278 'Some plants may be poisonous.' This is a speech that I had never really had much need to deliver before. As an avowed vegetable-phobic, Freddie had never shown any enthusiasm for putting plants in his mouth. But he had changed.

Jeffrey Steingarten, author of *The Man Who Ate Everything*, devised a Six-Step Programme to liberate his palate from irrational dislikes. He worked on the principle that what is learned can be forgotten. Freddie had clearly forgotten to be suspicious of vegetables on our very own alphabetical step programme. He had become 'The Boy Who Ate Everything'. Well, nearly everything. We hadn't yet reached P for Peas.

Freddie had no urge to try the nettles raw. Though I did tell him about the World Nettle Eating Championships, which are held annually in a small village in Dorset. Competitors gather at the Bottle Inn pub to see who can munch their way through the most nettle leaves. Anaesthetics are prohibited. Side effects include a black tongue and swollen lips. The competition lasts a masochistic hour after which the discarded stalks are measured and the winner declared. The world record is apparently 22.5 m (74 ft) of nettles. Eating through the A to Z of vegetables seems a remarkably sane project compared with that.

I turned our remaining cooked nettles into a variation on a Spanish tortilla, which everybody enjoyed. Freddie gave it 8 out of 10.

Nettle Soup

Freddie approached the soup with a brave face and a little trepidation. Despite the fact that the sting is removed through cooking, he thought he could still feel his lips stinging.

Serves 4
450 g (14 oz) potatoes, peeled and diced
50 g (2 oz) salted butter
1 medium onion, finely chopped
1 clove of garlic, crushed
1 apple, peeled, cored and chopped

250 g (8 oz) young nettle leaves, chopped
and tough stalks discarded
900 ml (1½ pints) chicken or vegetable stock
4 tbsp crème fraîche or double cream
A handful of chopped chives, to decorate
Salt and freshly ground pepper

1 Parboil the potatoes for 10 minutes. Drain.

2 In a large pan, melt the butter and sauté the chopped onions, garlic, apple and nettles for 10 minutes on a gentle heat.

3 Add the potatoes and continue to sauté for a further 5 minutes. Add the stock and bring to the boil. Lower the heat and simmer gently for 10 minutes.

4 Remove from the heat and allow to cool slightly. Add the crème fraîche and a little seasoning. Liquidise the soup in a blender and serve with a few chopped chives scattered on top.

If you can't get hold of nettles, a great alternative for this soup would be spinach.

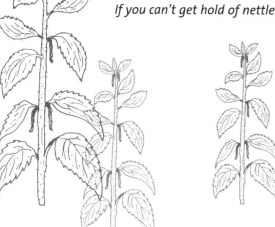

Nettle and Potato Tortilla

You can incorporate nettles into a tortilla in the same way that you might use kale or spinach leaves.

Serves 4
3 tbsp olive oil
2 red onions, thinly sliced
250 g (8 oz) potatoes, diced into small cubes
1 clove of garlic, finely chopped

200 g (7 oz) young nettle leaves, chopped
 and stalks discarded
6 large eggs
25 g (1 oz) freshly grated Parmesan cheese
Salt and freshly ground pepper

1 Use a deep non-stick frying pan about 23 cm (9 in.) in diameter. Heat two tablespoons of the olive oil in the frying pan on a medium heat and add the onions, potatoes and garlic. Stir well and cover with a lid or circle of foil and gently cook for about 15 minutes, stirring frequently to prevent sticking.
2 Add the nettles to the potato and onion mixture, stirring for 5 minutes on a medium heat. The nettle leaves will wilt. Remove from the heat.
3 Beat the eggs in a bowl with a pinch of salt and twist of ground pepper. Add the potato, onion and nettle mixture to the beaten eggs and stir.
4 Return the frying pan to a medium heat, add the remaining oil and heat. Pour the egg, nettle and potato mixture into the pan. Cook slowly, without a lid, on a low heat for about 20–25 minutes, depending on the depth of your tortilla.
5 Cook gently until the egg on the base sets and browns. Carefully draw round the edge of the pan with a palette knife, tipping any liquid edge left on the surface, down the sides. When there is no runny egg on top it is time to cook the other side. If you feel up to inverting the tortilla on to a plate and putting it back into the pan then go ahead. I know my limitations. I sprinkled a little Parmesan on top and put the pan under a preheated grill to cook the top.
6 To serve, slice into quarters or cut into 5-cm (2-in.) cubes as finger food.

tip

Substitute the nettle leaves for spinach, kale or Savoy cabbage, finely shredded. Steam the kale and Savoy cabbage for 2 minutes before adding to the tortilla.

N is for... NOPALES

'Can you visualise the cacti in cartoons? You know; the ones with the huge Bugs Bunny ears – well that's the kind of plant that nopales come from. You have got to think of nopales as Mexico's answer to the green bean.'

My nopales therapy session took place on the telephone with a Mexican food wholesaler. There I was kneeling on the kitchen floor, surrounded by an array of phone directories pursuing an edible cactus. It was Day Two of the Nopales Hunt. I hadn't even got dressed yet. Finally I had found someone who knew about nopales. Somebody with a kind voice who was prepared to give me a free thumbnail sketch. I caught sight of myself in the reflection of the glass roof, still in my nightie, on the floor and clinging to the phone as if my life depended on it. If anyone had seen me they would have thought I was being talked out of something by the Samaritans.

On Day One, I had walked round aisle after aisle in an endless series of strip-lit supermarkets. I had become expert at sniffing out the Mexican food row. I located the tacos and scoured the shelf for jars of nopales. There weren't any. My enquiries were met with blank looks. I registered my request with the inaccurately-named Customer Services Desk.

The man behind the desk disappeared to ask the manager. Twenty minutes later I was still waiting with a daft look on my face. The assistant had clearly decided to go on a tea break. He obviously thought I was one nacho short of a picnic. But my Mexican food wholesaler had saved me. 'I'm afraid we can't sell you any fresh nopales. We used to stock it but no one was buying it. But you can come along and buy some pickled nopalitos in jars.'

I was happy with a jar of nopalitos. Though I had been looking forward to buying a gourmet cactus thorn removal tool on the internet. On the way back from work I picked up my pickled nopalitos from the Mexican food shop. *Nopal* means cactus in Spanish and *nopales* (no-PAH-les) are cactus stems. Getting ever more diminutive, the *nopalitos* are the cactus pads once they have been cut up and prepared. And that is what I brought home.

'What are we having for supper?'
'A bit of cactus.'

Silence. In fact, I turned a bit of cactus into tacos filled with Mexican Chilli Beef with Nopalitos. Nopalitos taste very pleasant. I can't help thinking it would be more exciting to try them fresh but until then we can recommend them from a jar. The tacos scored 10 out of 10, sadly the nopalitos garnish was given a less confident 6.

Mexican Chilli Beef with Nopalitos

It's not every day that you can claim to have eaten cactus for supper – the perfect school-boy boast.

Serves 4
1 tbsp olive oil
1 green pepper, finely chopped
1 medium onion, finely chopped
500 g (1 lb) lean minced beef
1½ tsp Smoky Sweet mild Spanish chilli powder or Mexican spice mix
400 g (13 oz) tin of chopped tomatoes

3 tbsp tomato purée
2 small pieces of dark chocolate
4 taco shells

To fill the taco
Soured cream
Shredded lettuce
Nopalitos, 1 tbsp per taco

1 Heat the oil in a large pan and fry the pepper and onion for 2 minutes. Add the beef and the mild chilli powder.
2 Cook on a medium hot heat for 8 minutes. Add the tomatoes and tomato purée and stir. Reduce the heat and simmer for 5 minutes, stirring occasionally.
3 Add the chocolate. The liquid from the tomatoes should reduce, leaving you with a lovely rich filling for tacos.
4 Serve with shredded lettuce, a little soured cream and, of course, the nopalitos.

tip

Our blog readers came up with some great ideas for nopalitos. You can sauté some chopped onion, peppers and sweetcorn with the nopalitos and add to cooked rice with a little Mexican seasoning. Or try using them in cheese and nopalitos quesadillas. They can also be chopped up and added to scrambled egg.

If you can't get hold of nopalitos, we make another garnish for tacos from courgettes. Choose the smaller courgettes and, using a vegetable peeler or knife, make long thin ribbons. Steam them or stir-fry for a minute or two and serve with the tacos.

N is for... Nori

N vegetables needed a bit of coaxing. I sent a group email around the office to generate more inspiration. My colleagues were remarkably tolerant about my vegetable obsession.

Other group emails invite people to help with the washing up, share a pint in the pub or play a game of football. Mine had become rather narrow in their focus. But they were generous with their suggestions, which included neeps, nuts, nori and nopales. Nuts were thrown out as non-vegetable. The Scottish dish of neeps was set aside to feature later on in the challenge under S for Swede. But nori and nopales intrigued me.

Nori used to be a more general term for various kinds of seaweed but nowadays it usually refers to the thin dried seaweed sheets that are used in some sushi dishes. It starts off life as a reddish coloured plant that is made into these dark green paper sheets. In Japan, nori, also known as purple laver, even has its own designated day. We decided to hold our very own nori day.

I found a 'Make Your Own Sushi Kit' in a health-food store. 'Make Your Own' kits always make me nervous. It is never as easy as the label suggests. So I handed it over to Freddie and Alex who are far less jaded. The kit came complete with a bamboo sushi rolling mat, sushi rice and crisp paper sheets of nori. They made three fillings: cucumber, tuna mayonnaise and avocado. The end result was impressive for two first-time sushi chefs. And they enjoyed eating them.

When you hold a sea shell against your ear, you can hear the ocean. And when you eat nori, you can taste the sea. There is no better way of describing it.

Freddie's Favourite 10/10
Nori Ciabatta

I bought a bag of something marketed as 'Nori Sprinkles': crisp flecks of shredded seaweed. You can buy this from some supermarkets and health-food shops. I sliced some ciabatta bread, drizzled olive oil on each slice and sprinkled a couple of teaspoons of nori onto each one and toasted them in the oven until the bread was just golden brown. Nori Ciabatta is a perfect accompaniment to a bowl of soup. Alex and Freddie renamed Nori Sprinkles, Sea-glitter. They gave Nori Ciabatta 10 out of 10.

Try using thin slices of nori as a garnish for soup. One visitor to the blog explained that as the nori dissolves, it adds a lovely flavour to the soup. Or you can add nori sprinkles to brown rice as a side dish.

For Chris and Alex, as well as Freddie, The Great Veg Challenge was an adventure.

O is for... Okra

(or lady's finger)

Forget singles columns or online dating sites, vegetables are the next big thing in making relationships. Okra generated more conversations, more new friendships for me than any other vegetable in the challenge. But it wasn't romance I was after, just recipes.

Okra is also known as lady's finger, which I'm presuming is because of its slender green shape. It beckoned at me from the supermarket shelf and then pointed at the first of many people with whom I found myself discussing cooking methods. My first introduction, in the supermarket aisle, was to a woman from Syria. She insisted that the best okra are the smallest ones, and told me only to buy lady's fingers that are no longer than 10 cm (4 in.).

Later, at Shepherd's Bush Market, a Nigerian man insisted that the worst crime is to overcook them. Each time I went home with a fresh bag of okra and a fresh recipe. Okra made me work hard but I still didn't succeed in producing a dish that the family liked. The problem was the sliminess that oozes from okra when you cook it. This clear gooey secretion, which is great to thicken stews and gumbos, was off-putting.

The lady's finger then pointed me in the direction of the internet. I appealed for help on the blog and asked for assistance on food message boards. These message boards are the modern day equivalent of gathering round the campfire to chat. A man called Norm popped up in a box on the Martha Stewart community message board, telling me how his mom used to cook okra. The tips came thick and fast. I learnt that younger, smaller okra are best, never to soak it, always to tenderise it at a high heat, to cook it uncovered, soak it in milk. Overnight, the comment box on the blog was bursting with recipes from all over the world. People wanted us to enjoy okra. I took notes. This was the consensus on okra:

- Buy small and fresh.
- You must fry them.
- Bread them, then fry.
- Coat in cornmeal, then fry.
- Soak in buttermilk, then fry.
- Embrace the slime and make a gumbo.
- Oil and roast them.
- Spice them, then fry.
- Sauté them.
- Deep-fry them.

I got the message. OKRA NEEDS TO BE FRIED. I offered Freddie the gumbo option and he turned it down. Armed with this collective wisdom, I followed the path to zero slime. The most intriguing tip had been emailed by Cynthia Nelson from Barbados, who blogs 'Tastes Like Home'. She advised me to lay out my cut okra on a baking sheet and let them dry for an hour in the sun. London can't compete with sunny Barbados but I followed Cynthia's advice, shunting my baking tray around our tiny patio so that my okra could catch the weak September sunbeams.

I dipped them in beaten egg, then in seasoned flour and pan fried them. At supper, I left a bowl of sun-dried, fried okra on the table, turned round to fetch a jug of water and by the time I had sat down, it had all but disappeared. Freddie scored this 9 out of 10. I could hear all the lady's fingers around the world coming together and clapping. Okra was no longer a pariah. The slime was banished, all thanks to the Great Big Okra Convention.

The Russian scientist, Ivan Petrovich Pavlov, studied reflexes. He struck a bell when his dogs were fed. In time the dogs associated the bell with dinner and drooled in anticipation.

In our house the ping of a newly-arrived email has the same effect. The subject of one email was simple: 'Okra, the slimy one.' The email came from a lady in Athens. Kalli described how her friend cooks a delicious dish of chicken with okra and potatoes. I printed off the email and went to Olympia Butchers to buy chicken. Whenever I go to our Armenian butchers, I come away with much more than just meat.

'I'm cooking okra tonight, with a Greek recipe,' I told Sid, Ara and Rose. The chopping stopped and they turned round to discuss okra with me. The recipe was dissected, the methods debated. Eyebrows were raised when I mentioned that Kalli recommends soaking the okra whole in a vinegar and water mix to get rid of the slime. Ten minutes later, I left with a chicken and a heavily annotated email. At home I drew on all this expertise and adapted Kalli's recipe. Kalli had signed off, 'hope everything goes well!' It did go well. Chicken with Okra and Potatoes earned 8 out of 10.

Fried Spiced Okra

Originating in Barbados, this recipe brings a little sunshine into your day – and was demolished in seconds by Alex and Freddie.

Serves 4
450 g (14 oz) fresh okra
1 egg
1 tbsp water
75 g (3 oz) plain flour
½ tsp smoked paprika
½ tsp mild chilli powder
½ tsp ground coriander
3 tbsp olive or vegetable oil for pan frying
A generous pinch of salt and some freshly
  ground pepper

1 Slice the okra into 1-cm (½-in.) pieces. Dry with paper towels. Lay out on a baking tray in the sun, if there is any. (Some people suggest placing them in an oven at a low heat for 10 minutes to dry out.)
2 Beat the egg in a wide-rimmed bowl. Season the flour with the spices and some salt and pepper.
3 Dip the okra into the egg, then coat in the seasoned flour and pan fry in hot oil until crisp and golden brown.

Freddie scored this 9 out of 10. I could hear all the lady's fingers around the world coming together and clapping.

abcthedgreatebigfveggchallengehijklmn o pqrstuvwxyz

Chicken with Okra and Potatoes

This combined international effort from Greece and Armenia successfully banishes the slime.

Serves 4

375 g (12 oz) fresh okra
4–5 tbsp cider vinegar
500 g (1 lb) potatoes, peeled and chopped
3 tbsp olive oil
1 medium chicken, approx 1.6 kg (3½ lb), cut into pieces, or a selection of legs, thighs and breast
2 onions, roughly chopped

1 tbsp dried oregano
25 g (1 oz) chopped fresh parsley
2 x 142 g (4½ oz) can concentrated tomato purée
350 ml (12 fl oz) water
1 large tomato, chopped
1 tbsp freshly chopped small leafed Greek basil, or standard basil
Salt and freshly ground pepper

1 Soak the whole okra in a bowl of water with the cider vinegar for an hour.

2 Boil the potatoes in water for 10 minutes. Drain and put aside.

3 Preheat the oven to 190°C (375°F) Gas 5.

4 Heat the oil in a high-sided pan and sauté the chicken for 20 minutes on a medium heat. Add the onion, oregano and seasoning. Sauté for another 15 minutes until the onion is soft.

5 Add the tomato purée and chopped parsley and stir well. Add 200 ml (7 fl oz) of water and slowly bring to the boil. Reduce the heat and allow to simmer for 15 minutes or until the chicken is cooked. If you think the tomato and onion sauce is reducing too quickly, add a little more water.

6 Pour everything into a deep baking dish. Drain the okra and add to the chicken mixture. Add the chopped tomato and parboiled potatoes. Stir round so that everything is covered well with the sauce. Add the remaining 150 ml (¼ pint) of water.

7 Cover with foil and cook in the oven for about 35 minutes. Stir halfway through, checking to make sure the chicken doesn't dry out. Serve with some chopped Greek basil.

O is for... Onions

To make onion rings, I had to borrow a deep-fat fryer from my neighbour, Catherine. I cannot be trusted to have my own. And I suspect the reason lies deep in my childhood.

On the nights that my mother was working, my Dad would make our evening meal. Both of them were good cooks but he had learnt to make sweet and sour pork in batter and delicious chips; huge fried chunks of potato. But the cooking of chips and pork balls was carried out under a strict code of secrecy so that my mother, who wanted us all to eat healthily, wouldn't know. The chip pan, full of oil, was kept hidden in an outhouse. When the coast was clear it was brought into the kitchen. One of us would be given the job of cutting up the potatoes. As the oil heated up, the scent of our last clandestine meal would fill the kitchen: a delicious reminder of our past transgression.

We would eat our meal quickly and greedily without conversation. A cover-up operation followed. The chip pan with its cargo of forbidden oil was returned to the outhouse, plates were washed up and the door out of the kitchen opened wide. One of us would stand outside like a punka-wallah, flapping the door open and shut to waft away the scent of fried food. Deep-fried food became my forbidden fruit.

When we arrived at O for Onions, it was the perfect excuse to make deep-fried onion rings. These were, unsurprisingly, a great hit with Freddie and Alex who scored them 9 out of 10. And, knowing my weaknesses, I dutifully walked back down the street with my neighbour's deep-fat fryer and returned it.

'Let onion atoms lurk within the bowl,
And, scarce-suspected, animate the whole.'
(In Lady Holland *Memoir* **(1855) vol. 1 ch.11**
'receipt for a Salad.')

So said the 19th-century clergyman Sydney Smith. All through the Great Big Vegetable Challenge I have been using onions as an ingredient, 'scarce-suspected'. It's hard to imagine cooking without them. Without knowing it, Freddie, who used to scrape onion off pizzas, had been getting used to their taste and texture. Now it was time for them to come out of the shadows.

Caramelised onions require what seem like industrial quantities of sliced onions. It became a labour of love. Freddie and Alex left the kitchen, driven out by the smell of onions. What scientists in the journal *Nature* identified as the onion's 'irritating lachrymatory factor' reduced me to a sobbing wreck. I put on a pair of goggles which I keep in a kitchen drawer. These are the same goggles that rescued me from being blinded by horseradish fumes.

'Damn.'

I tried to put the goggles on without wiping onion juice in my eyes.

'Damn, damn, damn.'

Chris came in.

'Do you know what you look like?'

I swore at him and he retreated behind the glass doors. Through my plastic goggles I could see him looking into the kitchen, weeping with laughter. I knew why. My multi-tasking mode had gone into over-drive and I had dressed early for a concert. I was wearing high heels, a posh dress and a pair of child's goggles which were steaming up. The plastic goggles misted over, I misjudged the chopping and sliced at my thumb. Tears of pain joined the onion tears. Chris stopped laughing. There was a look of pity on his face. My mound of sliced onions was decorated with a swirl of red blood. He took the knife from me, removed the goggles and placed my bleeding thumb under running water.

'Would you like an early birthday present?'

'I'm not in the mood for presents.'

Chris doesn't normally buy me kitchen utensils for my birthday but after months and months of intensive vegetable preparation I had asked for a food processor. He unwrapped the box, plugged in the processor and in a flash produced a fresh mound of sliced onions. No more tears. The blood-contaminated onions were thrown out. With my plastered-thumb, I made Caramelised Red Onions served with sausages. The more you cook them, the better they taste. The children came back into the kitchen for supper and Freddie scored them 8 out of 10.

tip

When you are buying onions, look for ones that are firm and dry all the way round. Don't buy them if they are sprouting green shoots!

Deep-fried Onion Rings

This recipe was the perfect excuse to indulge my childhood weakness for fried food and proved a great hit with the next generation, too.

Serves 4
150 g (5 oz) plain flour
Cayenne pepper or paprika (optional)

150 g (5 oz) coarse breadcrumbs
2 eggs, beaten
2 large onions, sliced into 1-cm (½-in.) wide rings

Deep fat fryer

1 Add a pinch of cayenne pepper or paprika to the flour and sieve onto a plate.
2 Have a plate of breadcrumbs ready and a wide-rimmed bowl with the beaten egg.
3 Dip the onion rings into the seasoned flour, then into the egg and finally the breadcrumbs, making sure they are well coated.
4 When they are ready, fry them in small batches in hot oil in a deep-fat fryer for 2–3 minutes until golden brown.

Freddie, who used to scrape onion off pizzas, had been getting used to their taste and texture. Now it was time for them to come out of the shadows.

Caramelised Red Onions

If you wish to avoid the potential trauma of slicing so many onions, a food processor will make this job far less painful! It may seem like a lot of onions, but they reduce dramatically as they cook.

Serves 4 as a side dish
3 tbsp olive oil or unsalted butter
8–10 medium red onions

2 tbsp red wine vinegar
1–2 tbsp maple syrup
Salt and freshly ground pepper

1 In a large pan, heat the olive oil or butter. Add the onions and cook on a medium heat for 10 minutes, stirring to make sure they don't burn.
2 Add the vinegar, maple syrup and three tablespoons of water and stir well. Cover and cook for 25 minutes on a low heat.
3 Remove the lid and cook for another 15 minutes. The onions should reduce and will be a lovely golden brown colour. If it looks as if it is drying out, make sure the temperature isn't too hot and add a little more water if necessary. Season before serving.

tip

Caramelised onions are great as an accompaniment to sausages. You can cook the caramelised onions with the sausages in the oven in a large casserole dish with the lid on. If you want to do this, cook the caramelised onions following the recipe above for 35 minutes and precook the sausages for 15 minutes on the hob. Then put the onions and the sausages together in a casserole dish with four tablespoons of water and cook with the lid on for about 25 minutes in the oven at 180°C (350°F) Gas 4. The juice from the sausages seeps into the onion and vice versa.

You don't have to use red onions. Any kind will do for this recipe. They are also delicious mixed into mashed potato. See S for Sweet Potato on page 275, for another recipe.

P is for... Pak choi

Our first P vegetable was pak choi, also known as bok choy or Chinese cabbage. When I bring a new vegetable home I don't put it away in the fridge or hide it in the vegetable basket. I sit it on the scales in the centre of the kitchen, a vegetable on a throne.

And we all look at it like a curiosity and wonder how to eat it. When the pak choi came home, we were experiencing Britain's wettest summer on record. Entertaining children in the wet is never easy. We had watched our entire DVD collection, fallen out over Monopoly and visited all the museums.

As the rain pelted down on the roof of our kitchen, Alex and Freddie wrenched the Pak Choi from its throne and started to make faces out of vegetables. What started off as a desperate attempt to escape from grinding boredom, turned into entertainment. Pak choi adds a certain beauty to the vegetable faces, which we posted on the blog. Boredom must be a universal experience because within days, people were emailing us their vegetable faces. From across the four continents of the world, hundreds of people were sitting at their kitchen tables and piecing together a mosaic of vegetables.

The pak choi had prompted a mass movement in vegetable faces which were still arriving in their droves from Alaska to Beijing. I had imagined that pak choi was one of those vegetables flown an indecent number of miles to reach my local supermarket. But I was wrong. We were eating British-grown pak choi, a crop that is growing in popularity. And I can see why. It is versatile. You can steam it, quickly boil it or stir-fry it. And it has a mild sweet taste. We combined it with some other summer greens to make a salad that everyone enjoyed.

Pak Choi and Chicken Stir-fry

As well as making great hair and noses for vegetable faces, the pak choi was delicious in a stir-fry, which we had with our friends Kitty and Margaret, and Freddie scored it 7 out of 10.

Serves 4–6
400 g (13 oz) pak choi
4 tbsp toasted sesame oil
500 g (1 lb) boneless and skinless chicken fillet,
  cut into thin strips
25 g (1 oz) freshly grated ginger
2 cloves of garlic, crushed

½ red chilli pepper, deseeded and finely chopped
1 red pepper, deseeded and sliced into thin strips
200 g (7 oz) bean sprouts
2 tbsp soy sauce
1 tbsp sherry
1–2 tbsp sesame seeds

1 Prepare the pak choi by cutting off the leaves and cutting them into wide ribbons. Cut the stalks in half or, if they are larger, into quarters.
2 Heat half the oil in a wok or large frying pan on a medium-high heat. Add the chicken strips with the grated ginger and crushed garlic. Stir-fry for 3 minutes.
3 When the chicken is cooked through and golden brown, remove with a slotted spoon to a plate.
4 Add the rest of the oil to the wok, the pak choi stalks and leaves, chilli pepper, red pepper and bean sprouts. Stir-fry for 3 minutes on a high heat.
5 Put the chicken back into the wok and add the soy sauce and sherry. Stir-fry for a minute and sprinkle the sesame seeds on top. Serve with rice or noodles.

abcthedgreatebigfveggchallengehijklmno_pqrstuvwxyz

Pak Choi with Minted Greens

This refreshing summer salad was enjoyed by all – even the presence of peas did not deter Freddie from scoring it 8 out of 10.

Serves 4–6
200 g (7 oz) pak choi
200 g (7 oz) peas (frozen or freshly podded)
100 g (3½ oz) broad beans, podded

For the dressing
4 tbsp olive oil
2 tsp caster sugar
2 tsp dried chopped mint or 2 tbsp of freshly chopped mint
1 tsp Dijon mustard
2 tsp white wine vinegar

1 Bring a pan of water to the boil. Cut about 2.5 cm (1 in.) off the bottom of the pak choi so the leaves fall part and place them in a steamer over the boiling water for 2 minutes. (Or you can throw them in a big pot of boiling water for about 3 minutes.) Don't overcook them. Drain them and place them in a serving dish.

2 Steam or boil the peas and broad beans for 3 minutes. Drain and add to the pak choi.

3 Make the dressing by combining all the ingredients in a bowl or jug. Pour over the greens so that they are well-covered and serve.

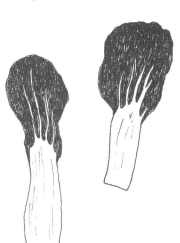

P is for... parsnip

When we arrived at P for Parsnips, I looked through old cookery books for inspiration. Some of these books put me in a particular frame of mind. I bought a 1933 edition of *Entertaining with Elizabeth Craig* in a car boot sale.

On the back page, the disembodied head of a nervous looking woman stares out. This is Elizabeth. Her kitchen is described as a model of perfection. 'The ideal kitchen of which every housewife dreams.' Her enigmatic smile has a touch of the Mona Lisa about it. As I leaf through the book, with its chapters on entertaining with or without maids and electricity, dealing with difficult guests and serving Tennis Tea, a wartime newspaper cutting falls out.

'Tonight's blackout starts at 7.36 pm and lasts until 6.22 am tomorrow.' Alongside the blackout instructions are recipes for 'cheap and energy-giving vegetables'. Parsnips, it says, can be roasted and mashed with banana essence. This is 'Mock Banana'.

I put on an apron. Elizabeth Craig always has this effect. I am entertaining with electricity, without a maid and some of my guests do have a tendency to be difficult, at least over vegetables. Freddie likes bananas and thankfully there are no shortages. We give the Mock Banana a miss and roast the parsnips conventionally, serving them with a leg of Welsh lamb for Sunday lunch. In their first outing, parsnips earned 8 out of 10.

It is said that fine words butter no parsnips. See how vegetables have woven their way into the English language. When it comes to vegetables, flattering words make no impression on Freddie, but butter: well now you are talking. Parsnips don't look very interesting. Their skin is pallid and they seem a little dowdy. Alex thought they looked like a carrot without a sun tan. So a little butter played its part in smoothing the introduction of our second taste of parsnips – a parsnip purée. Nuzzled up against a sausage, Freddie found it hard to resist and gave it 7 out of 10.

Roasted Parsnips with Honey

Accompanied by a decent serving of red meat, this first introduction to the parsnip scored highly with Freddie.

Serves 4
450 g (14 oz) parsnips
1 tbsp clear honey

1 tbsp sesame oil
1 tbsp sesame seeds

1 Preheat the oven to 200°C (400°F) Gas 6.

2 Cut each parsnip lengthways into quarters. If the core looks a little woody, cut it out. Cut each piece in half. Cook them in a pan of boiling water for 5 minutes. Drain well.

3 In a bowl, mix the honey, sesame oil and seeds with the parsnips so they are well coated. Put them in a non-stick roasting tin and roast in the oven for about 25 minutes. They should be tender and golden brown when ready.

Parsnips don't look very interesting. Their skin is pallid and they seem a little dowdy. Alex thought they looked like a carrot without a sun tan.

Parsnip Purée

This simple parsnip purée uses crème fraîche and a pinch of paprika for colour.

Serves 4 as a side dish
450 g (14 oz) parsnips, peeled and sliced
1 tbsp crème fraîche or single cream
1 tbsp milk

A knob of butter
A pinch of ground paprika
Salt and freshly ground pepper

1 Put the parsnips in a pan of boiling water and cook until tender. Drain well and put in a food processor or hand-blender. Blend to a purée with a little salt and pepper to taste.

2 Add the crème fraîche or cream, milk, butter and a little paprika. Process again and serve. It is great as an accompaniment to lamb or pork chops or sausages.

tip

Try combining different root vegetables in a purée. And if you know your child likes the taste of one vegetable you can use it to help introduce a new one. Just make sure you cook the different vegetables in separate pans as they take different times to become tender and you don't want to over- or undercook them. Then blend them together.

You can also use any of these root vegetable purées as a base for a simple soup. Just thin down the purée with a little milk and chicken or vegetable stock in a pan. Heat up and serve. You can try combinations of parsnip, celeriac, potato, sweet potato, carrot, yams, eddoes and Jerusalem artichokes.

abcthedgreatebigfveggchallengehijklmno*p*qrstuvwxyz

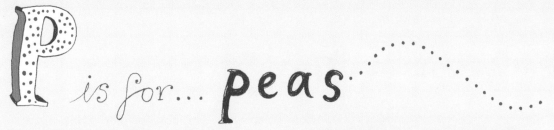

P is for... peas

As P for Peas was getting closer, Freddie had become a little nervous. Peas were Fred's nemesis. They had always been a source of anxiety. These little drops of squeaky greenness were in fact the reason we started the blog in the first place.

'Can we just do peas as quickly as possible?', Freddie pleaded.

I knew my work–life balance was out of kilter when I found myself propped up against the kitchen units at one in the morning, watching pea muffins rise. Chris had given up on me and gone to bed. But this violent hatred of peas demanded extra effort. We held a pea-tasting party: a party for pea-haters to challenge their fears. Freddie's friend Esme hates them, so she was invited. Alexandra and our neighbour Jack, love peas. The guest list was balanced. All I had to do was to create irresistible pea recipes.

The pea muffin was inspired by Garrett from Sacramento who writes a blog called Vanilla Garlic. He has a talent for creating exotic cupcakes: Tomato Soup; Butternut and Sage; Rhubarb and Ginger. A while back he had baked a sweet pea cupcake which was uncompromisingly green. I don't see why vegetables should be confined to savoury dishes. I experimented with the humble pea. The night before the party, the final version of the Petits Pois Muffin was ready.

Our guests arrived. Esme's face paled when she entered the kitchen, seeing a table full of food made with her vegetable enemy number one. I am adept at distraction. We kicked off with a pea-podding competition to see which team could pod the most peas in 2 minutes. The pea-haters, Esme and Freddie, won, which boosted their confidence.

The time to eat arrived. Surely the most important rule about party food is that you should be able to eat whatever you like in whatever order: jelly followed by hot dogs or Swiss roll with marmite sandwiches. Esme and Freddie bit into the least threatening option, which was cake. This was a good move. If I could hoodwink them, albeit in a sweet muffin, it was a start. I acted like a drug dealer, peddling in peas.

'I cannot believe these are made from peas. *No* way! Look Mum, I am actually eating peas,' said Esme. There was no going back. It is good to mix vegetable-enthusiasts with their opposites; a little of their enthusiasm rubs off. Jack and Alexandra consumed bowls of pasta with Pea Pesto. And the two pea-haters rampaged through everything, shedding their prejudices like two peas in a pod.

Petits Pois Muffins

Inspired by Garret of Sacramento's Sweet Pea Cupcake, I used petits pois to up the sweetness in these Kermit-coloured muffins.
(See www.vanillagarlic.blogspot.com)

Makes 12 large muffins
100 g (3½ oz) soft margarine or butter
2 eggs
200 ml (7 fl oz) milk
2 tbsp maple syrup
½ tsp vanilla essence

300 g (10 oz) self-raising flour
1 tsp baking powder
75 g (3 oz) caster sugar
200 g (7 oz) frozen petits pois
15 g (½ oz) butter
1 tbsp reduced-fat crème fraîche

12-hole muffin tin, lined with paper muffin cases

1 Preheat the oven to 200°C (400°F) Gas 6.
2 Gently melt the margarine or butter in a pan. Remove from the heat and set aside.
3 In a bowl, whisk the eggs. Stir in the milk, maple syrup and vanilla essence. Pour the melted margarine into the bowl and mix together with a fork.
4 Sift the flour and baking powder into a separate bowl. Add the caster sugar.
5 Cook the petits pois in boiling water for 5 minutes. These are smaller and sweeter than other peas. Drain and then purée in a food processor or hand-blender with 15 g (½ oz) of butter and the crème fraîche.
6 Add the pea mixture to the flour mixture and stir with a fork. Then add all the remaining ingredients and quickly mix until the flour is fully moistened. Don't over mix. The muffin batter will be a little lumpy.
7 Divide the batter between the muffin cases and bake in the oven for 20 minutes. The muffins will rise and be lightly golden when ready. Leave to cool in the tin for a few minutes before turning out onto a wire rack to cool completely.

abcthedgreatebigfveggchallengehijklmno**p**qrstuvwxyz

Pea and Basil Soup

Freddie gave this pea and basil soup a 9 out of 10 and it has become one of his favourite soups. The key to its success is the smoothness, so I ensure that the pea texture he dislikes is smoothed away. We serve it with hot rolls or croutons.

Serves 4–6
400 g (13 oz) fresh or frozen peas
1–2 tbsp olive oil
1 large onion, finely chopped

1 roasted garlic bulb (see page 115)
50 g (2 oz) fresh basil leaves
1.2 litres (2 pints) chicken or vegetable stock
2 tbsp crème fraîche or soured cream

1 Cook the peas in a pan of boiling water for 5 minutes. Drain.

2 Heat the olive oil in a pan and add the chopped onion with the soft contents of the roasted garlic. Fry for 5 minutes, stirring all the time until the onions are translucent and soft.

3 Put the peas, basil leaves and onions in a food processor or hand-blender and whiz until smooth. Little by little, pour in the stock until you have a lovely smooth pea soup mixture.

4 Finally, add the crème fraîche and process again until the soup is a smooth creamy consistency. Pour into a pan to warm through (do not boil) and serve.

These little drops of squeaky greenness were in fact the reason we started the blog in the first place.

Pea Pesto

Having hooked the pea-haters with cake, it was relatively easy to convert them to the joys of peas with this bright green pasta sauce.

Serve 4–6 as a pasta sauce
300 g (10 oz) dried pasta shapes
100 g (3½ oz) fresh or frozen peas
7 tbsp olive oil

1 clove of garlic, chopped
50 g (2 oz) freshly chopped basil
3 tbsp pine nuts
50 g (2 oz) finely grated Parmesan cheese

1 Cook the pasta according to the packet instructions.
2 Cook the peas in boiling water for 5 minutes and drain. Transfer to a food processor or hand-blender. Add the olive oil, garlic, basil and pine nuts and process until smooth. Stir in the finely grated Parmesan cheese.
3 Drain the pasta and coat thoroughly with the pea pesto. Serve.

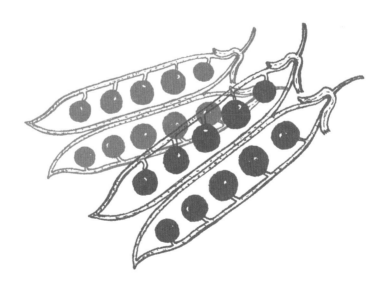

Pea and Ricotta Tarts

These little pea and ricotta tarts scored highly with half of my pea-tasters. Freddie gave them 8 out of 10. They are good for school lunchboxes and picnics.

375 g (12 oz) ready-made puff pastry
2 rashers of bacon
1 tsp oil
150 g (5 oz) fresh or frozen peas

1 clove of garlic, crushed
2 tbsp ricotta cheese
Salt and freshly ground pepper

7¹/₂ cm (3 in.) biscuit cutter
Baking tray lined with baking paper

1 Preheat the oven to 200°C (400°F) Gas 6.

2 Roll out the puff pastry until it is about 5 mm (¹/₄ in.) thick. Using a large biscuit cutter, cut out circles of pastry.

3 Using a palette knife, transfer the pastry circles onto the prepared baking tray. With a knife, lightly score an inner circle 1 cm (¹/₂ in.) from the edge on each pastry circle. This will form a ridge around each tart when baked.

4 Chop up the bacon into small pieces and fry in the oil for 5 minutes or until crisp.

5 Cook the peas in boiling water for 5 minutes. Using a food processor or hand-blender, purée the peas with the garlic and ricotta cheese.

6 Dollop one generous spoon of this mixture in the middle of each pastry circle. Add a piece of bacon on top. Bake in the centre of the oven for 15–20 minutes, or until the pastry is golden brown.

P is for... peppers

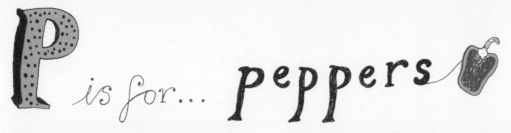

Peppers had a treacherous and slow journey climbing up our fridge. We call it the Naming and Shaming Fridge. There are three categories: 'Vegetables I hate'; 'Vegetables I am not sure about' and 'Vegetables I like'.

Freddie moves the vegetables up and down depending on how he rates a recipe. It appeals to his love for premiership football tables.

When we started the vegetable challenge, all but potato and sweetcorn sat in the 'I hate' category: a whole class of vegetable outcasts. As time passes, the fridge paints a different picture. Very few vegetables are hated. Many sit in a state of suspended hope, waiting to be loved. The golden ones look down from their exalted position, basking in the glory of being liked. Peppers started off in the 'I hate' category. Their journey upwards was not easy.

Peppers have several disadvantages. Freddie thought they were the same as ground black pepper, which he hates. He disliked the texture of their skin and thought they tasted bitter. The only thing they had going for them seemed to be their colour.

'They look like traffic lights,' he said. Alex has all the best ideas. She suggested we made traffic light burgers. We were helped by the presence of three star ingredients: beef, bread rolls and ketchup. We also favoured a little more red peppers, rather than the more bitter-tasting green. Reluctantly, Freddie moved them from 'I hate' to 'I am not sure about.' The pepper was now in purgatory. He scored his sister's Traffic Light Burgers 7 out of 10.

I went back to the supermarket for more peppers. I chose the mildest red chilli pepper to team up with the completely innocuous red Romano peppers. These are long, narrow and bright red. Under the grill, I blackened their skins, then rubbed them off under running water to reveal their sweet, succulent bright red flesh. I made Romano Pepper Houmous, with half a red chilli to add a hint of heat.

Back on the Naming and Shaming Fridge Freddie couldn't *quite* bring himself to move peppers into the 'I like' category. But he did score the houmous 9 out of 10. Prejudice is alive and well in the world of vegetables.

Traffic Light Burgers

Before we started, the one and only thing that Freddie liked about peppers was their colour.

Makes 4 large burgers or 8 smaller ones
1 red pepper
½ orange pepper
½ green pepper

450 g (14 oz) lean beef mince
1 egg, beaten
Salt and freshly ground pepper
Bread rolls, to serve

1 Cut the peppers in half and remove all the seeds. Take 2 red pepper halves and just one half each of green and yellow. Dice them very finely.

2 In a bowl, mix up the beef mince with the diced peppers by hand. Add a beaten egg and a little seasoning. Stir well with a fork.

3 Shape the mixture into four or eight evenly-sized individual burgers, depending on your preferred size. Lay them on a baking tray and chill for at least 30 minutes in the fridge.

4 Using a lightly oiled pan, carefully cook the burgers on a medium heat for 5–6 minutes. Turn over and cook the other side for a further 5–6 minutes. Serve in a roll.

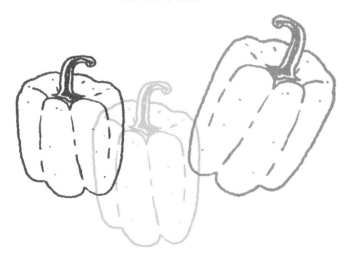

abcthedgreatebigfveggchallengehijklmno*p*qrstuvwxyz

Romano Pepper Houmous

The mild red chilli gives this houmous just a hint of heat – and raised no objections from Freddie, who gave it almost top marks, despite his reservations.

Serves 4
175g (6 oz) red Romano peppers, halved and deseeded
400 g (13 oz) tin of chickpeas, rinsed and drained
2–3 tbsp light tahini
Freshly squeezed juice of 1 lemon

Freshly squeezed juice of 1 lime
1 tbsp olive oil
½ mild red chilli pepper, deseeded and sliced (optional)
A pinch of smoked paprika

1 Place the pepper halves, skins facing up, on a flat baking tray under a medium hot grill. Allow the skins to blacken. You may need to move them around to make sure the skins blister evenly.

2 Run the cooked peppers under cold water. Wait until you can handle them and carefully rub off the blackened skins and rinse. Dry them well or the houmous will be sloppy in consistency.

3 In a food processor or hand-blender, process the chickpeas, tahini, lemon and lime juice, olive oil, peppers, red chilli pepper and a pinch of smoked paprika until smooth. Serve with flat breads or mini pitta.

tip

You can substitute ordinary red peppers for Romano peppers if you prefer.
For a different kind of houmous, try the Grilled Aubergine Houmous on page 22.
Try steaming some sweet potato, puréeing it and adding it to houmous as another alternative.

P is for... plantain

– looks like a banana but isn't

As the months passed by, the Great Big Vegetable Challenge made us all realise what we miss living in a city. We had pots of tomatoes and chilli peppers growing on our patio, mushroom kits sprouting under the kitchen sink and we were growing our own herbs.

But it isn't quite as good as having a vegetable garden. And it seems easier to get tickets to the FA cup final than reach the top of the local allotment waiting list. But when it comes to finding out about unusual vegetables like plantain, living in a city has its advantages. We took the bus to Notting Hill to enjoy the annual carnival and to have lunch.

In the streets off the main carnival route, hundreds of food stalls sell different Caribbean specialities. People turn their basements into makeshift kitchens. Freddie and Alex sucked on chunks of sticky sugar cane, drank jelly coconut juice, tasted goat curry and yam chips. It was our first introduction to plantain, which look like large green bananas. One stall holder explained that plantain can be eaten at different stages of ripeness. If kept at room temperature, the plantain goes through chameleon like changes: green to yellow, to brown and then black as it ripens, the flesh becoming sweeter. She handed Freddie a hot deep fried plantain, wrapped in waxed paper. He took a bite.

'This isn't as good as banana,' he said. His initial disappointment was down to the fact that plantain might look like a banana but it doesn't really taste quite like one. There isn't the same sweetness and the flesh is much firmer, not soft like a banana. He thought it was more like a sweet potato. He took another bite of the deep yellow plantain and started to like it, scoring it 7 out of 10. The cook who was frying the plantain came over and told us to try it with chicken.

I bought some plantains on the way home. Plantain is a staple African food and is also eaten throughout Tropical countries. It's a close relative of the banana. But it is more fibrous than a banana and has less sugar. As it ripens the starch turns to sucrose.

I spoke to my friend Grace to learn more. I have watched her fry huge pans of plantain at a parish lunch. You can fry, boil, mash and grill plantains in the same way as potatoes. She advised me to wait until the green plantain had ripened. As they ripen, they become more tender and creamier and easier to peel. Our first recipe was Plantain and Chicken Kebabs, which Freddie loved.

A few days later and our remaining bunch of plantain had ripened to become completely black. We peeled and sliced them into strips, then baked them in a delicious mixture of lime juice, brown sugar, ginger and cinnamon. We ate these with a dollop of crème fraîche and they were awarded 8 out of 10.

The following recipes are mostly specifically for plantain. But for the Plantain and Chicken Kebabs you could substitute the plantain with tinned artichoke hearts, halved, or slices of courgette.

The comment box on the blog filled up with comments from plantain officianados from around the world, who told us about the pleasures of tostone, or fried plantain chips. These might not be the healthiest way to cook plantain but they are delicious. You can make tostone by cutting the skinned green plantain into 3 cm (1¼ in.) disc shapes, frying them,

flattening them and then refrying them. These can be served as a snack. But Freddie's favourite, scoring the maximum 10 out of 10, was given for Tostone Dippers which we ate with Guacamole Dip.

A visitor to the blog, Carolina, told us about a plantain sandwich known as a jibarito, made by the Puerto Rican community in Chicago. Jibaritos (pronounced hee-bar-ree-toh) are like sandwiches made with slices of flattened plantain instead of bread. Inspired by this, we filled our jibaritos with strips of beef steak, onions, red peppers and lettuce. Freddie's score was 9 out of 10.

tip

Plantain will take a few days to ripen. Unripe ones are green, semi-ripe are a mottled yellow and black and the ripe ones are black.

If you want to speed up the ripening process of the plantains, try putting them in a brown paper bag with a very ripe banana. The ripening banana gives off the gas known as ethylene and this should accelerate the ripening of other fruit nearby. Incidentally this technique works well with ripening any fruit.

Plantain and Chicken Kebabs

The Notting Hill Carnvial provided the perfect opportunity for Freddie to get a taste for plantain and he enjoyed this recipe so much he awarded it 9 out of 10.

Serves 4–5
2 nearly-ripe plantain, skinned and chopped
  into 2.5-cm (1-in.) cubes
Freshly squeezed juice of 1 lime
4 boneless and skinless chicken fillets, cut into
  2.5-cm (1-in.) cubes

2 tbsp olive oil
1 tbsp jerk seasoning
1 clove of garlic, crushed
Salt and freshly ground pepper

6–8 wooden kebab skewers, soaked in water for 30 minutes

1 Put the plantain in a bowl and add the lime juice, then the chicken, olive oil, jerk seasoning and crushed garlic. Stir well. Cover with cling film and leave to marinate for an hour. At the same time soak the wooden skewers in water.

2 Thread the chicken and plantain onto the skewers and place on a baking tray. Pour over any remaining marinade. Cook under a hot grill, turning regularly for about 20 minutes. Make sure the chicken is thoroughly cooked before serving. You can also cook these on a barbecue.

tip
How to fry plantain

1 Peel four ripe plantains and slice 1.5 cm (3/4 in.) thick on a slant. Heat some vegetable oil in a frying pan. The oil should just cover the plantain.

2 When the oil is hot, add the plantain in a single layer. Fry them on both sides until they are deep yellow in colour and crispy. This should take about a minute.

3 Remove with a slotted spoon and lay on some kitchen paper to absorb excess oil. Season with some salt and pepper or if you prefer, with some ground cinnamon instead.

Baked Plantain with Lime and Ginger

This is not as sweet as baked bananas but works well either as a very simple dessert or a side dish to poultry or pork.

Serves 4
4 ripe (black) plantain
Freshly squeezed juice of 2 limes
1 tsp grated fresh ginger or 1/2 tsp ground ginger

3–4 tbsp brown sugar
1/2 tsp ground cinnamon
A knob of butter
Crème fraîche, to serve

1 Preheat the oven to 180°C (350°F) Gas 4.
2 Peel the plantain and slice in half lengthways, then cut each half into three. Lay in a shallow baking dish. Add the lime juice, ginger, brown sugar and cinnamon. Stir until evenly-covered. Add a knob of butter.
3 Cover with foil and bake for about 25 minutes. Serve with some crème fraîche.

Guacamole Dip

Green Pepper Tabasco sauce is milder than the normal Tabasco and adds just a little bite, without being too much for children.

Serves 4
1/2 onion, finely chopped
1 ripe tomato, peeled and chopped
Freshly squeezed juice of 2 limes

1/4 red pepper, diced
A splash of Green Pepper Tabasco sauce
2 large ripe avocados, destoned
2 tbsp soured cream

1 In a food processor, gently blend the onion, tomato, lime juice, red pepper and Green Pepper Tabasco sauce.
2 Scoop out the flesh of the avocados and pulse-blend with a hand-blender or in a food processor with the tomato mixture. Stir in the soured cream. Serve with Tostone Dippers (see page 210).

abcthedgreatebigfveggchallengehijklmnopqrstuvwxyz

Jibaritos

You can experiment with different cooked-meat fillings such as chicken or pork, together with your favourite vegetables.

Serves 4
4 green plantains
1 tbsp olive oil
½ onion, very finely chopped
4 cloves of garlic, crushed
½ red pepper, sliced into thin strips

1 tsp smoked paprika
1 tsp dried oregano
400 g (13 oz) beef steak, cut into thin strips
1 tbsp freshly squeezed lime juice
2 tbsp soured cream
½ round lettuce

1 Follow the instructions on page 210 to make Tostone Dippers. Keep them warm in a low oven.
2 Heat the olive oil in a shallow frying pan. Sauté the onion, garlic, red pepper, smoked paprika and oregano until the onion has softened.
3 Add the beef steak strips to the pan and sauté with the lime juice until the beef is cooked.
4 Take one tostone slice, spread with half a tablespoon of soured cream, scatter over a quarter of the beef, pepper and onion mixture, a lettuce leaf and top with another tostone slice. Repeat to make three more jibaritos. Serve immediately.

Plantain might look like a banana but it doesn't really taste quite like one.

Freddie's Favourite 10/10

Tostone Dippers

If you like, you can use these dippers to make a plantain sandwich known as a jibarito (see page 209).

Serves 4
Vegetable oil
4 large green plantains

1 Choose the greenest plantains you can find. Peel them with a knife and slice them in half lengthways.

2 In a large, deep frying pan heat up enough oil to cover the plantain slices. Add the plantain when the oil is hot and fry for 3–4 minutes, until they are a yellowy golden brown.

3 Take the frying pan off the heat and remove the plantain carefully. Use kitchen paper to absorb excess oil from the fried slices.

4 Find two large heavy chopping boards. If they are wooden, cover with cling film to protect them. Lay the plantain slices on one board, place the other board on top and press to flatten. Don't be too rough or the plantain will break.

5 When they are flattened, reheat the oil and add the plantain to refry for a minute. Remove the plantain slices, wipe with kitchen paper to absorb excess oil and keep in a warm place and use as dippers with Guacamole Dip (see page 208).

abcthedgreatebigfveggchallengehijklmno**p**qrstuvwxyz

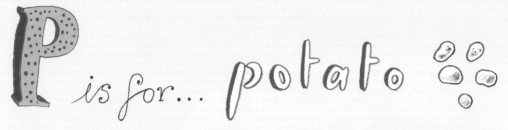

P is for... potato

Every summer we drive for five hours down to the south coast of Cornwall to stay in the same slate-hung cottage. Our first Cornish meal is always the same. After a long drive down a wooded lane to the ancient town of Lostwithiel, we pass over a 13th-century bridge and park near the bakery.

We buy four large Cornish pasties and sit on the river bank to eat them. Like all traditional dishes, the ingredients of an authentic Cornish pasty are often argued about but potato is central.

'Do you think that we could learn to make our own this holiday?' said Alex.

'Let's do it for P for Potatoes.' We finished our pasties and went back into Lostwithiel bakery to ask if we could watch them being made. I used to be too embarrassed to ask people how they cooked something. But where vegetables are involved, I had become shameless. I had chatted, quizzed, gossiped and sometimes interrogated people during our journey through the alphabet. More than 45 vegetables into the challenge, I had developed a thick skin.

'You really ought to come back and learn from Ruth,' said Christine Green, who owns the bakery with her husband, Barry.

Four days later we turned up for our date with one of Cornwall's most experienced pasty makers, Ruth Dungey. Ruth greeted us with floury hands and explained that she had been making pasties for over 55 years. She had learnt from her mother and grandmother, baking her first pasty when she was five years old. She took Freddie and Alex under her wing and showed them how to create their favourite Cornish meal.

In the middle of a circle of pastry they placed flakes of uncooked potato, swede, very finely chopped onion and a handful of raw beef skirt, diced into small cubes. They copied her as she brushed round the edges of the circle and folded the circle in half, crimping the seam of the pastry together to seal it. Seeing Ruth crimping the pastry reminded me of expert knitters. Lightning fast, the forefinger and thumb of each hand worked in formation, pressing and folding over the pastry to create what looked like a plaited edge. A smooth, co-ordinated movement in her hands, became a fumbling, jagged mess in mine. Like any craftswoman, she made something difficult look very simple. She patiently helped us as we made our pasties. Freddie and Alex brushed their pasties with beaten egg and watched as Barry slid the tray into the oven.

Traditionally, Cornish housewives used to mark the pastry with their husband's initials so that at lunchtime there was no confusion. An hour later, when our creations were cooked, they were easily identifiable next to Ruth's perfectly crimped pasties. We ate them on the banks of the River Fowey. Pasties are best eaten outdoors, preferably with a beautiful view of the British countryside to look at.

'I am going to give these pasties eleven out of ten,' said Freddie.

I went to an all-girls' secondary school in the days when Home Economics was compulsory. For three years, I learnt to cook, sew and keep my fingernails clean. I was a chaotic cook, dangerous with a needle and my nails were always dirty. My main problem in cookery was that I was out of synch with the schedule. I brought the ingredients for Christmas cake in the week we were making Quiche Lorraine; Bolognese sauce when it was Chelsea Buns. I thank my Home Economics teacher, Mrs Thomas, for my encyclopaedic knowledge of cooking terminology. Week after week, my punishment for bringing the wrong ingredients was to copy out the list of definitions. Béchamel, blanch, bouillon,

chaud-froid, croutons: I can recall the glossary like the shipping forecast. Mrs Thomas's kind eyes would look at me with pity as I sat in her office, scrawling out lists as everyone else cooked. Things improved after half-term when I managed to resynchronise. We were taken back to basics and I learnt how to cook boil, roast, bake and, of course, mash potatoes.

We experimented with combining other vegetables with mashed potato. The Great Big Mash Up turned our kitchen into a laboratory. We sautéed beetroot with rosemary, boiled carrots, parsnips, swedes, chopped spinach and chives, roasted garlic and made pesto sauce. This was bangers and mash with a difference. Freddie's favourite combination was the Beetroot and Potato Mash, which was a beautiful pink colour. Alex loved the carrot combination.

tip

Ruth explained that as all the ingredients cook inside the pasty, it is important that they are finely flaked so that they cook better and evenly.

If you are making pasties as a starter or for smaller children you can make eight small pasties instead, using a saucer as a template.

Cornish Pasties, inspired by Ruth

We were lucky enough to enjoy a masterclass first-hand in the home of the pastie, but these can be recreated anywhere.

Makes 4 pasties
500 g (1 lb) ready-made shortcrust pastry

For the filling
2–3 large potatoes
150 g (5 oz) swede

1 onion, finely chopped
300 g (10 oz) beef skirt, diced into small cubes
A knob of butter for each pasty
Beaten egg, to glaze
Salt and freshly ground pepper

1 Preheat the oven to 200°C (400°F) Gas 6.

2 Peel the potatoes and the swede. Using a potato peeler or the coarse side of a grater, cut the potato and swede into small potato flakes.

3 Roll out the pastry so that it is about 5 mm (¹/₄ in.) thick. Cut round a plate to make four circles, approximately 22–24 cm (8¹/₂–9¹/₂ in.) in diameter.

4 Divide up the potato, swede, onion and beef into four equal parts. In the centre of each pastry circle, spoon the potato, then the swede and onion. Then add the beef skirt on top.

5 Season with salt and ground pepper and Ruth recommends placing a knob of butter on top. Brush round the edge of the circle with warm water and bring together the two sides of the pastry circle to make a parcel with the filling in the centre. Crimp the edges of the pastry together to seal it using your thumb and forefinger. With a knife, slash a small slit in the side of the pasty to let the steam out. Brush with beaten egg to glaze.

6 Place on a baking tray in the preheated oven for 45 minutes until golden brown.

Great Big Mash Up

Plain mashed potato can be transformed by any number of ingredients and is the perfect understated partner for allowing other vegetables to take the limelight.

Serves 4
1 kg (2 lb) floury potatoes, such as King Edwards, Maris Piper, Desiree

150 ml (¼ pint) full fat milk
A knob of butter
Salt and freshly ground pepper

1 Peel the potatoes and cut into similar-sized pieces so that they cook at the same rate. Add the potatoes to a large pan of salted water. Bring to the boil and then simmer until the potatoes are soft but not mushy. Drain well. Put the lid back on and leave for 4 minutes.

2 Mash the potatoes, adding the milk, butter and seasoning.

Beetroot, Rosemary and Potato Mash

Sauté 3–4 cooked, diced beetroot with the leaves from a sprig of rosemary in a little olive oil for a few minutes. Purée in a blender. Add the beetroot purée to the mashed potato.

Roasted Garlic Mash

Follow the recipe for mashed potato. See page 115 for how to roast a whole garlic head. Squeeze the soft contents of the roasted garlic into the mashed potato, mixing in with a fork.

abcthedgreatebigfveggchallengehijklmnopqrstuvwxyz

Carrot and Cumin Mash

Take 3–4 large carrots, scrub them and slice them. Cook in boiling water until soft. Drain and mash up with the potato, adding half a teaspoon of ground cumin. Any root vegetable will work well combined with potato. Try celeriac, sweet potato, parsnip or swede. Just remember to boil the different vegetables in separate pans as they cook at different rates.

Chive Mash

Stir in three tablespoons of chopped fresh chives into the mashed potato. Or try fresh basil leaves instead. If you like the flavour of basil, add two teaspoons of basil pesto.

Kale and Onion Mash

Take 115 g (3½ oz) of shredded kale leaves and cook in boiling water for 3 minutes. Drain well. Peel and thinly slice an onion and gently sauté in a little olive oil until it is translucent. Add the kale and onion to the mashed potato. Or if you prefer, try this with Savoy cabbage leaves instead for a simple colcannon.

tip

As with the League of Lettuce, you can have some fun trying out the different tastes of potatoes. There are hundreds of varieties of potatoes with distinct tastes and textures. They are perfect for a taste-testing session, encouraging children to learn to explore food. Remember to avoid buying potatoes that are turning green or starting to sprout.

P is for... PUMPKIN

I brought a pumpkin home and everyone decided it looked like a friendly vegetable: its warm colour, comforting plump shape, even the name gave it a touch of the fairy tale. To arrive at the name pumpkin, this poor vegetable has been the subject of a thousand year game of Chinese whispers.

When the ancient Greeks really liked someone they would call them 'my little ripe melon' or 'Pepon', which passed to the Romans and then mutated into 'pompon' in France, who whispered it to their English neighbours. They added a little English vowel-flourish with 'pumpion'. The whispering carried pumpion across the Atlantic where it landed in Colonial America with a bounce, becoming pumpkin. Well, more or less. Now it has become the Mr Happy of vegetables. You can see why the Fairy Godmother chose to turn a pumpkin into Cinderella's coach. The pumpkin is obliging.

The feelgood factor continued when I roasted our pumpkin to make some soup. Roast Pumpkin Soup with a dash of maple syrup earned a top scoring, 10 out of 10, propelling the pumpkin up the fridge league table to 'Vegetables I like.'

'To dream of pumpkins is a very bad omen.'
Richard Folkard, *Plant Lore* **(1884)**

I was beginning to dream of pumpkins. As with the daikon, the giant radish, I felt that there was a never-ending supply of pumpkin flesh to consume. Even with a modest-sized pumpkin you need several recipes up your sleeve. At school, Freddie showed me the pumpkins they were growing in their edible garden. We planned a pumpkin feast, a night where every recipe would feature this orange beast. My stepson Leo joined us for supper. I warned him that the meal might be a little one-note. We roasted pumpkin seeds, made pumpkin and smoky bacon risotto, with sweet pumpkin pie for dessert.

Freddie's Favourite 10/10

Roasted Pumpkin Soup

This is the first new vegetable we have tried where there was unbridled enthusiasm from Freddie.

Serves 4–6
1 medium pumpkin, approximately 1.5 kg (3^1/$_2$ lb)
2–3 tbsp olive oil
Sprigs of rosemary
2 onions, chopped finely
1 clove of garlic, crushed

2 medium potatoes, peeled and finely diced
750 ml (1^1/$_4$ pints) vegetable or chicken stock
1–2 tbsp maple syrup
2 tbsp crème fraîche
Salt and freshly ground pepper

1 Preheat the oven to 200°C (400°F) Gas 6.
2 Cut the pumpkin in half, scrape away the seeds and white pith and rub olive oil over the flesh inside. Season and then place the two halves of the pumpkin with the cut side facing down, on to a baking tray.
3 Put a sprig of rosemary under each half and bake in the preheated oven for 45 minutes, depending on the size of the pumpkin, or until the flesh is soft.
4 Scoop out the flesh into a bowl. In a large pan, sauté the chopped onions, crushed garlic and potatoes in a tablespoon of olive oil for about 5 minutes.
5 Add the pumpkin flesh and stock. Bring to the boil and then turn down the heat to low and simmer gently for 15–20 minutes.
6 Remove from the heat and allow to cool a little, then pour into a food processor and blend until smooth, adding the maple syrup and crème fraîche.

tip
How to roast pumpkin seeds

Scoop out the stringy pulp from the centre of the pumpkin and pick out the seeds. Don't wash them, just pick off the strings and lay the seeds on a baking tray, lined with parchment paper. Lightly spray with cooking oil and add a little salt to taste. You can add a little seasoning if you like – try half a teaspoon of mild chilli powder, smoked paprika or cinnamon. Bake in a preheated oven at 180°C (350°F) Gas 4, for about 20–25 minutes, until browned and crisp.

Pumpkin and Smoky Bacon Risotto

Risotto is a warming, comforting dish and is an ideal vehicle for the equally mild-mannered and friendly pumpkin.

Serves 4
400 g (13 oz) pumpkin flesh, skinned and diced into small cubes
2–3 tbsp olive oil
12 thin rashers of smoky bacon, chopped

2 onions, chopped
325 g (11 oz) arborio risotto rice
1 litre (1¾ pints) chicken or vegetable stock
Freshly grated Parmesan cheese
Salt and freshly ground pepper

1 Steam the diced pumpkin for about 10–15 minutes, until softened.
2 In a large pan, heat the olive oil on a gentle heat and sauté the onion and bacon for about 3 minutes. Add the rice and stir until the grains are transparent.
3 Stir in the pumpkin. Then add the stock, one ladle at a time. As it is absorbed, gently stir and add more stock. This should take about 20 minutes. The rice should be creamy in texture but not sticky.
4 Stir in some freshly grated Parmesan, season and serve.

You can see why the Fairy Godmother chose to turn a pumpkin into Cinderella's coach. The pumpkin is obliging.

Freddie's Favourite 10/10

Sweet Pumpkin Pie

It's not often that you can employ a vegetable in a dessert, but pumpkin pie is a classic exception. Freddie is always delighted to see a vegetable used in a dessert and his first taste of pumpkin pie was a great success. He was so proud of it, we took some round to share with his friend Molly, who comes from America, where pumpkin pie is a traditional dish.

Serves 4–6
2 eggs
200 ml (7 fl oz) evaporated milk
3 tbsp golden syrup
½ tsp ground ginger
½ tsp ground allspice
½ tsp ground cinnamon
400 g (13 oz) cooked pumpkin purée (see tip below)
Ready-made sweet shortcrust pastry case (about 23 cm/9 in. in diameter, 3–4 cm/½ in. deep)

1 Preheat the oven to 180°C (350°F) Gas 4.
2 In a bowl, whisk the eggs with the evaporated milk. Whisk in the golden syrup and spices. Stir in the pumpkin purée so that it is well combined.
3 Pour the pumpkin mixture into the ready-made pastry case and bake for about 40 minutes until the filling is set. Serve warm or cold with a dollop of crème fraîche or vanilla ice cream.

tip
How to make pumpkin purée
Cut the pumpkin in half, scoop out the seeds and stringy pulp and drizzle a little olive oil on the flesh of each half. Put flesh-side down on a baking tray in a preheated oven at 180°C (350°F) Gas 4, for about 40–45 minutes until the orange flesh is soft. Remove from oven, scoop out the flesh and purée in a food processor.

Q is for Quick Veg.

I took the Number 10 bus home. At rush hour this is a tedious journey and people pass the time reading newspapers, plugged into their iPods and making phone calls. It is hard not to listen in. At 6.45 pm, when all I want is to be back home, tuning into other people's noisy calls passes for entertainment.

'Now look here, listen to me. Don't say that. I had to stay late, I didn't have any choice. I think you are being a little unfair,' blurts out a man in a suit. Other similarly harassed men look on sympathetically.

Next to me a woman opens her bag and takes out a Tupperware box. She prises the lid open. Steam bursts out and the bus fills with the smell of Thai green chicken curry. She places it on her lap, takes out a plastic knife and fork and eats. She looks as if she could be at home on the sofa. Then her phone rings. She wedges the Tupperware box between her legs and answers.

'Hello?' she says, forking khaki-green chicken into her mouth. 'No, don't worry about me. I don't need anything to eat. I'm not really hungry. I'll see you later after I've been to the gym.'

I turn away from the stench. Next to me is a woman in her early forties, wearing a city suit. She is barking instructions into her phone.

'Hello Viola, it's me. I'm on the bus coming home. Would you heat some fishfingers up for Oscar and do his reading with him. Oh, and defrost the butternut squash purée for the baby. I want them fed and watered and in bed by the time I get home.'

I picture Viola, who I imagine is the nanny, feeding and watering these two children as if it were a formula one wheel change. And I think of all the mealtimes I have rushed with my own children. That evening I joined the Slow Food movement. This is a worldwide group which aims in its manifesto to banish the effects of fast food. And this doesn't mean labouring over a stove for hours on end making complicated meals. There is nothing wrong with making good food fast but rushing the whole experience of preparing food and eating means missing out on some of the greatest pleasures in life.

Dr Edouard de Pomiane wrote a book, *La Cuisine en Dix Minutes, ou l'Adaptation au Rythme Moderne*. This was translated into English as *Cooking in Ten Minutes, or Adapting to the Rhythm of Modern Life*. This was back in the 1930s and in France. Who said that convenience food is a modern phenomenon? The difference is that Docteur de Pomiane was teaching people how to cook real French food, quickly. In the time that it takes to remove the packaging, pierce a cellophane lid, microwave, stir and serve a ready-made meal to the family, we could be munching on Pig's Ears in Egg and Breadcrumbs or rustling up Hare à la Crème.

Here is our modest attempt at slow food in a fast world; some of the quicker vegetable recipes that we have enjoyed:

Asparagus dipped in egg (page 16)
Broccoli Pesto (page 35)
Chard and Basil Fritters (page 65)
Bruschetta with Courgettes (page 79)
Mangetout Noodle Stir-fry (page 161)
Deep-fried Onion Rings (page 187)
Pea Pesto (page 199)
Samphire with Poached Egg (page 253)
Spinach and Feta Toasties (page 262)
Spaghetti with Spinach and Bacon (page 263)
Pan Con Tomate (280)
Watercress Quesadillas (page 297)
Yam Rosti with Poached Eggs (page 305)

tip

If you want to learn how to counteract fast food and fast life, you can always join the slow food movement.
www.slowfood.com
www.slowfood.org.uk

R is for... RADICCHIO

Radicchio was our first R vegetable. Freddie suggested that it must be the radish's Italian cousin. In fact they aren't related. Radicchio is a red-leaved chicory. There are different types, named after the regions of Italy from where they originate. I found them in a grocer's shop.

There were three red-headed divas on offer: the Chiogga, the Treviso and the Castelfranco. We chose the Chiogga, which was round and the leaves are compact.

'It tastes quite bitter,' warned the grocer. 'Try grilling it with some olive oil.'

'Use it as an "accent",' barked a rather grand lady who was buying fancy mushrooms.

I didn't want to reveal my ignorance. 'Oh yes, of course, an *accent* vegetable,' I muttered.

When it comes to vegetables, what exactly is an 'accent'? There are some vegetables that feel too grand for our family mealtimes and this had to be one of them. The Chiogga radicchio came home with us in a brown paper bag, no doubt complaining bitterly that it had to travel on the bus. I figured that the posh lady's use of the word 'accent' was more akin to interior decoration. The radicchio needed to be given a decorative role. I quartered it once and then again, coated it with olive oil, balsamic vinegar, a little salt and grilled it. The bright red pigment rapidly ages in the heat and turns a rather distinguished mottled brown. Radicchio isn't in the same bitterness league as the karela, or bitter gourd (see page 144), but it is still challenging. The grilled Chiogga was arranged on oven-warmed foccacia bread with a slice of ripe Brie. The grand lady would have been proud of me. I warned Freddie and Alex about the bitterness. Bolstered by the Brie, it scored 7 out of 10.

When I went back to the grocers to buy more radicchio, the grand lady wasn't there. This time we picked out the Treviso and decided to forget any thoughts of 'accents'. Freddie had enjoyed chicory gratin so we adapted the recipe to suit its red-headed cousin. Braised in chicken stock and then enveloped in a cheese sauce, the radicchio was tamed. The bitterness didn't seem so obvious.

Freddie thought it was delicious, which might have been more to do with the fact that he was about to watch a crucial football match on the television. On the other hand, his plate was empty and he gave this radicchio recipe 9 out of 10.

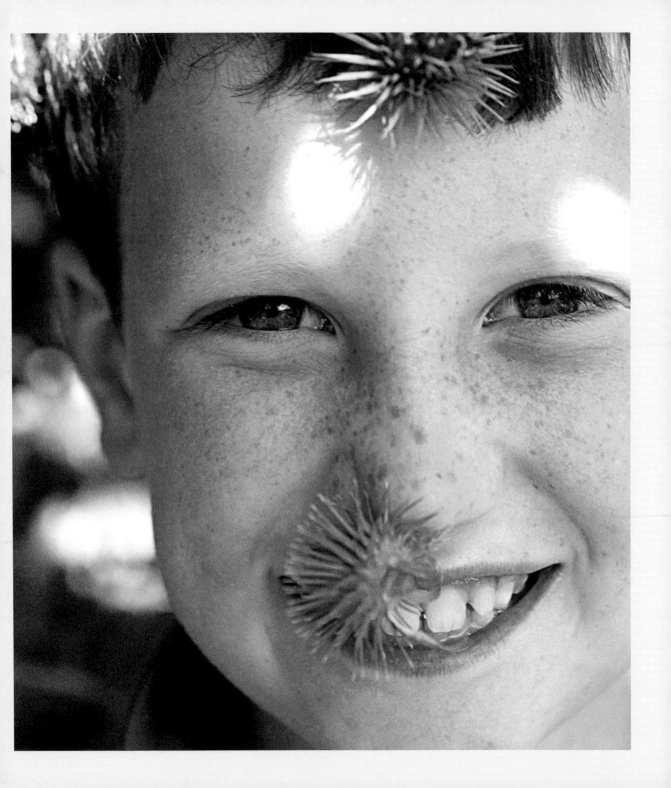

Grilled Radicchio and Brie on Foccacia Bread

We teamed this rather grand vegetable with a suitably posh cheese to make an upmarket sandwich with an 'accent'.

Serves 4
1 head of radicchio
2 tbsp olive oil
2 tbsp balsamic vinegar

Foccacia bread rolls
115 g (3½ oz) Brie
Sea salt

1 Trim the stem of the radicchio and cut the head into eight pieces. Toss the radicchio in the olive oil and balsamic vinegar and sprinkle on a little sea salt.

2 Lay the radicchio pieces flat on a baking tray and place under a medium grill for about 15 minutes. Turn them halfway through, adding a little drizzle of olive oil if needed. Make sure the leaves don't burn.

3 Warm the foccacia bread rolls in the oven. Cut in half and add a slice of Brie to each, then a few radicchio leaves, followed by another slice of Brie. The heat of the bread and radicchio will make the Brie melt a little.

When it comes to vegetables, what exactly is an 'accent'? There are some vegetables that feel too grand for our family mealtimes and this had to be one of them.

Radicchio Gratin

This recipe brings the noble radicchio down to earth and in so doing, tames its bitterness with a good degree of success.

Serves 4
2 heads of radicchio
300 ml (½ pint) vegetable or chicken stock
40 g (1½ oz) butter
1½ tbsp plain flour

175 ml (6 fl oz) milk
115 g (3½ oz) mature Cheddar cheese, grated
50 g (2 oz) coarse breadcrumbs
Salt and freshly ground pepper

1 Preheat the oven to 180°C (350°F) Gas 4.

2 Trim the stems and quarter the radicchio. Pour the stock into a large frying pan and bring to the boil. Reduce the heat. Add the radicchio and simmer for 15 minutes with the lid on. Drain the stock into a measuring jug. Remove the radicchio and lay them out in a deep baking tray.

3 Melt the butter in another pan on a low heat and stir in the flour so it forms a paste. Add the milk, 75 ml (3 fl oz) of the reserved stock and bring it to the boil, whisking all the time.

4 Add the grated cheese, whisk the sauce and season with salt and pepper. Pour over the radicchio and sprinkle the breadcrumbs on top.

5 Cover with foil and bake in the preheated oven for 25 minutes. For the last 10 minutes of cooking time, remove the foil so that the breadcrumbs crisp up.

R is for... Radish

'We are going to try radishes tomorrow,'
I announced.

'But I think I'm a Supertaster,'
said Freddie as he sat in front of the
television, watching a BBC documentary
about fussy-eaters. I had in mind a caped
crusader saving the world by taking
huge bites out of mounds of food.

'I may have an extra powerful tongue for
tasting,' he elaborated, 'and that's why
supertasters don't like things like vegetables.'

I looked up at the television to hear more.
Apparently, supertasters are not caped but
they do have an unusually high number of
taste buds, making them taste food more
keenly. Freddie was convinced of his
supertaster status. I wasn't so sure.

Scientists at Yale University of Medicine
have found that 25 per cent of people are
supertasters. On the internet there is even
a simplified version of their taster test. So
we tried it out. We punched a 5 mm (¼ in.)
hole in four small squares of paper. Out came
the blue food colouring which we swabbed

on to the tips of our tongues. The tiny papillae
that house the taste buds don't absorb the
blue dye, so they show up under a magnifying
glass as tiny pink circles. You place the paper
with the punched out hole onto the tip of
the tongue and count papillae through a
magnifying glass. Over 35 within the circle
and you could be a supertaster.

We stood in a line with our blue-swabbed
tongues hanging out in expectation. Our
kitchen has a glass roof. I looked up to see
a neighbour looking down. I grinned back in
embarrassment. After intensive examination
with a magnifying glass, we discovered that
in the taste stakes we were all profoundly
average. No excuses for Freddie. No avoiding
the radishes.

The Roman poet Horace wrote a long
list of foods that would wake up a weary
stomach. Radishes are on his list. And there
is nothing more weary than the stomach
of a fussy-eater. I bought a bunch of French
breakfast radishes in the supermarket. These
are slightly elongated with bright pink skin
that fades to become white at the tips. As

far as I know the French do not eat radishes for breakfast but they do serve them thinly sliced on crusty bread with a little sea salt on the side to sprinkle on top, as an hors d'oeuvre, 'radis au beurre.' These French breakfast radishes tasted milder than the smaller English version but they do still have quite a kick. Alex loved them. Freddie found them a little too hot but the bread and butter helped to earn this dish a modest 6 out of 10. On the Naming and Shaming Fridge, the radishes remained in the 'I hate' category.

'Can't you DO something with the radishes? You didn't exactly change them to make them taste any better,' said Freddie.

He was right. Radishes suffer from a rather limited public image: always the bridesmaid and never the bride. They are treated as a glorified garnish. On 23 December each year in Oaxaca in Mexico, they hold a Radish Night where people compete to create the most elaborate radish sculptures. Forget the tame radish roses that decorate salads. If you are a Mexican radish, La Noche de Rábanos is bigger than the Oscars. In the months leading up to the big night, radishes are lovingly cultivated and fertilised to grow to huge proportions. They are then carved into animals, dancers, entire scenes from the Nativity. There is nothing the good people of Oaxaca can't make with a radish.

I toyed with the idea of carving a face in a radish and then came to my senses. For our very own 'Noche de Rábanos', I roasted the radishes. I bought bunches of beautiful multicoloured Summer Blush radishes, coated them in seasoned olive oil and put them in the oven. I served them to Freddie and Alex with some roast chicken.

'What sort of potatoes are these?' asked Freddie. Once roasted, the radishes become quite tender and they lose some of their fiery taste. I told Freddie he was eating radishes. He stood up, walked over to the fridge and with a flourish, pushed 'radish' up from 'I hate' to 'I am not sure about this.' It was a small gesture but no doubt a moment of pride for the radish. His score for roasted radishes was 8 out of 10.

Radis au Beurre

Served in France as an hors d'oeuvre, this simple treatment doesn't disguise the fiery taste, but the butter does help to soothe the senses.

Serves 4
1 crusty French baguette
Unsalted French butter

1 bunch of French breakfast radishes
Sea salt, to sprinkle

1 Slice the crusty bread at an angle to make longer slices. Wash the radishes and remove the green leaves at the stalk. Thinly slice them.
2 Butter the bread and cover with the radish slices. Put some sea salt on the side to serve. (If you prefer salted butter, you won't need the added salt.)

As far as I know the French do not eat radishes for breakfast but they do serve them thinly sliced on crusty bread with a little sea salt on the side They taste milder than the English version, but do still have quite a kick.

Roasted Radishes

Rather than resorting to carving faces or animals from the radishes, I roasted them to bring out their gentler side.

Serves 4 as a side dish
750 g (1½ lb) radishes, halved
6 cloves of garlic, peeled
2–3 tbsp sesame oil

½ tsp mild chilli powder
½ tsp smoked paprika
A pinch of sea salt

1 Preheat the oven to 190°C (375°F) Gas 5.
2 Place the radish halves in a deep baking tray. Add the whole cloves of garlic, then cover in the sesame oil, mild chilli powder and smoked paprika. Add a pinch of salt. Stir well to make sure they are coated in the oil and seasonings.
3 Roast in the oven for 30 minutes. Halfway through, stir them round to make sure they are evenly cooked. Serve hot.

tip
If you like, you can substitute the radishes in this recipe for baby white turnips and roast them in the same way. Both are delicious.

R is for... Rhubarb

There are some vegetables that sit on the fence: rhubarb is one of them. We treat rhubarb as if it was a fruit but as we eat the stems of the plant, it is in fact a vegetable. It has a rich history in Britain. For some reason the Bermuda triangle is far more famous than England's rhubarb triangle.

Ships don't disappear but something far stranger happens. In a triangle of farmland bordered by Leeds, Wakefield and Bradford, rhubarb growers harvest their prize produce in sheds lit by candlelight. Cosseted in the dark warmth, the rhubarb can focus its efforts on producing long sweet stalks rather than wasting its efforts on leaves to absorb sunlight. This is 'forced' rhubarb and West Yorkshire used to produce 90 per cent of the world's winter rhubarb. The train transporting tons of rhubarb down to London was known as the Rhubarb Express.

When we reached R for Rhubarb we were in the middle of the summer rhubarb season, when it grows happily outdoors. We travelled down to Wiltshire to stay with friends and enjoy their rhubarb.

Our friends live in a Georgian house where the cliché 'time stands still' is deserved. The original servants' bells hang in rows in the kitchen. A door leads into the old scullery with vast ceramic sinks. To the left is the larder with wooden vegetable racks, mesh-fronted cupboards and meat hooks hanging down from a beam.

Our friend Colette took Freddie through these rooms to the walled kitchen garden, bordered by apple, plum and damson trees. Left to its own devices, rhubarb produces flamboyant green and red-veined leaves, which also happen to be poisonous. Freddie helped to pick the stems and ran off to build a den with his friend Matthew. In many parts of the world, rhubarb is used like a vegetable in meat stews. We were in need of something sweeter. 'We don't eat enough puddings,' complained Freddie. 'Can you make a rhubarb crumble?'

So I did, using a recipe from Colette's family recipe book. The crumble topping is made from oats, rather than flour and helped to ensure that rhubarb scored 9 out of 10.

When we came home, a neighbour had posted a small green pocket book through the letterbox with a post-it note stuck to one page. The book was Ethelind Fearon's *Hot and Cold Sweets*, written in 1956. You don't mess with Ethelind. 'I shall expect some slight co-operation from the reader,' she warns. No gentle hand-holding here. Ethelind took me by the scruff of my apron, poked me with her wooden spoon and barked at me to get on with cooking rhubarb fingers. This recipe was sandwiched between 'Puffs, Jugoslavian' and 'Rice Caramel.' As I dusted the counter with flour, rolled out my rough puff pastry and dipped my rhubarb sticks in melted butter, a wave of 1950s nostalgia passed over me.

Freddie came down and started to play marbles on the kitchen floor. Alex came into the kitchen and joined in. For a split second (if I ignored the iPod plugged into her ears) we looked like an illustration from a Ladybird book. You know the sort of thing. Jane and Peter are playing in the kitchen whilst Mummy cooks and Daddy is cleaning the car. Then I stepped on a marble, flipping a sugar-coated, butter-dripping rhubarb stick across the room. Mummy never swore in Ladybird books. Ethelind tutted disapprovingly and I pulled myself together, wrapped my rhubarb sticks in their puff pastry blankets and placed them in the oven.

When they emerged, some had split. These looked the most appetising, offering a flash of pink rhubarb. Freddie and Alex had no problem consuming a handful of rhubarb fingers and gave them 8 out of 10. I leave the last word to Ethelind who suggests that having worked steadily through her book, 'you should be capable of devising your own variations on this delectable theme and have no need of advice from anyone at all.'

I hope she would approve of the recipe that she inspired.

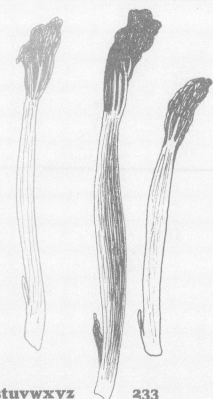

Rhubarb and Oat Crumble

Eating pudding in a vegetable challenge is not an everyday occurence and I was more than happy to oblige with the willing rhubarb.

Serves 6
75 g (3 oz) caster sugar
Finely grated zest and juice of 1 large orange
1 kg (2 lb) rhubarb stalks, cut into 3-cm
   (1¹/₄-in.) pieces

For the topping
175 g (6 oz) butter
1 tsp ground cinnamon
175 g (6 oz) brown sugar
225 g (7¹/₂ oz) whole porridge oats

1 Preheat the oven to 180°C (350°F) Gas 4.
2 Place the caster sugar, orange juice and zest with the rhubarb pieces in a pan over a medium heat, stirring for 3–4 minutes. Pour into an ovenproof dish.
3 To make the topping, melt the butter in a large pan. Remove from the heat and stir in the cinnamon and brown sugar. Then add the porridge oats and stir so they are well-coated.
4 Evenly spread the oat topping over the rhubarb and bake in the oven for 35–40 minutes. The topping should be golden brown and the rhubarb bubbling. Serve with a dollop of ice cream, cream or yoghurt.

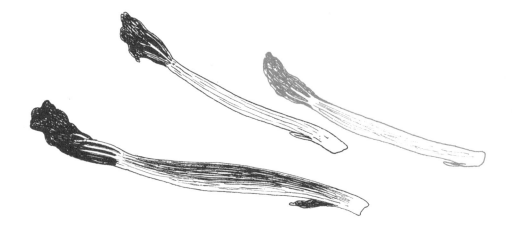

Rhubarb Fingers with Ginger

Here, rhubarb is wrapped in puff pastry blankets to bring a cosy feel of fifties nostalgia to your kitchen.

Serves 4
400 g (13 oz) rhubarb stalks, cut into
   finger-sized pieces
50 g (2 oz) butter

50 g (2 oz) soft brown sugar
½ tsp ground ginger
500 g (1 lb) ready-made puff pastry
1 egg, beaten

1 Preheat the oven to 190°C (375°F) Gas 5.

2 Gently melt the butter in a saucepan. Take off the heat. Put the sugar and ground ginger on a plate, mixing the two ingredients together.

3 Put the rhubarb stalks in the melted butter and one by one, take them out and roll them in the ginger and sugar so they are well-coated.

4 Roll out the puff pastry on a floured service into a large oblong the depth of 5 mm (¼ in.) or the thickness of a pound coin. Cut out smaller rectangles of pastry just big enough to wrap around each small stick of rhubarb. Using a little water on a pastry brush, dampen the edges of the pastry and seal around the sides and top of the rhubarb. Make sure there are no holes. Repeat for each rhubarb stick.

5 Lay them out on a baking tray on top of a piece of non-stick baking paper. Brush each one with a little beaten egg.

6 Bake in the preheated oven for about 20–25 minutes until the pastry is golden brown and well-risen.

Rhubarb and Strawberry Compote

Freddie greeted rhubarb and strawberry compote with a little suspicion. He didn't enjoy the texture of stewed rhubarb but when he stirred it into some Greek yoghurt things improved and he gave it a cautious 6 out of 10. Alex, however, gave this full marks.

Serves 4
Zest and juice of 1 large orange
250 g (8 oz) rhubarb stalks, cut into 3-cm
(1¼-in.) pieces

250 g (8 oz) strawberries, hulled and halved
75 g (3 oz) caster sugar

1 Add the orange juice and zest to a pan with the rhubarb, strawberries and sugar.
2 Gently heat all the ingredients together until the juice starts to run from the strawberries.
3 Cook on a medium heat for 10 minutes, stirring. The rhubarb will become tender. Serve with Greek yoghurt, vanilla ice cream or custard.

Rhubarb growers harvest their prize produce in sheds lit by candlelight. Cosseted in the dark warmth, the rhubarb can focus its efforts on producing long sweet stalks.

R is for... Rocket

Rocket isn't just a vegetable: it's a social climber. She can be found appearing under the more exotic names of Roquette and Rucola. In America, she dances under the soubriquet Arugula: the epitome of gourmet food. Like Eliza in *Pygmalion*, she's acquired airs and graces.

In reality, rocket is nothing special and has been a feature of British cookery since the 16th century. There is even a variety, known simply as 'London Rocket', that was noticed by botanists flourishing in the ruins after the 1666 Great Fire of London. I suspect that Miss Roquette learned very early on that to survive, she had to reinvent herself. Nowadays rocket is definitely seen as posh food and with its peppery, zesty flavour, certainly not something that you would give to the children. But I had to go to France to have my mind changed.

We flew to Nantes to see my brother marry his French girlfriend. Now I know that when it comes to valuing and producing good food, France has always occupied the high ground. And watching the way that local delicacies and wines were woven into the day-long celebrations, I can see why.

Freddie and Alex were involved in all this ceremony, summoning the guests with drums and banners into a huge circus tent. They sat with other children and enjoyed the same food as the adults. Between the courses the children danced, fought, chased each other, covered themselves in mud and behaved like children anywhere. But when the next course arrived, they returned to their seats and ate well. At midnight, a flaming brioche processed through the room and I found Freddie asleep with his head on the table, still holding a spoon next to a plate of half-eaten patisseries. Good food and fun were intertwined and it is easy to see why the children enjoyed both.

We stayed in Nantes for the rest of the weekend. La Cigale is a famous brasserie in the centre of the city. They offer a children's taster menu for only 7.50 Euros. In Britain, most childrens' meals offer a variation on chips, beans, sausages and chicken nuggets. The smarter menus appease parents with organic chicken nuggets and sausages. The occasional pasta and pizza option appears with a few vegetables thrown in for good measure. It is as if children require entirely different food to adults.

At La Cigale, the '*Initiation au Gout*' is exactly that. Children are introduced to tastes. They are treated as equals. Freddie and Alex were handed a children's menu that was entirely grown-up. The dishes were simplified versions of what we were eating. Warmed goats' cheese, smoked salmon, sardines were tasted. They tried a roquette and tomato salad and we ordered six snails. 'As long as you don't think that they are snails, they taste fantastic,' said Freddie.

Alex, who has long since refused childrens' menus in Britain, was impressed with the French version. The waiters were relaxed and there was nothing stuffy about the restaurant. We were surrounded by French families having Sunday supper. And there wasn't a chicken nugget in sight. The next day we flew home. Freddie had decided in France that he liked the peppery taste of rocket so I made a Warm Potato and Rocket Salad. He scored it 9 out of 10.

Warm Potato and Rocket Salad

Sometimes it takes a little bit of international travel to nudge children towards accepting new tastes. After our trip to France, rocket became a firm favourite with Freddie and Alex.

Serves 4–5
200 g (6 oz) smoked bacon lardons
500 g (1 lb) baby new potatoes
2 tbsp olive oil
1 tbsp freshly squeezed lemon juice

1 tsp clear honey
1 tsp Dijon mustard
65 g (2½ oz) rocket leaves
2 tbsp freshly chopped chives

1 Dry-fry the bacon lardons in a non-stick frying pan until they begin to crisp. You shouldn't need to add any oil to do this – they will cook in their own fat.
2 Boil the potatoes for 15–20 minutes, until tender. Drain and halve them.
3 Whisk together the oil, lemon juice, honey and mustard in a small jug.
4 Wash and dry the rocket leaves and put them in a large salad bowl. Add the chopped chives, cooked potatoes and lardons. When you are ready to eat, toss the salad with the dressing and serve.

abcthedgreatebigfveggchallengehijklmnopq^rstuvwxyz

Rocket Noodles

Freddie loved the combination of the peppery rocket, salmon and Parmesan stirred into noodles and gave this recipe 8 out of 10. Smoked salmon trimmings are cheaper than sliced salmon and perfect for this meal.

Serves 4
375 g (12 oz) dried egg noodles
1–2 tbsp olive oil or 1 tbsp of melted butter,
   if preferred
115 g (3½ oz) rocket leaves

150 g (5 oz) smoked salmon trimmings,
   cut into strips
3–4 tbsp freshly grated Parmesan cheese
Freshly ground pepper (optional)

1 Cook the noodles according to the packet instructions.
2 Drain the noodles and add the olive oil, stirring it round. Quickly stir in the rocket leaves which will wilt in the heat of the cooked noodles.
3 Add the smoked salmon strips. Sprinkle some freshly grated Parmesan on top and add a little ground pepper, if liked.

tip

If you find rocket too peppery, you can combine it with baby spinach leaves or lambs lettuce which have a much milder taste. Rocket can be added to pasta, scattered on bruschetta and you can use it to make a tangy pesto sauce. If your family really enjoy the peppery taste, then choose wild rocket as it has a stronger flavour.

 S is for... Salad Days

'My salad days, when I was green in judgement' (William Shakespeare, *Anthony and Cleopatra*)

When Freddie was little he was invited to a birthday party at an extremely smart house in Kensington. This was a house where an only child had not one but two nannies. Caterers had been brought in for the fourth birthday party. There were no sausage rolls, no crisps, no jelly or sweets. Instead, the mother looked on as tables of small children were served with salads and what can only be described as canapés for infants. The mothers and nannies became competitive.

'Come on now Peter, you know you like tomatoes.'

'Lucinda, try those lovely asparagus tips.'

Most of the kids went on strike. Some of them crawled under the table and started fighting. Even the birthday child refused to play ball. They held out until the cake arrived and then fell on it like vultures.

It has taken five more years to entice Freddie to eat a salad. I experimented with ingredients and dressings. After months of intensive research, we stumbled on a successful formula; give complete control to the child and make the salad bowl edible.

This is the ultimate do-it-yourself salad. Alex called the final product, made from tortilla wraps, 'Salad Shells'. This lifted the humble salad from being simply a side dish and turned it into something that Freddie awarded an astonishing 9 out of 10.

tip
How to make a tortilla salad shell

Metal tortilla shell makers or ovenproof glass bowl
Cooking oil spray
Medium tortilla wraps

You can buy specialist tortilla shell makers online and from cookware shops. These are simply flat-bottomed non-stick metal shells. If you can't get hold of one, try using an ovenproof glass bowl with a flat bottom.

Method for tortilla shell maker
1 Preheat the oven to 180°C (350°F) Gas 4.
2 Spray the inside of the shell pans lightly with cooking oil spray. Place a tortilla in each shell pan, making sure it fits the shape of the pan.
3 Bake in a preheated oven for 8–10 minutes. Cool for 5 minutes before removing from the pan.

abcthedgreatebigfveggchallengehijklmnopqr tuvwxyz

Method for ovenproof bowl

1 Preheat the oven to 190°C (375°F) Gas 5.
2 Lightly spray both sides of the tortilla and smooth with kitchen paper.
3 Drape the tortilla evenly over an upturned ovenproof bowl, place it on a baking sheet and bake in a preheated oven for 6–8 minutes. Allow to cool before removing.

Salad shell fillings
To fill 4 salad shells

Salad leaves
Choose your favourite salad leaves. Wash them and make sure they are thoroughly dry. You don't want the tortilla bowl to become soggy when filled with a salad.
🍴 Lamb's lettuce, Little Gem, Iceberg, round lettuce or baby spinach leaves work well.

Vegetables
🍴 Take 150 g (5 oz) of fresh or frozen edamame beans. Heat 1 tablespoon of olive oil in a wok with half a teaspoon of mild chilli powder. Stir-fry for 2 minutes.
🍴 Take 200 g (7 oz) of chopped asparagus tips. Heat 1 tablespoon of sesame oil in a wok with a tablespoon of sesame seeds. Add the asparagus and stir fry for 1–2 minutes.
🍴 Put 250 g (8 oz) of baby corn in a pan of boiling water for 2 minutes. Drain well. Or you can stir-fry them in a wok for 2 minutes with a little olive or sesame oil.
🍴 Add 150 g (5 oz) of mangetout, either raw or stir-fry them for 1 minute in a teaspoon of olive or sesame oil.
🍴 Halve and deseed one red or yellow pepper and cut into strips. Stir-fry with a chopped clove of garlic for 2 minutes in olive oil. Or you can offer them raw but make sure they are very thinly sliced.
🍴 Boil 350 g (11 1/2 oz) of small new potatoes until they are just soft. Cut them in half. Add a little knob of butter and some chopped fresh mint. Season with salt and pepper.
🍴 Wash and dry 250 g (8 oz) button mushrooms and chop in half. Either offer them raw or stir-fry them in sesame oil for 1 minute.
🍴 Grated carrot and celeriac, mixed together. Add a squeeze of lemon juice to stop the celeriac from going brown.
🍴 Halve a butternut squash. Scoop out the seeds and drizzle with a little olive oil and season with salt and pepper. Bake face down in a preheated oven at 200°C (400°F) Gas 6

for about 35 minutes, until the squash is soft and lightly browned. Carefully peel off the skin and cut the flesh into cubes. You could prepare some pumpkin or acorn squash in the same way.

 Choose whatever selection of vegetables your family enjoys.

Toppings

 Roast chicken breast, cut into strips.

 Stir-fry strips of beef fillet with a little vegetable oil, grated ginger and soy sauce.

 Rashers of crispy streaky bacon.

 Tinned tuna, well drained or cooked tuna.

 Smoked salmon pieces.

 Any hard cheese, grated: Emmental, Cheddar or Gruyère.

 Mixed seeds to sprinkle on top: sesame, sunflower, pumpkin or pine nuts.

 Raisins and sultanas.

 Offer a bowl of couscous or quinoa. Quinoa (pronounced 'keen-wah') is a tasty alternative to rice and takes less time to prepare. The Incas used to refer to it as the mother of all grains. It isn't a true grain as it doesn't belong to the grass family but is related to beets, spinach and chard. You can buy it in health-food shops and supermarkets. Cook according to instructions.

Dressings

Provide a choice of shop-bought or home-made dressings. The creamy dressings work better as you don't want the tortilla shell to become soggy.

 Creamy Lime Dressing. Grate the zest and squeeze the juice of the lime into a bowl. Add 4 tablespoons of mayonnaise and 2 tablespoons of crème fraîche. Hand whisk until it is smooth and creamy. You can substitute with reduced-fat versions of mayo and crème fraîche.

 Yoghurt and Herb Dressing. Beat 250 g (8 oz) plain smooth (not set) yoghurt with 2 teaspoons of lemon juice, 1 teaspoon of Dijon mustard, 2 teaspoons of chopped basil leaves and 2 teaspoons of chopped fresh mint.

 Mint Dressing. Take a clean, empty jar with a lid. Pour in 4 tablespoons of olive oil, 2 teaspoons of caster sugar, 2 tablespoons of finely chopped fresh mint, 1 teaspoon of Dijon mustard and 2 teaspoons of white wine vinegar. Put the lid on the jar and shake until well mixed.

 Simple Blue Cheese Dressing. In a food processor, put 75 g (3 oz) of blue cheese such as Roquefort or Gorgonzola. Add 150 g (5 oz) of soured cream or Greek yoghurt, 1 tablespoon of lemon or lime juice and blend until smooth.

S is for... Salsify

'Salsify is the forgotten vegetable,' said the grocer. 'It's as if people don't know that it exists and wouldn't know what to do with it.'

He was right. When I put the word salsify in the search engine, there were countless entries from seed companies. Yet they hardly ever appear for sale. I had seen them for sale in France and Italy but much of Britain seems to have chosen to neglect them. The grocer was delighted to be able to sell me salsify. I took the bus to his shop in Turnham Green Terrace where there were bundles of what looked like stumpy black wands stacked on display. This was black salsify, also known as scorzonera. A small pink label told me it came from a farm in Belgium.

Salsify and scorzonera are both long tapering root vegetables. One is long and thin with light-brown whiskery skin and has the nickname 'vegetable oyster'. It is related to scorzonera, which has much darker roots with skin that looks like bark. I went to pick Freddie up from school. A small crowd of children gathered round the scorzonera.

'They look like daggers,' said Freddie's friend, Eleanor. Freddie took one look and asked if I had any biscuits. After artichokes, daikons, eddoes and karela, he doesn't bat an eyelid at strange-looking vegetables.

I looked through my older cookery books to learn what to do with my forgotten salsify. Constance Spry writes that in France, authorities on the subject classify both types of salsify as one category 'salsifis'. She also praises the black salsify for its superior taste. I had nothing to compare it with as the lighter-skinned salsify proved impossible to find. What she didn't say was that the scorzonera has a strange habit. As it waited on the kitchen counter, a sticky white milk started to ooze from its skin. This stuck to my fingers and was impervious to scrubbing. When I searched on the internet to find out more, I discovered that this milk is in fact latex. Salsify is apparently a member of one branch of the *Asteraceae* family, which includes dandelions. And this particular family group known as the *Cichorieae*, share this distinguishing feature.

When I returned to prepare the scorzonera, I wore gloves. There was another unpleasant family characteristic that we were all to discover later on that evening. Jerusalem artichokes also belong to the *Asteraceae* family and contain inulin, which has earned them the nickname 'fartichokes'. Inulin also appears in salsify and scorzonera with much the same effect when eaten. You have been warned. Not surprisingly the genteel Ms Spry hadn't mentioned this problem.

When trying a new vegetable it is normally best to keep it simple. All of my older cookery books recommended boiling or steaming the scorzonera and serving it with browned butter and freshly chopped herbs. So this is what I did. You have to have ready a large pan of cold water with plenty of lemon juice before you start. The salsify is a sensitive vegetable and once exposed to the air, its white flesh starts to turn brown. The lemon juice prevents this.

With my gloves on, I scrubbed the roots clean, peeled them and placed them in the water with lemon juice. I boiled them until they were tender – soft but not mushy. Browning butter is easy – unless you use a dark-coloured pan. Unable to see how the butter was browning, I burnt it. I switched to a white pan and started afresh.

This was the first time any of us had tasted any kind of salsify. We tried to describe it. Alex thought it was like a mild turnip, Freddie compared it to Jerusalem artichokes, Chris thought it was a little like asparagus. None of us felt that it tasted like its nickname, oyster. Freddie gave it 7 out of 10.

tip

Salsify is in season from October through to spring. When you are buying salsify, try and choose roots that are less whiskery and if you can find them, still have their green tops. Choose the firm roots and don't buy them if they are flabby or look a bit tired.

Scorzonera with Browned Butter and Herbs

Freddie is now unfazed by even the most unusual looking vegetables, and it adds to their appeal if they look like weapons.

Serves 4 as a side dish
1 kg (2 lb) scorzonera
Freshly squeezed lemon juice
115 g (3½ oz) butter

Generous handful of freshly chopped chives
 and parsley
Freshly grated Parmesan cheese, to serve
 (optional)

1 Clean the roots under running water, peel them and then put them into a large pan with some lemon juice added. Make sure they are covered by the water or they will brown.

2 Cut the roots into smaller pieces and slice them at an angle, into pieces the same size as penne pasta. Bring a pan of water with lemon juice to the boil and add the scorzonera. Simmer for about 25–30 minutes or until the roots are tender. There seems to be a huge difference in the recommended cooking time for this root vegetable. Some say that 10 minutes boiling is enough – we found that it took over 25 minutes. Use your judgement. They are ready when they are tender and just soft – but not mushy. Drain well.

3 In a small light-coloured pan, melt the butter and stir until it starts to turn a golden nutty brown. Stir in the chopped herbs.

4 Put the scorzonera in a serving dish and pour over the browned butter with the chopped herbs. Serve immediately. If you like, you can add some freshly grated Parmesan cheese.

S is for...

'Half-way down lies one that gathers samphire, dreadful trade!'
(William Shakespeare, King Lear)

I made the mistake of eavesdropping on a pub conversation whilst on holiday in Cornwall. Someone was claiming to have found samphire growing in a nearby estuary. Samphire is a succulent wild green plant that you find growing on coastal marshes around Great Britain. It is also delicious.

The next day I went on a wild goose chase to find it. The children looked on as I stepped out purposely into the mud, grasping what I thought was the perfect foragers' basket. I had thoughts of returning, the basket brimming over with poor man's asparagus. When you go foraging you have to be optimistic. The mud started to creep over the top of my wellington boots. I clung to my wicker basket and squelched around. Never believe anything you hear in a pub. There was no samphire. Or at least if there was any, it was hidden by mud. I thrust my hand into the mud and pulled out weeds. It started to rain heavily and then thunder. Alex and Freddie shouted at me to get out and come home. Walking back was impossible. With each step the boots became stuck. In order to scramble out, I let go of the basket. I climbed up on all fours, mud-drenched. Slowly and with considerable pathos, the foragers' basket sank into the mud. With one final glug, the wicker handle was subsumed and a spray of tiny bubbles rose to the surface. My image as an intrepid samphire forager was in tatters. Freddie took me by the hand and led me home. Samphire makes you do strange things.

Hundreds of years ago samphire gatherers risked their lives to pick strands of the rarer rock samphire. At times, children were tied with rope and dangled over the cliff edge. This is the 'dreadful trade' that Shakespeare refers to in *King Lear*. Having failed with my foraging, Freddie and Alex went, unroped, to Fowey Fishmongers and bought back a bag of marsh samphire and some smoked mackerel.

Samphire is known as sea asparagus or poor man's asparagus. It looks like tiny strands of cacti. Like asparagus, it tastes good having been quickly boiled and served with a little melted butter or some extra virgin olive oil and lemon juice. Early on in the vegetable challenge, Freddie had discovered the joys of asparagus and he decided that he also loved the samphire, awarding it 8 out of 10.

The samphire season in Britain lasts between June and September. The North Norfolk coast is famous for this delicacy. When we came home to London, our local fishmongers was selling some that had come from Brittany. Our second samphire recipe was another very simple dish: samphire with poached eggs on toast. The poached eggs must not be overcooked. What makes this taste irresistible is the combination of runny egg yolk and samphire. Alex and Freddie consumed this so quickly by the time Chris and I had sat down to eat our meal, they were already asking for seconds. Samphire with poached egg on toast scored the maximum 10 out of 10.

If you can't get hold of samphire for the Samphire with Poached Egg on Toast recipe, you can substitute it with spinach, but sauté it first in a teaspoon of butter for a few minutes.

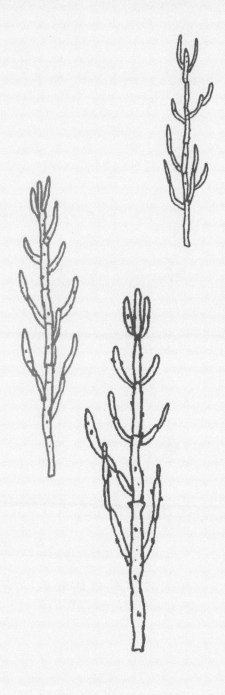

Samphire with Lemon and Butter

Boiling samphire quickly gives it an intense bright green colour which has great visual appeal. It's also a great 'hands-on' vegetable, requiring you to hold the roots with your fingers as you suck the flesh from the stalks.

Serves 4

1 bunch marsh samphire, washed and rinsed thoroughly

Unsalted butter or extra virgin olive oil

Freshly squeezed lemon or lime juice

1 Bring a pan of water to the boil and add the samphire to the boiling water and cook for 3 minutes. If you prefer, you can steam it instead.

2 Drain and add a knob of butter, douse with lemon juice and serve immediately. I recommend using unsalted butter if you have some, because the samphire is naturally salty in taste.

Samphire is known as sea asparagus or poor man's asparagus. It looks like tiny strands of cacti.

Freddie's Favourite 10/10

Samphire with Poached Egg on Toast

Having discovered that he already loved asparagus, Freddie also gave top marks to this 'sea asparagus', consuming this dish in record time and giving it a record top score.

Serves 4
4 eggs
350 g (11½ oz) marsh samphire, washed and rinsed thoroughly

4 large slices of crusty country bread
25 g (1 oz) unsalted butter
A handful of freshly chopped chives

1 Poach the eggs, making sure they aren't overcooked as the yolk inside should be runny.
2 Toast the slices of crusty country bread under the grill.
3 Bring a large pan of water to the boil and add the samphire, cooking it for about 3 minutes. Drain and add a small knob of unsalted butter.
4 On each plate, place a slice of hot toast, rubbed with a little unsalted butter, a mound of samphire and top it with the poached egg. Sprinkle some finely cut fresh chives on top. Serve immediately. Prepare to be asked for seconds.

tip

Samphire is only in season for a short time from the end of May to the end of August. You can buy it at fishmongers and it is found growing in coastal mudflats. The North Norfolk Coast is famous for its samphire but it can also be found in other places across Britain such as Cornwall, Essex and other parts of East Anglia. When the British stocks are unavailable, fishmongers will sell samphire from further afield, such as France and Israel.

It is often quite expensive but if you use it with other simple ingredients that are less costly, it is worth the effort. Keep it simple. Serve it with fish or toss some into linguine with a little olive oil and Parmesan. As it doesn't stay fresh for long, try and use it the day you buy it so that it is at its best.

S is for... Sorrel

In the back garden of a small Cornish cottage in Lostwithiel we took our first lesson in foraging. This is the home of Marcus Harrison's Wild Food School.

'This is like the herbology class at Hogwarts,' whispered Alex as we were led into a back garden packed full of man-sized weeds. Except, when you looked closer, the weeds were lined up in ordered rows and as Marcus explained, his back garden is an encyclopedia of wild edible plants. In this living classroom, he introduced us to plants like burdock, edible thistles, rosehips, borage and sorrel. For two children who have grown up in an urban jungle, this was a whole new world. Freddie, who had already eaten dandelions, nettles and cactus, covered himself in burdock seeds and safely sampled petals, stalks and leaves under the expert guidance of Marcus.

After our back garden lesson, he took us out into the Cornish countryside to hone our foraging skills. We found watercress swirling in a brook, brushed past ground elder and walked along a river bank where clumps of sorrel leaves were growing. We scrabbled along the bank, filling a basket with the sorrel. It had a sharp lemony taste. It is more of a cross between a herb and a vegetable and you can use the young leaves in salads. Having seen cultivated sorrel for sale at great expense in smart food shops, it was satisfying to pick it for free. Before we said goodbye to Marcus, he told us how to use sorrel in omelettes, quiches, soups and how to make trail food, sautéing it quickly with a little olive oil, a sprinkling of caster sugar, with some raisins, pine nuts and a dollop of crème fraîche.

Sorrel is a pretty shade of green but once cooked it rapidly turns an unsettling shade of khaki. Freddie closed his eyes to taste the trail food. 'If I had to eat it to stay alive I suppose I would,' he said.

When the holiday ended we took home with us a small bag of sorrel. I made a simple sorrel sauce and served it with haddock and new potatoes. On the fridge, sorrel crept up to join the elite vegetables in the 'I like' category.

tip

Wild plants can be unsafe for children, people with certain medical conditions, or pregnant women. But there are lots of opportunities for families to learn more about wild food under expert guidance from various organisations across Britain. Try the following:
Marcus Harrison's Wild Food School
The Forestry Commission
The National Trust

Sorrel and Potato Soup

In wild, hunter-gatherer mode, we tracked and picked our own sorrel from the Cornish countryside and turned it into this delicious soup.

Serves 4
1 tbsp olive oil
1 large onion, peeled and sliced
2 large potatoes, peeled and diced
1 litre (1¾ pints) vegetable stock

250 g (8 oz) sorrel leaves
Crème fraîche or plain yoghurt, to serve
A handful of chopped chives, to serve
Salt and freshly ground pepper

1 Heat the olive oil in a pan and gently sauté the onions and potatoes for 20 minutes until the onions are translucent and the potatoes softened. Season.
2 Add the vegetable stock and bring to the boil. Reduce the heat and gently simmer for 15 minutes until the potatoes are soft.
3 Stir in the sorrel leaves for a minute and then use a hand-blender or food processor to purée the soup. The heat of the soup will cook the sorrel.
4 Serve with a dollop of crème fraîche or yoghurt and sprinkle with chopped fresh chives.

Freddie closed his eyes to taste the trail food. 'If I had to eat it to stay alive I suppose I would,' he said.

Creamy Sorrel Sauce

We were on a roll after our successful Wild Food experience, and Freddie enjoyed this so much that he confidently moved sorrel into the 'I like' category in the vegetable league.

Serves 4
A large bunch of sorrel leaves, approximately
    80 g (3 oz)

A knob of butter
200 ml (6½ fl oz) thick single cream

1 Heat the butter on a medium heat in a pan with a teaspoon of water. Add the sorrel leaves and stir. They will quickly wilt and start to turn a khaki colour. Keep stirring.

2 After 2 minutes, turn off the heat and stir in the cream. Use a hand-blender to purée the sauce. Serve with chicken or fish or you can stir it into new potatoes.

S is for... Spinach

I like what the chef Robert Carrier wrote about spinach in his cookbook. 'An exotic from Persia, it was brought by the Moors to Spain, by the Spaniards to the Low Counties, by Flemish refugees to England.

And after that great pilgrimage, we plunge it in cold water, boil it, and then force it on our children.'

Spinach is one of those vegetables that seems to have been forced on generations of children, presumably because of its reputation as an iron-rich wonder food. The trouble is, in our house, the 'this is good for you' approach is the kiss of death. In fact, the iron in spinach can easily be lost in cooking. Clearly Popeye was popping far more than spinach to get those bulging biceps.

All Freddie cares about is that his vegetables *taste* good. So we took a brave step. The Great Big Vegetable Challenge went on the road to test out our spinach recipe with the gardening club at Freddie's school. On a small patch of land in front of the school, the children and their teachers have created their very own Garden of Eden. They dig, sow and weed with devotion, oblivious to the distant hum of the Great Western Road, a major carriageway that cuts through West London. There are beetroot, corn, tomatoes, potatoes, rhubarb, pumpkins, chard and spinach.

Little notices announce the progress of the garden. It reminds me of the official notices posted on the gates of Buckingham Palace. 'It is with great sadness that we announce the passing of a runner bean that succumbed to a green fly infestation' or 'the tallest sunflower broke all school records.' People stop and admire the vegetables. There is something uplifting about a vegetable garden in the middle of a city.

With the school gardeners, I made Rainbow Chard Pizzas and Spinach Fritters. They picked the chard and spinach leaves and washed them in the kitchen. The braver ones munched on the raw spinach leaves, flexing their biceps like Popeye. I learnt that once heated, spinach has Houdini like qualities. You think you've put a huge quantity of bright green leaves into a pan and within seconds in a cloud of steam the leaves disappear, leaving behind a dark green stringy slime. It is the escapologist of the vegetable kingdom. I wanted to avoid any sliminess. With the spinach fritters, I cut the freshly picked leaves into thin strips, added them to the batter and quickly cooked them in a little oil in a hot pan.

abcthedgreatebigfveggchallergehijklmnopqr**s** tuvwxyz

The young gardeners waited by the cooker like hungry dogs. They took their hot fritters out into the rain to enjoy, surrounded by their beautiful vegetables. Judging by the speed with which they were consumed, spinach fritters passed the taste test with flying colours. And there was no hint of slime, the spinach staying bright green and succulent inside the fritter. Freddie's score was 10 out of 10. The gardening club gave me all the leftover spinach to take home. I made a simple spinach omelette that evening. The following day we had Spinach and Feta Toasties. Freddie gave them both 8 out of 10.

Some days I feel as if I could do with support from the Army Catering Corps. The nights when we all arrive home late, drenched in rain and exhausted by work, school and football fixtures. There are instant demands for food. I fend them off with a drink of squash and a biscuit but that only buys a few minutes' grace. The demands become more aggressive.

An unexpected side effect of the Great Big Vegetable Challenge was that I became far better at looking at the fridge and coming up with fast food, incorporating vegetables. I made spaghetti with baby spinach leaves, bacon and pine nuts. The pine nuts, or pine kernels, are oily and can be toasted very quickly in a dry pan. The meal takes as long to make as it takes to cook the spaghetti. The baby spinach wilts in the heat of the cooked pasta. The film star Sophia Loren said, 'Spaghetti can be eaten most successfully if you inhale it like a vacuum cleaner.' We were all so hungry, we followed her advice. Freddie's score for this meal was 9 out of 10.

tip

When you buy spinach, choose the freshest leaves. Whether you use baby spinach or larger leafed spinach, make sure it is crisp and bright green and not discoloured. It deteriorates quickly and smells bad. Look at the packet carefully and don't buy it if you can see any hint of brown sliminess. Try to eat it within a couple of days. Wash it well and use a salad spinner to dry.

Freddie's Favourite 10/10

Spinach Fritters

This recipe not only won Freddie over to the scourge of children everywhere, but was a huge success with the school gardening club, too.

Serves 6–8
4 eggs, separated
225 g (7½ oz) self-raising flour
350 ml (12 fl oz) milk
75 g (3 oz) butter, melted

2 tsp caster sugar
115 g (3½ oz) fresh spinach leaves, finely
   chopped into thin strips
1 clove of garlic, finely chopped
Cooking spray oil or 2–3 tbsp olive oil

1 Put the yolks in a large bowl and beat. In another bowl whisk the egg whites until they form soft white peaks.

2 Sift the flour into the bowl with the egg yolks, add the milk, melted butter and caster sugar. Mix together with a wooden spoon until it forms a smooth batter.

3 Add the spinach to the batter along with the garlic. Then gently fold in the egg whites.

4 Make the fritters in batches of four in a large frying pan. You may need to have a piece of kitchen paper to hand to clean the pan of any burnt oil in between batches. Spray the frying pan with cooking oil or add 1 tablespoon of olive oil and heat the pan. When the oil is hot, drop in 4–5 dollops of batter, spacing them apart in the pan.

5 Cook for 2 minutes and when you see the edges begin to brown, flip them over to cook the other side. Wipe the pan with kitchen paper and add a little fresh oil for each batch. Serve immediately.

abcthedgreatebigfveggchallengehijklmnopqr **s** tuvwxyz

Spinach Omelette

Eggs and spinach have a certain affinity, so an omelette is a winning combination that can be served in minutes.

Serves 3–4
6 eggs
225 g (7½ oz) baby spinach leaves, washed
and dried

1 tbsp butter, for cooking spinach
2 tbsp butter, for cooking omelette (use a cooking
spray if you prefer a lower-fat option)
Salt and freshly ground pepper

1 Break five of the eggs into a bowl. Separate the remaining egg. Add the yolk to the other eggs and mix them together gently with a fork. With the one egg white, whisk in a separate bowl until it forms soft peaks. Gently fold in to the beaten eggs. Don't beat it or you will lose the lightness.

2 In a pan, heat the butter and stir in the spinach leaves, allowing them to wilt for about a minute. Take off the heat and season.

3 Melt the butter in an omelette pan until it starts to foam. If the pan is too large the omelette will be too thin. If it is too small, the omelette will be too thick and tough to fold over. Pour in the eggs and the spinach leaves. Stir them round with a fork. Tilt the pan so that the egg is evenly distributed. The eggs will start to set after 20 seconds. Redistribute any runny egg by tilting the pan. With a fork, trace round the edge of the omelette.

4 When the egg is nearly set, fold the omelette in half in the pan using a spatula. Leave it to cook for nearly a minute. The remaining runny egg will set. Slide the omelette out of the pan and serve.

tip

You can substitute spinach for kale leaves in this recipe if you like. Shred them into smaller strips and steam them before adding them to the omelette. You can try kale as a substitute in the fritter and toastie recipes, too.

Spinach and Feta Toasties

This may not be haute cuisine but it is delicious, good fast food.

Makes 4 toasties
125 g (4 oz) baby spinach leaves, washed and dried
A handful of fresh basil leaves

200 g (7 oz) feta cheese
8 slices of sliced brown bread
Butter or margarine, for spreading

Sandwich toaster

1 Using a food processor or hand-blender, blend the spinach and basil with the feta cheese until it is a smooth paste.
2 Follow the instructions for the sandwich toaster, using the feta and spinach as your filling. Serve immediately.

The school gardeners picked the chard and spinach leaves and washed them in the kitchen. The braver ones munched on the raw spinach leaves, flexing their biceps like Popeye.

abcthedgreatebigfveggchallengehijklmnopqr tuvwxyz

Spaghetti with Spinach and Bacon

This recipe came together from an assortment of things that I found in the fridge, under great pressure to feed hungry mouths at the end of the day.

Serves 4
400 g (13 oz) spaghetti
4–5 rashers streaky bacon
4 tbsp pine nuts

2 tbsp olive oil
250 g (8 oz) baby spinach leaves, washed and dried
Freshly grated Parmesan cheese
Salt and freshly ground pepper

1 Cook the spaghetti according to the packet instructions until al dente.
2 Cut the streaky bacon into squares and dry-fry in a non-stick pan. You shouldn't have to add any extra oil as it should cook in its own bacon fat.
3 Toast the pine nuts by scattering in a small pan and stirring them on a medium heat for a minute or two until they turn golden brown.
4 Drain the pasta well and put back in the pan. Immediately add the spinach leaves and put the lid on for 2 minutes, allowing the heat of the spaghetti to wilt the spinach leaves.
5 Add the olive oil, bacon and pine nuts with a pinch of salt and freshly ground pepper. Toss the pasta so that it is evenly coated. Serve with some freshly grated Parmesan cheese.

tip

Try replacing the spinach leaves in this recipe with other green-leafed vegetables. It works well with rocket and dandelion leaves. Or you can try it with chard leaves cut into thin strips. We enjoy combining two or three different types.

S is for... Squash

Squashed

As the autumn begins, one family of vegetables start to appear on market stalls and in the supermarkets. Like a collection of jewels, mounds of brightly-coloured squash compete with each other for attention from the shopper.

They do this in two ways; flaunting their flamboyant colours and muttering their elaborate names. The Red Kuri, also known as the Baby Red Hubbard, jostles with the Yellow Patty Pan, Gem Squash, Golden Acorn, Turk's Turban, Crown Prince and the Butternut Squash.

After a game of squash boules on the kitchen floor, two were singled out for special treatment. Freddie picked butternut squash and acorn squash to make Spicy Roasted Squash. Freddie gave this 8 out of 10. The best thing about this dish is that you can combine any number of different squash together.

Tasting all the different roasted squash gives you an idea of their individual qualities. The butternut squash was the most popular with its sweet taste and soft melting texture. So I bought some more and made a Butternut Squash and Coconut Soup. Freddie awarded this soup 8 out of 10. Our pile of squash was getting smaller but we still had the Patty Pan and Red Kuri waiting for their moment in the limelight. Patty Pan has a pretty shape, like a cut diamond, its flesh is pale white and floury in texture. By contrast the Red Kuri has intense orange-red flesh.

I went to Ara and Sid at Olympia Butchers. They cut some cubes of pork shoulder to cook on skewers with the squash, saying that it would keep nice and moist. I cooked the kebabs with a ginger and teriyaki marinade. Freddie's score rose to 9 out of 10.

At work the next day I chatted to a South African colleague, Frik. He told me about a gem squash recipe that his mum made for him when he came home from school. I took notes and brought his mum's recipe to life, for my children.

When Freddie asked what was for supper, he looked a little disappointed. 'Is there no meat or fish in this recipe?' he moaned. But when he tasted it, he smiled. 'Tell Frik this is really good. And tell him his squash recipe gets the highest score.'

Baked Butternut Squash and Coconut Soup

Because it is so smooth, butternut squash makes a perfect soup, particularly for those with a hatred of 'bits'.

Serves 4
1 medium butternut squash, approximately
    1.2 kg (2³/4 lb)
Olive oil
2 sprigs of fresh rosemary
1 onion, chopped
1 clove of garlic, crushed

1 potato, diced
1 carrot, diced
50 g (2 oz) sachet of creamed coconut
1 litre (1³/4 pints) vegetable stock (bouillon
    powder is good)
3 tbsp crème fraîche
Salt and freshly ground pepper

1 Preheat the oven to 180°C (350°F) Gas 4.

2 Cut the butternut squash in half lengthways and scoop out the seeds. Rub a little olive oil and a pinch of salt into the flesh of the squash and place flesh-side down on a baking tray. Place a sprig of rosemary under each half. Bake in the oven for about 40 minutes, until the flesh is soft.

3 Remove and scoop out the flesh into a large pan. Discard the rosemary.

4 Sauté the onion, garlic, potato and carrot in a pan in a little oil for 5 minutes.

5 When they are soft, add to the baked squash with the creamed coconut and vegetable stock. Stir well. Bring to the boil and then reduce the heat and simmer gently for 20 minutes.

6 Remove from the heat, stir in the crème fraîche and use a hand-blender or food processor to purée the soup. Serve with warm crusty bread.

tip

You can substitute different squash in these recipes. Use pumpkin or acorn squash in the soup or combine all three.

Baked Gem Squash with Cheese and Corn

This childhood recipe came from my South African colleague, Frik, whose mum made it when he came home from school. A few decades and a continent later, it can still work its magic on a starving school boy.

Serves 2 as a main course or 4 as a starter
2 gem squash
250 g (8 oz) tinned sweetcorn (drained weight)
   or creamed sweetcorn

115 g (3½ oz) Cheddar cheese, grated
4 tsp freshly grated Parmesan cheese

1 Bring a large pan of water to the boil. Add the whole gem squash. Simmer for 20–25 minutes. Remove and dry.

2 Preheat the oven to 180°C (350°F) Gas 4.

3 Cut the squash in half and scoop out the seeds. Place the four halves in a roasting tray. If you have some, the gem squash can be baked in ramekins.

4 If not using creamed sweetcorn, blend the sweetcorn kernels until smooth in a food processor, adding a tablespoon of milk.

5 Spoon some creamed corn into the centre of each gem squash. Then divide the grated Cheddar between the four halves and sprinkle on top. Add a teaspoon of grated Parmesan to each.

6 Bake in the preheated oven for 25 minutes. The cheese will be golden brown and the squash soft. Serve immediately.

Squash and Pork Kebabs in Teriyaki Marinade

I gave these kebabs a Japanese twist, inspired by the oriental variety Red Kuri. Try experimenting with different combinations of squash.

Serves 4–5

625 g (1¼ lb) assorted squash (kuri, patty pan, acorn, butternut squash), peeled and cut into 2.5-cm (1-in.) cubes
2 tsp freshly grated ginger
1 clove of garlic, crushed

2 tbsp teriyaki marinade
1 tbsp sesame oil
750 g (1½ lb) pork shoulder, cut into 2.5-cm (1-in.) cubes
Salt and freshly ground pepper

8 wooden skewers, soaked in water for 30 minutes

1 Cook the cubed squash in boiling water for 3–5 minutes until tender but not too soft. Drain well and allow to cool.

2 In a large bowl, mix together the grated ginger, garlic, teriyaki marinade, sesame oil and season with a little salt and pepper.

3 Add the pork cubes and stir so that it is well covered. Add the squash cubes and stir well, taking care not to damage them. Cover with cling film and leave for an hour in the fridge.

4 Thread the meat and squash cubes alternately onto the skewers. Lay on a foil sheet on a baking tray and cook under a medium hot grill for about 6–8 minutes, turning regularly until the pork is well cooked. Serve with rice and salad. The kebabs can also be cooked on a barbecue.

Spicy Roasted Squash

This is delicious served with lamb or pork chops.

Serves 4 as a side dish
1 butternut squash
1 acorn squash
250 g (8 oz) baby corn
2 courgettes, sliced into wedges

3 tbsp olive oil
1–2 tsp mild chilli powder
1 roasted garlic bulb (see page 115)
Sea salt and freshly ground pepper

1 Preheat the oven to 180°C (350°F) Gas 4.
2 Use a potato peeler to remove the skin of the squash. Cut them in half and scoop out all the seeds. Cut into wedges. Place on a lightly oiled baking tray.
3 Add the baby corn and courgette wedges. Sprinkle over the olive oil and mild chilli powder, according to taste. Squeeze in the roasted garlic bulb.
4 Turn the vegetables in the oil to make sure they are evenly coated. Bake for about 50 minutes to an hour. Stir the vegetables halfway through cooking.

S is for... Sweet potato

(not just ordinary potato with sugar on top)

When I was a child, I spent a year living in the United States, in Philadelphia. We arrived in 1976, a pale-faced English family with exemplary bad timing. This was the bicentennial year of the American Declaration of Independence from the British Empire.

The celebrations were in full swing and to cap it all, my brother's name was Benedict. As he soon learnt in school, Benedict Arnold was the infamous traitor of the American revolution.

We spent our first week at a university in Washington DC, undergoing 'acclimatisation'. Whilst my parents sat through lectures on how to use the telephone, drive on the right-hand side of the road and dial 911 (preferably not all at once), I drank coke, ate hot dogs and played chase with the other British kids, high on sugar.

My own acclimatisation was rapid. I settled into my American school. Within a few months I stood on stage, belting out songs of the American revolution whilst trussed up in a Betsy Ross outfit. She was the woman who was said to have sewn the first American flag. I tasted sweet potato mash for the first time and learnt how America's first president, George Washington, grew them on his farm in Virginia. I hadn't come across sweet potatoes before. Nowadays they are in most supermarkets. Despite its name, sweet potato is not related to the ordinary potato. It is a sweet-tasting root vegetable which, when cooked, has the texture of a potato crossed with a carrot. They are easy to use; you can boil, bake, steam, mash and fry them.

Freddie's first taste of sweet potato was a success. I baked them in their skins, in the same way as you might a potato, served with a little butter and black pepper. The mash from the sweet potato tastes delicious with caramelised onions. He scored this simple meal 8 out of 10. 'I think I want to do some of the cooking now with the sweet potatoes,' suggested Freddie.

Using a pizza base mix, he made calzone, which are like folded pizzas, filled with sweet potato, Brie and basil. Like quesadillas, calzone are a good way of serving vegetables. I have noticed that whenever Freddie is involved in the cooking, his scores are much higher. Sweet Potato Calzone were given 10 out of 10.

The kitchen-takeover continued. Most children love roasted potato wedges so Alex made a spicy marinade for Sweet Potato Wedges; another dish that scored a maximum 10 out of 10. Sweet potato had charmed its way into our kitchen. And because of its versatility, became a firm favourite.

abcthedgreatebigfveggchallengehijklmnopqr tuvwxyz

As dusk fell, I led the children to the perfect picnic spot to enjoy home-made tomato soup from a flask.

Sweet Potato, Brie and Basil Calzone

Freddie wanted to get stuck into the cooking himself and this version of a pizza gave him the perfect opportunity to enjoy creating something and then consuming the fruits of his labours.

Makes 4 calzone
300 g (10 oz) pizza base mix
300 g (10 oz) sweet potato, finely diced
2 tbsp pesto sauce

175 g (6 oz) Brie, cubed
Generous handful of fresh basil leaves,
    roughly chopped
Salt and freshly ground pepper

1 Preheat the oven to 220°C (425°F) Gas 7.

2 Make the pizza base mix according to the packet instructions. Knead the dough and divide into four equal pieces.

3 Boil or steam the sweet potato for about 8 minutes until tender, but not mushy. Drain well. Place in a bowl and stir in the pesto.

4 Flour a clean surface and roll out each piece of dough into a 23-cm (9-in.) diameter circle. On one side of each circle of dough, spoon some sweet potato, Brie and add some basil leaves. Season. Don't put the filling too near the edge.

5 Using your fingertips or a pastry brush dipped in water, slightly dampen round the circumference of the dough. Fold the dough over the side that is piled with the filling, matching up the two edges. Seal the edges firmly together by pinching and twisting the dough together. Twist the dough into a little point at each corner.

6 Dust a baking sheet with flour and place the calzone on top. Bake in the oven for about 12–15 minutes. When ready, the calzone are very lightly browned. Take care when serving – they can be piping hot inside.

Sweet Potato Wedges

For this recipe Alex devised a spicy marinade, thus ensuring yet another resounding top score for the sweet potato.

Serves 4 as a starter
500 g (1 lb) sweet potatoes
1 tbsp sesame oil
1 tbsp vegetable oil

½ tsp ground paprika
½ tsp curry powder
½ tsp mild chilli powder
Soured cream or plain yoghurt, to serve

1 Preheat the oven to 220°C (425°F) Gas 7.
2 Scrub the sweet potatoes clean but don't peel. Cut them in half lengthways and then cut each half into four.
3 In a bowl, add the oil and spices and mix together well.
4 Lay the sweet potato wedges on a non-stick baking tray and brush them with the spiced oil. Make sure all sides are coated. Put them in the preheated oven and bake for 20 minutes. Serve with a bowl of soured cream or yoghurt for dipping.

Beef Hot Pot with Sweet Potato Topping

You can use sweet potato to top all kinds of pies and hot pots. This recipe for beef hot pot is a great family meal for a cold day and Freddie gave it 9 out of 10.

Serves 4

500 g (1 lb) beef braising steak, cut into
  2.5-cm (1-in.) cubes
2 tsp freshly grated ginger
3 tbsp olive oil
1 clove of garlic, crushed
1 tsp dried oregano
1 tsp dried thyme
1 tbsp plain flour

300 g (10 oz) shallots, peeled
400 g (13 oz) sweet potatoes, peeled and
  thinly sliced
150 g (5 oz) celeriac, finely diced
2 large carrots, finely diced
600 ml (1 pint) beef stock
140 g (4½ oz) tin double concentrate tomato purée
1 glass red wine
Salt and freshly ground pepper

1 Put the beef in a large bowl and add the grated ginger, one tablespoon of olive oil, the garlic, oregano, thyme and flour. Season with salt and pepper. Stir until well coated. Cover with cling film and leave in the fridge for an hour to marinate.

2 Heat the remaining 2 tablespoons of olive oil in a large pan on a medium heat. Add the meat and brown it for about 5 minutes, turning it regularly with a wooden spoon.

3 Add the shallots to the meat and cook together for 5 minutes. Add the carrots and celeriac to the pan with the beef stock, tomato purée and red wine. Bring to the boil and then reduce the heat to low, cover with a lid and simmer for 1 hour. Stir occasionally.

4 Ten minutes before the cooking time is complete, preheat the oven to 190°C (375°F) Gas 5.

5 Carefully cook the sweet potato slices in boiling water for 2 minutes. Don't overcook them. Drain.

6 Transfer the beef hot pot to a large casserole dish. Arrange the sweet potato slices overlapping on top of the beef. Brush with a little olive oil and place in the middle of the oven. Cover with foil and bake for 40 minutes. For the last 15 minutes of cooking time remove the foil. Serve with a green salad.

abcthedgreatebigfveggchallengehijklmnopqr tuvwxyz

Sweet Potato Mash with Caramelised Onion

This combination of flavours earned an 8 out of 10 from Freddie, and confirmed his love for the vegetable.

Serves 4
3 medium sweet potatoes
A knob of butter

Salt and freshly ground pepper
Caramelised onions (see page 188)

1 Preheat the oven to 180°C (350°F) Gas 4.
2 Bake the sweet potatoes for 50 minutes to an hour depending on their size. Bake them in the same way you would a potato.
3 When they are ready, slice open the skin and scoop out the contents into a bowl with a small knob of butter and season with salt and pepper. Mash well. Stir in the caramelised onion and serve immediately.

Sweet potato charmed its way into our kitchen.

T is for... tomato

I know that a tomato is officially a fruit but it's treated like a vegetable so I felt I couldn't not include it. What's more, it probably makes the most well-loved soup around …

Everyone should have a tomato soup memory. My aunt and uncle were responsible for providing me with a whole album full. I would visit them during my school holidays. Maybe children remember things in a different way to adults but I can recall the smell of my aunt's house; a combination of cooking gas and Imperial Leather soap. They had exciting things that we didn't have at home; an Edwardian pianola, variety packs of breakfast cereals and best of all, a pale blue Volkswagen Camper Van. When I wasn't clinging onto the sides of the piano stool, pedaling my way through 'The Toreador', my aunt and uncle would drive us around the country sightseeing in this van. Wherever we were, the routine was the same. I loved that.

Inside the camper van were secret shelves and drawers. The cream formica top in front of my seat would lift up to reveal a little sink with a tap that you pumped up and down to get water, and even more exciting – a Calor gas stove. Wherever we were, my aunt would unpack marmite sandwiches and heat up a tin of tomato soup on the stove. We would park in fields, on hard shoulders and at stately homes. One day she drove us into the centre of London to visit the Science Museum. The camper van was parked right in front of the museum in Exhibition Road. The little gas stove was ignited and the obligatory tin of tomato soup opened. My brother, my aunt and I sat in the camper van, with the slide doors open, sipping our tomato soup from a mug as all the tourists filed past into the museum.

I have passed on this love of creamy tomato soup to my own children. I don't yet have a camper van but on holiday in Cornwall I bought a small gas camping stove. I bought the tomatoes from an honesty box with a difference. On the front door of a house in Lostwithiel, someone had pinned bags of vegetables grown in their garden with an instruction to put the money through the letter box.

I brought the tomatoes home and made my own creamy tomato soup. To make it really smooth, I pushed the soup through a sieve, smoothing the tomato and potato mixture through the metal mesh with a wooden spoon.

And late that evening we all walked up to the top of a hill by the cottage where there is a beautiful view of Lantic Bay. We lit up the

abcthedgreatebigfveggchallengehijklmnopqrs $_t$ uvwxyz

gas stove and heated the tomato soup, which we sipped from mugs, looking out over the sea as the sun went down. One of many tomato soup memories that I hope my children will have forever.

I thought I knew that tomatoes were red, unless of course they were unripe, in which case they are green. But all my certainty disappeared when I went to the supermarket. The tomatoes were competing with the lettuces in the variety stakes. Next to the conventional red ones were crates of yellow, purple, black and green tomatoes. And they boasted their own sign: 'Heirloom Tomatoes'.

Now when I think of heirlooms I imagine grandfather clocks or boxes of old photographs. But these jewels of the tomato world have exquisite names: the glamorous Eva Purple Ball, the exotic Green and Red Zebras, the esoteric Dr Wyche's Yellow and the voluptuous French Marmande. It was a cast of tomatoes that boast good old-fashioned breeding. I politely invited them home to take part in a tomato tasting session.

Inspired by Amanda who blogs about Mediterranean food at 'Figs, Bay, Wine', I prepared Spanish Tomato Toast, or Pan Con Tomate, for everyone. Up until now, Freddie had not eaten raw tomatoes, only consuming them puréed in tomato soups or pasta sauces.

Pan Con Tomate has a great trick up its sleeve: it allows children to take charge of the meal. You simply give them huge tranches of toasted country bread, a little dish of olive oil, halved cloves of garlic, a little sea salt and a selection of ripe tomatoes cut in half.

Freddie didn't even recognise half of them as tomatoes with their mottled black, yellow and purple skins. Strictly speaking, tomatoes are fruit, not vegetables, and eaten like this you can see why. They are sweet and delectable. Freddie and Alexandra squeezed, squelched and drizzled their way through plates of well-bred tomatoes. Freddie was creative with his scoring. 'Its 10 out of 10 as a way of getting people interested in eating raw tomatoes and about 7 out of 10 for taste.'

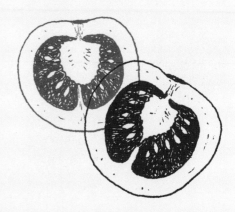

Creamy Tomato Soup

Even without a VW camper van, this delicious soup can transport me back to happy childhood memories.

Serves 4
900 g (2 lb) ripe tomatoes
2 tbsp olive oil
1 medium potato, peeled and finely diced
1 small onion, sliced
1 clove of garlic, crushed

1 tsp ground paprika
4 tbsp tomato purée
1 tsp caster sugar
750 ml (1¼ pints) chicken or vegetable stock
200 ml (7 fl oz) single cream or reduced-fat cream
Salt and freshly ground pepper

1 Bring a large pan of water to the boil. Add the whole tomatoes. Turn off the heat and allow to sit for a few minutes. The skins of the tomatoes will split. Drain them and peel off the skins. Chop the skinned tomatoes.

2 Heat the olive oil in a large pan on a medium-low heat. Add the potato, onion and garlic and sauté for 3 minutes until the onion and potato have softened. Don't allow it to burn.

3 Add the paprika, tomatoes, tomato purée, caster sugar and stock. Bring to the boil, stirring well. Then lower the heat and allow to simmer for 20 minutes.

4 Remove from the heat and using a wooden spoon, smooth the soup through a sieve. If you prefer, purée in a food processor or hand-blender. Return to the pan and add the cream, stirring over a low heat. Season and serve.

abcthedgreatebigfveggchallengehijklmnopqrs_tuvwxyz

Pan Con Tomate

This is a traditional Catalan dish and is so simple. The garlic-smeared bread is the perfect foil for all sorts of ripe and colourful tomatoes. (See www.figsbaywine.blogspot.com)

Serves 4
1 large loaf of crusty country bread or ciabatta
Extra virgin olive oil
3 large ripe tomatoes, cut into quarters

4 cloves of garlic, peeled and halved
Sea salt
Serrano ham (optional)

1 Cut the bread lengthways to make long slices. Toast both sides under the grill.
2 For each person, arrange a little dish of olive oil, a few halved garlic cloves and some quarters of ripe juicy tomatoes and a few flakes of sea salt. You can add slices of Spanish Serrano ham if you like. Everyone can rub their toast with garlic, ripe tomato flesh, sprinkle a little salt and drizzle it with olive oil.

tip

Like the League of Lettuce, tomato bread-tasting is a good way of encouraging children to try out the taste of raw tomatoes. Children enjoy meals where they can assemble their own dish of food. The tomatoes are best eaten in season in the summer when they are at their sweetest. They are also easy to grow in containers or tomato bags, even if you only have a small patio or balcony. In the days when Freddie refused to eat vegetables, I always felt it was good that he at least enjoyed growing them for the family.

Fresh Tomato Sauce

If you have heard about the invisibility cloak in *Harry Potter*, this pasta sauce has the same qualities. Under the cover of fresh tomato, interlopers such as celery, carrot and courgette can hide, unnoticed.

Serves 4 as a pasta sauce
1 tbsp of olive oil
1 medium onion, finely chopped
1 large celery stalk, finely chopped
1 large carrot, peeled and finely chopped
1 courgette, finely chopped

2 cloves of garlic, crushed
1 kg (2 lb) tomatoes, skinned
1 tbsp sugar
A generous bunch of basil leaves
Freshly grated Parmesan cheese, to serve

1 Heat the oil and gently sauté the onion, celery, carrot, courgette and garlic for about 3 minutes. Add the tomatoes with the sugar and some salt and pepper to taste.

2 On a medium-low heat, simmer and stir for around 5 minutes or until the vegetables are softened. Add the chopped basil leaves.

3 Remove from the heat and use a hand-blender or food processor to blend into a smooth sauce. Serve with pasta and Parmesan cheese.

T is for... TURNIPS

Before we started on turnips, we had to clear up some confusion. Are turnips different to swedes? After consulting several gardeners I was told that the swede is in fact a Swedish turnip, known in America as rutabaga.

To add to the confusion, in Scotland the swede is often referred to as a turnip or neep. According to Marwood Yeatman in his book, *The Last Food of England* (2007), swedes are 'the product of an accidental cross with cabbage' and arrived in England in the 18th century. Freddie and Alex were relieved as this means we felt we could deal with swede turnips at the same time as any other turnips: two for the price of one. Freddie and I went to the supermarket to buy our turnips. We took a strong hessian bag and planned to take the bus back home. We were thinking big.

The first 10 years of my childhood were spent in Scotland. At Halloween, we would buy large 'neeps' from the grocers and carry them home in our bike baskets. My father would slice off the tops and scoop out the hard flesh, cutting out eyes, a nose and mouth.

My mother would cook this with potato to make 'tatties and neeps.' Dad threaded a wire through the turnip and hooked it on to a stick. We walked around the garden in the dark, scaring ourselves with turnip lanterns.

When we eventually found our turnips, Freddie and I were a little taken aback. These were dainty little creatures, with pale skin and a tinge of purple around the top and they were small enough to fit in the palm of Freddie's hand. We bought a bag full. Next to them were the larger, dark yellow swedes. Even they looked small compared with the cannon balls I remember as a child.

For our first turnip I used the swede. Freddie had tried swede before and hadn't liked it. So I had to be clever about this. I cut the swede into thin sticks, like French fries, tossed them in olive oil and a little sea salt and baked them in the oven for 20 minutes.

There is a point every evening, about 20 minutes before supper is ready, when the children come in and start looking for snacks. I shoo them out of the kitchen. They distract me and sneak back into the cupboards to find biscuits.

But that night I made the swede fries, arranged them in a ramekin and left them on the kitchen table. At snacking time, Alex and Freddie came in. They scurried around like mice looking for scraps and discovered the swede fries. Freddie thought they were potato fries. I said nothing and pretended not to notice. When they were finished I asked him for his score. 'Those were made from swede?' said Freddie. 'That is definitely 10 out of 10.' It clearly works to serve your vegetables as if they were fast food.

The night after our successful swede fries, I turned to the small white turnips with their bright purple tops. When the children were younger we used to read them a story about a gigantic turnip. It involved a long cast of characters pulling an enormous turnip out of the ground. Freddie always used to worry about how the farmer and his family were going to finish all that turnip. I felt a little like that when I looked at my bag of small turnips.

I promised to try and make these miniature versions as appetising as possible. I combined them with shallots, which look like little onions with a tapered end. In fact they are a species of their own. They belong to the allium family which include garlic, leeks, chives and, of course, onions. Shallots taste like a cross between a sweet onion and garlic. The turnips and shallots were combined with sprigs of thyme and cloves of garlic in a deep baking tray and roasted in the oven. Nothing was going to live up to the high-scoring swede fries but our miniature turnips, served with salmon fillets, were given 7 out of 10.

tip

The best-tasting turnips are the smaller ones and they don't need to be peeled. Older, larger turnips should be peeled before cooking. You can cook and eat the turnip leaves. Try them steamed or boiled or add to a stir-fry. Try cutting your swede or turnips into cubes, boiling it until tender and combining it in a mash with other root vegetables like potatoes, sweet potatoes, celeriac or carrots.

Oven-baked Swede Fries

Disguised as French fries, the children devoured these swede nibbles in minutes.

Serves 4 as a side dish
2 swedes or rutabaga
2–3 tbsp olive oil

1 tsp sea salt
A handful of fresh thyme sprigs, chopped

1 Preheat the oven to 200°C (400°F) Gas 6.

2 Peel the swedes and cut in half. Slice each half into even slices, 1.5 cm (3/4 in.) thick. Then slice those into sticks, like French fries.

3 Place them on a baking tray and add the olive oil. Mix around with your hands so that the swede sticks are well-coated. Sprinkle the sea salt over evenly with the thyme. Place in the oven and bake for approximately 20 minutes. Halfway through cooking, turn the sticks so that both sides cook. Take care to make sure the fries become crispy but do not burn. Serve hot with some ketchup for dipping.

It clearly works to serve your vegetables as if they were fast food.

Roast Turnips with Shallots and Thyme

We enjoyed this with salmon fillets, but they would also complement a roast or lamb chops.

Serves 4 as a side dish
750 g (1¼ lb) small turnips, halved or quartered
300 g (10 oz) shallots, peeled and halved
5 cloves of garlic

A handful of fresh thyme sprigs, chopped
½ tsp sea salt
1 tbsp olive oil

1 Preheat the oven to 180°C (350°F) Gas 4.

2 Put the turnips, shallots, whole cloves of garlic in their skins and thyme in a deep-sided roasting or baking tray. Add the olive oil and mix round with your hands to make sure everything is well covered. Sprinkle with sea salt.

3 Place in the oven and cook for about 40–45 minutes, until the turnips are golden brown and tender inside. Halfway through cooking, turn them over so that they cook evenly.

4 When they are cooked and ready to eat, pick out the garlic cloves and squeeze the soft roasted garlic out and mix it around to flavour the turnips and shallots. Serve immediately.

abcthedgreatebigfveggchallengehijklmnopqrs t uvwxyz

Tatties and Neeps

As children, my Mum made us this simple recipe for tatties and neeps. On Burns Night, we would eat it with haggis and with sausages at other times of the year.

Serves 4
625 g (1¹/₄ lb) floury potatoes (Maris Piper, King Edwards, Desiree), peeled and cubed
625 g (1¹/₄ lb) swede, peeled and cubed

50 g (2 oz) butter
A pinch of grated nutmeg
Salt and freshly ground pepper

1 Put the potato and swede in a large pan of water. Bring to the boil and simmer for about 20–30 minutes until the swede and potato are tender.
2 Drain well. Add the butter and mash until smooth. Add a pinch of grated nutmeg and season with a little salt and ground pepper.

When the children were younger we used to read them a story about a gigantic turnip. Freddie always used to worry about how the farmer and his family were going to finish all that turnip. I felt a little like that when I looked at my bag of small turnips.

V is for Vegetable Kebabs

Each year we measure the success of the spring and summer by counting how many days it was warm enough to eat outdoors. As a family we are easily pleased, willing to set up a picnic in a chill wind or risk trekking out into a field even though the skies are turning grey.

We argue about most things; what to watch on television, who finished the biscuits, what flavour of ice cream to buy; but when it comes to eating outdoors we are all addicted.

With the Great Big Vegetable Challenge well established, vegetable kebabs replaced sausage rolls and ham sandwiches and became a new feature of our picnics. Freddie's favourite, which scored 10 out of 10, is Lamb and Artichoke Kebabs. Alex is our chief kebab maker, creating the mushroom and halloumi cheese skewers. Halloumi is traditionally made from ewes' or goats' milk. Jammed up against different sorts of mushrooms and brushed with teriyaki sauce, these were delicious.

For the mixed vegetable kebabs, use your favourite vegetables and marinade for at least 2 hours, even overnight if you can plan ahead. Then wait for the sky to turn a menacing slate grey, pick up a disposable barbecue and head outdoors! Alternatively, all of these kebabs work well indoors cooked under the grill.

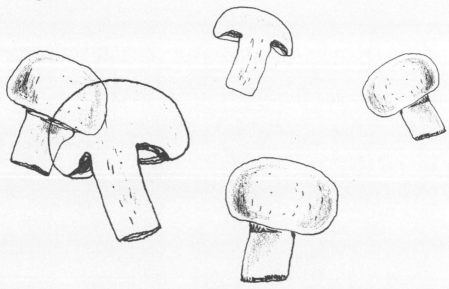

Lamb and Artichoke Kebabs

Combining a hearty helping of red meat with one of Freddie's new-found fave vegetables, made this an instant hit.

Serves 4
625 g (1¼ lb) lamb neck fillet, cut into 4-cm (1¾-in.) cubes
400 g (13 oz) tin of artichoke hearts, drained and halved

2 tbsp olive oil
1 clove of garlic, crushed
2 tbsp fresh rosemary
Salt and freshly ground pepper

6–8 wooden skewers, soaked in water for 30 minutes

1 Put the lamb and artichokes in a bowl and add the olive oil, garlic, rosemary and season with salt and pepper. Mix so that everything is well coated, cover with cling film and marinate for 1 hour.

2 Thread the lamb and artichoke pieces onto the skewers. Brush with any remaining marinade. Cook on a barbecue or under a hot grill, turning frequently until the meat is well cooked.

Mushroom and Halloumi Skewers

In Lebanon, halloumi is known as kebab cheese as the outside browns and crisps whilst the centre melts.

Serves 4
2 tbsp sesame oil or olive oil
1 clove of garlic, crushed
2 tbsp teriyaki sauce
250 g (8 oz) halloumi cheese, cut into 3-cm
   (1½-in.) cubes

12 chestnut mushrooms
12 button mushrooms
125 g (4 oz) Shitake mushrooms

6–8 wooden skewers, soaked in water for 30 minutes

1 In a bowl, mix the oil, garlic and sauce. Add the mushrooms and cheese, cover with cling film and marinate for 1 hour.
2 Thread alternate pieces of cheese and whole mushrooms onto a skewer. Brush with any remaining marinade. Place the skewers under a hot grill or on a barbecue, turning regularly for about 5–6 minutes.

Wait for the sky to turn a menacing slate grey, pick up a disposable barbecue and head outdoors!

Mixed Vegetable Kebabs

These colourful kebabs can be made with any combination of your favourite vegetables.

Serves 4
2 cobs of sweetcorn
1 red pepper
1 yellow pepper
2 courgettes
8 small button mushrooms
8 cherry tomatoes

3 tbsp olive oil
1 clove of garlic, crushed
3 tbsp chopped fresh basil
2 tbsp freshly squeezed lemon juice
1 tbsp Dijon mustard
1 tbsp white wine vinegar
Salt and freshly ground pepper

6–8 wooden skewers, soaked in water for 30 minutes

1 Cut each sweetcorn cob into 8 pieces. Halve and deseed the peppers and cut into 2.5-cm (1-in.) strips. Cut the courgettes into 2.5-cm (1-in.) slices. Halve the mushrooms. Leave the cherry tomatoes whole.

2 Make the marinade in a large bowl, mixing together the oil, garlic, fresh basil, lemon juice, Dijon mustard and white wine vinegar. Season.

3 Add the vegetables and mix together really well so that everything is evenly coated. Cover the bowl with cling film and place in the fridge to marinate for 2 hours.

4 Thread the different vegetables onto the wooden skewers. Brush with the remaining marinade. Put onto the barbecue or under a hot grill and cook for about 10–12 minutes. Turn regularly and brush with the marinade until the vegetables are gently browned and ready to eat.

W
is for

When we reached W, we drove south to visit the watercress beds at the village of Abinger Hammer in Surrey. Watercress is a semi-aquatic plant and a member of the mustard family. Its proper botanical name is *Nasturtium officinale*. In Latin this means something that twists or tortures the nostrils.

Watercress has been cultivated since Roman times but the first recorded watercress farm in England dates back to 1808. There is a stream of chalk that runs through England, threading up to Lincolnshire. This chalk acts like a giant sponge, holding water which breaks out and comes to the surface. Wherever there was this bountiful supply of pure spring water, watercress farms started to appear.

Barrie Arminson has been growing watercress at Kingfisher Farm for over 50 years. There have been beds on the site since 1850, when the farmer dug a deep bore hole to tap into a sand bed, releasing a source of pure spring water. Over 150 years later the cultivation of watercress has hardly changed. Barrie showed Freddie around the long rectangular gravel beds where the watercress swirls, flushed by this constant fresh supply of spring water. These beds yield a million bunches of watercress each year. Together they hand cut some watercress and bunched it up. It is impossible not to enjoy watercress once you have seen it growing in these bright green beds. Over the months of the Great Big Vegetable Challenge, Freddie had developed an unexpected taste for strong-tasting green-leafed vegetables; Savoy cabbage, rocket and spinach became favourites. Now it was the turn of watercress to be sampled. Freddie and Alex enjoyed its peppery bite.

We took an autumn picnic with us, featuring watercress. On the village green we ate Watercress and Mozzarella Quesadillas, which Freddie scored 9 out of 10. The Red Leicester and Watercress Calzone scored the same but the triumph was the Watercress, Potato and Pea Soup which they drank from a thermos flask. This earned the maximum 10 out of 10. Watercress might be nose-twisting but that didn't deter Freddie.

tip

Watercress perishes easily so only buy it if the leaves look deep green, crisp and fresh. Keep in a refrigerator in a plastic bag. Or you can put the stems in a glass of water, the leaves covered very loosely by a plastic bag. Use within a few days, preferably the same day so that it is at its freshest. Wash and shake dry before eating.

Watercress Quesadillas with Mozzarella and Pine Nuts

Wrapped up with creamy mozzarella and crunchy pine nuts, the peppery watercress can be tamed and enjoyed.

Makes 1 quesadilla
15 g (½ oz) pine nuts
1 tortilla wrap
75 g (3 oz) mozzarella cheese, thinly sliced

25 g (1 oz) watercress, roughly chopped
Cooking spray oil
Salt and freshly ground pepper

1 Toast the pine nuts by heating up a small pan on a medium heat, sprinkle on the pine nuts and stir them around constantly for a minute or so until lightly browned.

2 Spray a large non-stick frying pan with a little cooking oil. Heat on a medium heat and put a tortilla in the pan, and turn over a few times with a fish slice. It will bubble up slightly.

3 First, scatter the mozzarella cheese evenly over the surface of the tortilla. Add the watercress and then the pine nuts. A quesadilla should be quite flat so don't overdo the filling. Then using the fish slice, carefully fold the tortilla in half so that the two edges match up with the filling in the middle. Gently press down so that the melting cheese sticks the tortilla together.

4 Turn over to cook the other side. Don't let the tortilla burn. Flip it over so that each side becomes a crisp golden brown. Serve with a little green salad or with soup.

tip
If you find watercress too peppery, you can substitute baby spinach leaves.

Watercress Mash with Baked Chicken

With the watercress we cut at Kingfisher Farm, I made a mash with potato and sweet potato and served it with baked chicken. For children who find watercress too peppery, they might prefer it combined with a mash. Freddie gave this 8 out of 10.

Serves 4–6
For the Watercress Mash
4 large floury potatoes (Maris Piper or Desiree), peeled and diced
1 large sweet potato, peeled and diced

A knob of butter
115 g (3½ oz) watercress, washed, dried and chopped
1 tbsp crème fraîche
Salt and freshly ground pepper

1 Put the potatoes and sweet potatoes in a pan of boiling water. Simmer until they are soft but not mushy. Drain well.

2 Mash the potatoes with a knob of butter and a spoonful of crème fraîche. Add the watercress to the mash and stir in well. Season with a little salt and pepper. Serve immediately with baked chicken.

For the Baked Chicken with Ginger and Spring Onions
2 tbsp freshly grated ginger
5 spring onions, finely chopped
2 cloves of garlic, crushed

1–2 tbsp olive oil
1 tsp mustard powder
8 chicken thighs
Salt and freshly ground pepper

1 Mix the ginger, spring onions and garlic together in a large bowl, with the olive oil and mustard powder. Add the chicken thighs and stir until the chicken is well-coated in the marinade. Cover with cling film and leave to marinate in a cool place for 2 hours.

2 Preheat the oven to 200°C (400°F) Gas 6.

3 Put the chicken thighs in a baking tray and bake in a preheated oven for 50 minutes. Serve with the watercress mash.

Watercress, Potato and Red Leicester Calzone

This calzone recipe was inspired by recipes at the website of the watercress alliance which has lots of good ideas for using watercress. (www.watercress.co.uk)

Makes 4 calzone
300 g (10 oz) pizza base mix
1 large potato, peeled and diced
Vegetable stock cube

115 g (3½ oz) watercress, washed, dried and chopped
125 g (4 oz) Red Leicester cheese, grated
Salt and freshly ground pepper

1 Preheat the oven to 220°C (425°F) Gas 7 and make the pizza base mix according to the packet instructions. Knead the dough and divide into four equal pieces.
2 Boil the potato for about 4 minutes with a few crumbs of a vegetable stock cube crumbled into the water for flavour. Cook until tender, but not mushy. Drain well.
3 Add the chopped watercress to the drained potato and put the lid on the pan. Allow the heat from the cooked potato to wilt the watercress for a few minutes.
4 Flour a clean surface and roll out each piece of dough into a 23-cm (9-in.) diameter circle. On one side of each circle of dough, spoon some potato, watercress and Red Leicester. Season with a little salt and ground pepper. Don't put the filling too near the edge. Using your finger tips or a pastry brush dipped in water, slightly dampen round the circumference of the dough. Fold the dough over the side that is piled with the filling, matching up the two edges. Seal the edges firmly together by pinching and twisting the dough together. Twist the dough into a little point at each corner.
5 Dust a baking sheet with flour and place the calzone on top. Bake in the oven for about 12–15 minutes. When ready, the calzone are very lightly browned. Take care when serving, especially with children as the calzone can be piping hot inside.

tip
If you are feeding smaller children you can divide the dough into six or eight pieces to make mini-calzone. These are great warm from the oven but can also be taken on picnics or used for school lunchboxes.

Freddie's Favourite 10/10

Watercress, Potato and Pea Soup

Having overcome his fear of peas, this soup combines their flavour and colour with the watercress to come out on top.

Serves 4

2 large potatoes, peeled and cut into small cubes
1 large onion, finely sliced
1 tbsp olive oil
900 ml (1½ pints) chicken or vegetable stock

1 tbsp apple balsamic vinegar or cider vinegar
175 g (6 oz) watercress, washed, dried and
 finely chopped
115 g (3½ oz) fresh or frozen peas
142 ml (4½ fl oz) carton of single cream

1 Sauté the potatoes and onions in the olive oil in a large pan on a medium heat for about 8 minutes, until the potatoes are softened and the onions translucent.
2 Add the stock and vinegar and bring to boiling point. Turn down the heat to low and simmer with the lid on for 5 minutes.
3 Add the watercress and peas and simmer for another 15 minutes.
4 Remove from the heat and allow to cool a little. Using a hand-blender or food processor, blend the soup until smooth. Return to the pan and stir in the cream. Warm through without boiling and serve.

Y is for yams

There is a stall in our local market that sells exotic fruit and vegetables. On our first visit it was like visiting a zoo and not being able to recognise any of the animals. But after months and months of cooking vegetables, they were no longer strangers.

Freddie was circling the stall pointing at each vegetable saying, 'I've eaten that', 'Tried that', 'Hated that', 'Loved that.' Children have always enjoyed collecting football cards, stamps or sticker books. This market stall had become his own personal vegetable collection.

Freddie stopped at one huge pen of vegetables and called me over. There was tray after tray of huge boulders; a Jurassic Park of vegetables. They looked like nests of dinosaur eggs and Freddie was in awe. The price label said yams. On sale were Cocoa yams, white yams from Ghana, yellow yams, gigantic yams labelled Puna yams and Brazil soft yams, oozing sticky white milk. We wondered if they might hatch if we took them home.

I dithered over what to buy, my confidence waning. Freddie picked up one of the biggest boulders with skin like tree bark. It was time to employ some of my investigative skills honed throughout the Great Big Vegetable Challenge. Approaching strangers is one technique. It takes fearlessness, optimism and rhino-thick skin. This is vegetable cold-calling. I sidled up to a woman in the local fruit and vegetable market. The position is crucial. I leant against a huge wooden tray of yams.

'It is warm today isn't it?' I commented. The weather is usually a good starting point.

She looked at me, smiled nervously and ran off. I waited for another victim.

'Glad there is a bit of sunshine today,' I commented.

'Yes, but on the radio they say it's going to turn cold tomorrow,' answered my prey.

'That's why I am buying some yams. I want to make a nice warm stew.' I am nervous. Will my target take the bait?

'I was just thinking that yams are what I need right now. You know, they boost your immune system,' said my prey. It was too easy. I quizzed her on cooking techniques and how to prepare the different varieties.

'Are you feeding a lot of people?' she asked.

'No, just the four of us.'

'Well, if you want to use it to put in a beef stew, then buy white yams. They can be a little bit hard but they are good in a stew. The easiest thing is to make mash. But if you want to make a really soft mash that little children will like, try the soft yam,' she advised, pointing at the yam oozing white milk.

Yams can be used like potatoes or sweet potatoes. In America, sweet potatoes are often called yams but they aren't related. I have tasted them before, cooked by my friend Grace. We met up at church. As Freddie kicked a ball about with her son Delassi, she taught me more about yams. Grace grew up on the south coast of Ghana, her family belonging to the Ewe tribe. By the age of 10 she had learnt how to cook by watching and helping her mother and aunt. Grace explained that yams cook far quicker than potatoes. You can mash them, make yam porridge, deep-fry them or chop them up and use them in meat and fish stews. She advised me not to add the diced yams until later on in the recipe so that they wouldn't overcook. That evening we made our first Beef and Yam Stew, using fresh ginger, garlic and ground cloves. Freddie and Alex enjoyed their warm beef stew and they liked the crisp texture of the white yams. Freddie scored the stew 8 out of 10.

The following day we had yams for breakfast. We used the soft yam. When I cut into it and peeled it, it became very sticky and moist. I grated it into a bowl. By now the yam was soft and sticky and clung together. It was as if some kind of chemical reaction was underway. The yam rapidly turns an unpleasant grey colour if you don't add some lemon juice. Using a tea towel, I squeezed some of the moisture out of the grated yam and spooned it into little mounds to fry as rosti. They need to be seasoned with some salt and pepper as yam does not have a very strong taste of its own. Freddie and Alex, who have tasted rosti made from potato and sweet potato, thought the yams were just as good. They earned 9 out of 10.

tip

The yam is the swollen underground stem tuber of a sprawling vine. Each variety of yam differs in its texture, sweetness and moistness. The skin should be peeled and boiled before eating, apparently to destroy some poisonous oxalic acid present just beneath the skin. My friends, who regularly cook yams, don't seem bothered by this but it's probably a good idea to peel and boil all the same.

If you are buying yams from a market stall, you buy by weight. Pick a yam that doesn't look too wrinkly with firm skin. The stall holder will chop off a section of the yam for you depending on how much you want. Check that the flesh is nice and white without brown spots running through it.

Beef and Yam Stew

Yams do not have a strong flavour and are better if they can soak up the flavours of meat and spices.

Serves 4

1 large onion, chopped
3 cloves of garlic
½ tsp ground cloves
½ tsp ground cinnamon
½ tsp mild chilli powder
25 g (1 oz) freshly grated ginger

2–3 tbsp vegetable oil
500 g (1 lb) stewing steak, cubed
1 large carrot, finely diced
500 g (1 lb) carton of tomato purée or passata
400 g (13 oz) tin of chopped tomatoes
400 g (13 oz) white yam
Salt and freshly ground pepper

1 Put the onion in a food processor with the garlic cloves, spices and ginger. Blend together.

2 In a large pan, heat two tablespoons of oil and add the cubed stewing steak, browning the meat for 3 minutes, stirring with a wooden spoon. Add the onion and ginger mixture and stir into the meat. Cook for 10 minutes, stirring frequently. If the meat is very lean, you may want to add another tablespoon of oil to the pan.

3 Add the carrot with the tomato purée or passata. Reduce the heat to medium low and simmer for 10 minutes, so the sauce reduces. Stir occasionally.

4 Add the tin of tomatoes and stir in. Simmer for another 10 minutes, stirring every now and again.

5 Peel the yam and rinse it well under water. Cut into small cubes. Add to the pan and stir. Cook for another 15 minutes. Serve with rice or flat bread.

tip

If you like, you can substitute the yam in this recipe for another root vegetable, such as sweet potato or potatoes. They will need to be introduced into the recipe earlier on to give them enough time to cook properly, as yams cook very quickly.

abcthedgreatebigfveggchallengehijklmnopqrstuvwx^yz

Yam Rosti with Poached Eggs

It's not often that you can introduce vegetables at breakfast, but a rosti with poached egg is a great way to start the day.

Serves 4
450 g (14¹/₂ oz) yam, peeled and grated
Freshly squeezed juice of ¹/₂ lemon

2 tbsp olive oil or knob of butter, to fry
4 eggs, poached
Salt and freshly ground pepper

1 You will need to squeeze some lemon juice into the grated yam as it discolours very quickly. Using a clean tea towel, squeeze the moisture out of the grated yam. Add some salt and freshly ground pepper. Stir together.

2 Heat the olive oil or butter in a large frying pan. Put four tablespoons of grated yam spaced apart in the pan. Carefully flatten them down with a fish slice. Fry for 1–2 minutes. Use a fish slice to turn over each rosti. Make sure both sides are golden brown and crisp.

3 Keep the cooked rosti warm in a dish in a low oven while you cook the remainder.

4 Serve with a poached or, if you prefer, a fried egg on top.

tip

Different kinds of yams will have a slightly different texture. The soft yams work well because they stick together well as you fry them. But it works just as well with a normal white yam. Traditionally, rosti are made from potatoes. But there is no reason why other root vegetables can't be prepared in this way. You can combine potato with grated beetroot or carrot and sweet potato. Add a little paprika or mild chilli powder for flavour. Or add some dried herbs, crushed garlic or grated onion.

Freddie's Favourite 10/10

Cinnamon Yam Mash

This recipe is very simple but Freddie loved its taste and texture which he described as 'floury'. This is good with sausages, lamb or pork chops or you can serve it with the Beef Stew recipe (page 304), having the yams in a mash rather than in the stew. If you want, you can substitute sweet potatoes or potatoes.

Serves 4–5
1 kg (2 lb) white yam, peeled
Freshly squeezed juice of ½ lemon
150 ml (¼ pint) milk

A generous knob of butter
½ tsp ground cinnamon
Salt

1 Rinse the peeled yam well. Chop into smaller chunks and add to a pan of water with the lemon juice. This will help to prevent discolouration. Bring the pan of water to the boil. Turn the heat down to medium and allow it to simmer for 25–30 minutes or until you can easily pass a skewer through the yam and it is soft.
2 Drain well and then mash, adding the milk, butter and ground cinnamon. Season with a little salt according to taste.

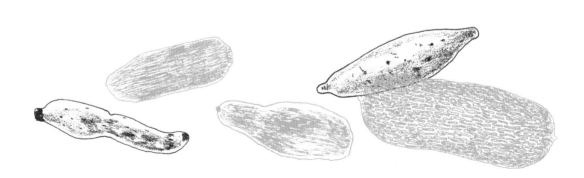

Freddie was a powerful adversary for The Great Big Veg Challenge - there had to be something he would like. As it turns out, there was.

Z IS FOR Zucchini

an American courgette

'What we call the beginning is often the end. And to make an end is to make a beginning.' (TS Eliot)

The finale of the Great Big Vegetable Challenge came suddenly. As we travelled to the very end of the alphabet, vegetables became scarce. We had to leapfrog over U, V and X, until we arrived at the letter Z, the full stop for our adventure. We sat mournfully around the kitchen table and discussed what we should do.

'I loved it like this, trying all these new vegetables. I want it to carry on,' said Alex.

'At least we won't have to wait until you have photographed each meal before we can eat it,' said Chris, trying to lift the mood.

'I was thinking it would stop halfway through – that you would give up,' said Freddie. 'Why don't we have a party to celebrate reaching the end of the alphabet?'

So we held a Z for Zucchini party. Zucchini was the only Z vegetable we could find and a bit of a cheat, having already tried it under its English alter ego, the courgette. From California, a fellow blogger Garrett, created a zucchini muffin recipe for Freddie. I made Zucchini Turkey Burgers and Leeky Sausage Rolls. Alex and Freddie chose their favourite vegetable recipes from our year of eating adventurously and invited some friends round. We made Courgette Quesadillas, Petit Pois Muffins, Herby Burgers, Artichoke Pizzas, Asparagus Twists, Vegetable Kebabs and the delicious Beetroot and Chocolate Cake.

We decorated the kitchen with vegetables. Artichokes, radishes, corn cobs and aubergines hung from strings around the room, looking like the signal flags on a ship. From the look on some of the children's faces, they might have spelt out 'SOS!'.

At most kids' parties, parents offer carrot sticks or cherry tomatoes as a nod to healthy eating. They are normally ignored and thrown away. But at this party, the vegetables were the stars. Those with a fear of vegetables were entering enemy territory. There was a table full of food, but would they denounce it as fake party food? There were no cheesy wotsits, no bowls of iced gems or sausages on sticks. A year before and the sight of all these vegetables would have made Freddie swoon. But he reassured his guests and recommended his favourite food. He had become a vegetable ambassador.

Before long, Eleanor and Jack were enjoying Leeky Sausage Rolls, Molly and Esme were munching their way through a mound of

Artichoke Kebabs and Bertie was biting into Zucchini Burgers. Alex and Elizabeth demolished a plate of Asparagus Twists. They played 'Name that Veg', identifying all the weird and wonderful vegetables hanging from the ceiling. I stood at the oven, flipping over zucchini burgers and taking orders for more quesadillas. The mound of food disappeared, along with my nervousness. Instead of party bags, Freddie handed out vegetables with recipes attached; an invitation to join his adventure.

And fuelled by a final slice of Beetroot and Chocolate Cake, they all ran off to the park and played football until the light started to fade. We traipsed home, slumped down in front of the television and put our feet up.

'What's for dinner Mum?' asked Freddie. And that is how The Great Big Vegetable Challenge came to an end. Except it isn't really an end but a new beginning.

Zucchini Turkey Burgers

Zucchini, as courgette is known in international circles, put in a final appearance in these burgers which were heartily enjoyed at our vegetable celebration.

Makes 18 mini burgers
250 g (8 oz) zucchini (courgette), finely grated
500 g (1 lb) turkey mince
½ tsp ground turmeric

½ tsp ground paprika
1 clove of garlic, crushed
Cooking spray oil
18 mini burger buns or mini panini

Ridged griddle pan

1 In a bowl, mix together the finely grated zucchini, turkey mince, turmeric, paprika and crushed garlic. The easiest method is to use your hands to do this.
2 Shape the mixture into small balls that fit in the palm of your hand. Flatten them slightly to make a burger. Making them small is perfect for parties.
3 Lightly spray a griddle pan or large flat frying pan with oil and heat to medium high. When the griddle is hot, place the burgers in the pan. Cook them for at least 3 minutes each side, turning them over carefully with a fish slice. When the meat is cooked through, serve in a mini burger bun.

tip

You can use grilled red peppers and mozzarella to give the burgers extra colour and flavour. Grill some red peppers until the skins are blackened. Rub off the skins under cold running water. Using a cookie cutter, cut out small rounds of red pepper flesh or cut out heart shapes. Slice some mozzarella and cut out a round with a cookie cutter. Put the red pepper and mozzarella on top of a hot burger and serve.

Leeky Zucchini Sausage Rolls

Classic party food can be given a healthy twist with a sneaky vegetable or two.

Makes 20 small sausage rolls
375 g (12 oz) ready-rolled puff pastry
1 small leek
1 medium courgette

450 g (14½ oz) pork sausage meat
1 tsp dried sage
1 egg, beaten

1 Preheat the oven to 200°C (400°F) Gas 6.

2 Roll out the puff pastry into a large rectangle. Cut in half lengthways so that you have two long rectangles.

3 Remove the tough outer leaves of the leek and trim top and bottom. It is important to slice the leek very finely, chopping those slices into even smaller bits.

4 Chop off the stalk end of the courgette. Finely grate and then squeeze out any excess moisture with your hands.

5 In a bowl, with clean hands, mix together the sausage meat, sage, chopped leek and grated courgette.

6 Divide the mixture in half and roll each part into a long even-shaped sausage, the same length as your pastry rectangles.

7 Place the sausage along the length of the pastry rectangle and fold the pastry over so that it covers the sausage meat. Seal the sides together firmly so that it doesn't split open when cooking.

8 Repeat with the other half of the sausage meat and pastry rectangle. Brush beaten egg over the pastry to give it a golden glaze.

9 Cut each of the pastry rolls into 10 little sausage rolls. Place on a baking tray and bake in the middle of the oven for about 25 minutes. Halfway through, turn the baking tray around so that they cook evenly. The pastry will have risen and be golden brown. The sausage meat must be properly cooked through. Serve hot or cold.

Zucchini and Raisin Muffins

This recipe was adapted from a recipe by Garrett from the Vanilla Garlic blog. (See www.vanillagarlic.blogspot.com)

Makes 18–20 muffins
375 g (12 oz) plain flour
3 tsp baking powder
275 g (9 oz) dark muscovado sugar
2 tsp ground cinnamon
115 g (3½ oz) butter, melted

4 eggs
1 tsp vanilla essence
150 ml (¼ pint) apple juice
115 g (3½ oz) raisins
200 g (7 oz) zucchini (courgette), finely grated

12-hole muffin tins lined with paper muffin cases (these are larger than standard cake cases)

1 Preheat the oven to 180°C (350°F) Gas 4.

2 In a large bowl, mix together the flour, baking powder, sugar and cinnamon. Make a well in the centre.

3 Allow the melted butter to cool slightly. In a smaller bowl, whisk together the melted butter, eggs and vanilla essence. Add to the flour and stir well until it is evenly combined.

4 Add the apple juice and stir, then stir in the raisins and grated zucchini. Spoon the batter into paper cases in a muffin baking tray. They should be about half-full.

5 Bake in a preheated oven for between 20–25 minutes. Halfway through cooking time, turn the baking tray around so that they cook more evenly. To test if they are ready, push a clean skewer or wooden cocktail stick into the centre. If it comes out clean, the muffins are ready. Leave to cool in the tin for a few minutes before turning out onto a wire rack to cool completely.

Conclusion

'Until we have learned to explore, our tastes are so limited, our experience is so narrow, that we can make no valid comparisons, can found no true judgements. So it is with food. We must learn to eat first.' (The Robert Carrier Cookbook)

If learning to eat is such a basic skill, why is it that so many of us have children who are fussy-eaters? As a Mum I started to write the the Great Big Vegetable Challenge blog because I couldn't work out where I was going wrong. Why would five peas (or any other vegetable) provoke a tantrum? How could I change my vegetable-phobic son? What I hadn't realised then, is what Robert Carrier explains so clearly. As a child, you can't learn to eat or to taste unless you have learned to explore.

For Freddie and the rest of our family, the Great Big Vegetable Challenge has been an adventure, an exploration of vegetables. We have tried out recipes and cooking tips left on the blog by people from all over the world. I learnt about mushrooms in the school queue, about sorrel whilst sitting on a river bank, discussed okra at the butchers and carrots whilst standing in the queue for a bus.

Another thing that I learnt was that change takes time. When we embarked on the Challenge, Freddie's experience of eating vegetables was limited to potatoes and sweetcorn. Everything else would cause him to panic. My attempts at introducing him to new tastes were short-lived. I would take his rejections personally and give up, going back to the default position of feeding him in rotation, peas, carrots and broccoli. He would in turn reject peas, carrots and broccoli. It was vegetable stalemate.

Eating through the alphabet of vegetables enabled us to escape this stalemate. There was a ready-made timetable with a beginning, middle and end for our journey. This gave us a momentum for change and it was wrapped up in the rhythm of family life. The Naming and Shaming Fridge, the scoring system, meant that Freddie had a voice and was in charge of the adventure. It was no longer about me and my cooking but about exploring vegetables and recipes

abcthedgreatebigfveggchallengehijklmnopqrstuvwxyz

suggested by people visiting the blog. I was simply the facilitator. And as the months went past and we consumed our alphabet, the whole thing became a normal part of family life. Change happened without us knowing. Freddie stopped being so suspicious about food. He didn't feel threatened by new foods. He started comparing the tastes of all these new vegetables. Before, he had hated all vegetables. Now he had a list of favourites.

I have probably changed as much, if not more, than Freddie. I learnt to teach him how to explore the food we were trying out, to taste it and make comparisons. I stopped taking his rejection of a meal as a personal slight. Trying each vegetable in at least three different ways meant that I had to learn to do more than simply tip a bag of frozen peas into boiling water. Family meals became far more fun and more relaxed. There had at times been a two-tier system of catering in our home. There was food for the children and then something different, more sophisticated for the parents. We were prepared to sit round a television together but bizarrely we often opted out of eating the same meal together. That changed and we all enjoy the same food together now.

Most days, through the blog, I get emails from parents of fussy-eaters. They normally start like this: 'Dear Charlotte, my son/daughter refuses to eat any vegetables and bursts into tears/kicks and screams when we serve her/him a carrot/pea/green bean. What did you do to Freddie to make him eat vegetables?'

I'm not cut out to be a vegetable agony aunt. Every family is different, every child unique and every fussy-eater needs a slightly different approach. But the truth is I didn't make *Freddie* do anything. I made *myself* learn to cook a wider repertoire of vegetables and keep up the momentum. I tried to think what would make him want to explore new foods and try out new tastes and turned it all into a game. And I have been very lucky that the Great Big Vegetable Challenge has turned him from a vegetable-phobic into a boy who will try anything (apart from five plain green peas on a plate).

How to embark on your own Great Big Veg Challenge

🌿 You don't have to eat through the entire alphabet. You can make it simpler. Take the letters in your child's name or the name of their favourite football team and try out vegetables starting with those letters.

🌿 Cook and taste each vegetable at least three different ways so that you explore together how the taste varies.

🌿 Encourage your child to give each dish a mark out of 10.

🌿 Work out what it is about a vegetable that your child dislikes. Is it the taste, the texture or the colour? You might be able to combine it with something that improves the taste or make a smooth soup if it is a problem with the texture.

🌿 Try out tasting sessions for vegetables like lettuces, squash or tomatoes where there are lots of different varieties. Look at the Lettuce League Tables, the Great Big Mash Up or Party for Pea-Haters for ideas (see pages 154, 216 and 195).

🌿 If you can, visit farms and farmers' markets where the growers will show your child how the vegetables grow. They will also give you cooking tips and ideas.

🌿 Take children to markets and supermarkets to involve them in choosing which vegetables to eat, seeing what is in season.

🌿 Try not to mirror the behaviour of the fussy-eater by offering them only a narrow range of vegetables. It might just be that they don't like peas and carrots but could develop a taste for green beans and artichokes. Try not to rotate the same old narrow selection of vegetables, regularly introduce new ones to try.

🌿 Don't assume that the vegetables you like or dislike will be the same for your children. Let them find their own favourites.

🌿 Try peer pressure. If there is a recipe your child's best friend likes, then mention it, get them round and see if they will try it together.

🌿 Chat to other parents and share your knowledge about cooking vegetables. The school queue is the original information superhighway. Share recipes with other parents or ask them if they will teach you how to cook a dish they grew up with.

🌿 Grow your own. Even if you don't have a garden, your child might enjoy growing some herbs in a pot on the patio or window sill and cooking with them.

abcthedgreatebigfveggchallengehijklmnopqrstuvwxyz

Index

abcthedgreatebigfveggchallengehijklmnopqrstuvwxyz

Acknowledgements

To the hundreds of fellow bloggers, food-lovers on the Martha Stewart and BBC food message boards, people at the supermarket checkout, the cafe, the grocers, bus stops and of course the original information super highway, Mums and Dads in the queue at the school gate. Thank you for sharing your love of vegetables with us.

abcthedgreatebigfveggchallengehijklmnopqrstuvwxyz